D1556396

FINANCIAL
RISK
ANALYTICS

FINANCIAL
RISK
ANALYTICS

A TERM STRUCTURE MODEL APPROACH FOR BANKING, INSURANCE AND INVESTMENT MANAGEMENT

**DONALD R. VAN DEVENTER
AND KENJI IMAI**

Professional Publishing

Chicago • London • Singapore

Library of Congress Cataloging-in-Publication Data

Deventer, Donald R. van 1997
    Financial risk analytics: a term structure model approach for banking, insurance and investment management / Donald R. van Deventer, Kenji Imai.
      p. cm.
    Includes index.
    ISBN 0-7863-0964-4
    1. Asset-liability management.   2. Risk management.   I. Imai, Kenji, 1963– . II. Title.
    HG1615.25.D49   1997
    332.1′068′1 — dc20   96-36236

Printed in the United States of America
   3 4 5 6 7 8 9 0 DO 3 2 1 0 9 8

For Jin-sa,
who gave birth to lovely Ella
in the middle of Chapter 6,

and

For Yasuko, Tomoki, and Anna

ACKNOWLEDGMENTS

So many people have contributed to the thinking behind this book that space doesn't permit us to thank everyone personally. Still, we would be remiss if we didn't make an attempt to make special mention of some of our friends and colleagues who supported us through this effort. Our friend and colleague Bob Jarrow at Cornell has been a major inspiration when it comes to the practical implementation of financial theory to real-world problems. Oldrich Vasicek at KMV Corporation, who is responsible for a lot of the theory in this book and the proof in Chapter 2, has been much too modest regarding his contributions to the advances in fixed-income analytics over the years. David Shimko, formerly of the University of Southern California and now with J. P. Morgan, has consistently been able to point us in interesting directions from both a practical and a theoretical point of view. Junji Hatano, deputy president of Tokyo Mitsubishi Securities, has long shared our enthusiasm for the profitability of first-class financial theory. His support has been invaluable. David Zweiner, now Chief Financial Officer at ITT Hartford Insurance Company, has kept us focused on "accuracy rather than precision." Mark Railston at Westpac Banking Corporation in Sydney, David Tanner at Toronto Dominion, and Robert Selvaggio at Chase Manhattan have been enthusiastic advocates for better risk analytics, and we appreciate their support. Volf Frishling at Commonwealth Bank in Australia deserves credit for the improved proof in the appendix to Chapter 2, having pointed out an error in the earlier version. Dennis Colwell and Debbie Asetta at People's Bank and Ed Grubb at Transamerica Corporation have substantially improved the contents of this book with penetrating questions and insights.

Finally, we owe a large debt to our Kamakura Corporation colleagues who have implemented all of the concepts in the following pages: Nicholas Benes, Jonathan Levin, Kenneth Adams, William Hall, Reg Henderson, K. Hirose, Taiichi Hoshino, Chieko Aizawa, Mika Tsumura, Sarei Mieki, Chiang-ying Li, Mari

Morimura, Susie Gin, David Milstein, and Yoko Ito have our special thanks. Naohiko Tejima, who recently changed his PhD studies from mathematics to German literature, probably did so as a
result of checking every formula in this book. We are grateful to
him for his special effort, but we point out that all the remaining
errors are ours alone.

CONTENTS

Chapter 6

Risk-Neutral Interest Rates and European Options on Bonds   151

Chapter 7

Forward and Futures Contracts   175

Chapter 8

European Options on Forward and Futures Contracts   191

Chapter 18

Alternative Term Structure Models   333

Chapter 19

Estimating the Parameters of Term Structure Models   351

Chapter 20

Hedging and Risk Measurement 369

FINANCIAL
RISK
ANALYTICS

INTRODUCTION

In the summer of 1992, one of us spoke to a gathering of risk management experts from 80 European and American financial institutions. Part of our presentation was designed to encourage the bankers who had assembled to be more proactive in implementing powerful and eminently useful financial techniques that had been sitting on the academic shelf for more than 20 years. The technique we discussed that day was the use of options theory to measure credit risk, an approach Robert Merton first published in 1974. The question we asked the audience that day was a simple one. Why did it take almost 20 years before intelligent bankers started paying attention to Merton's brilliant insight? Over the last two decades, both of us marveled at the difficulties that our major bank employers were having with the concept of duration, an idea that was already 40 years old at the time and later became the regulatory risk management standard in the United States. Even the Black-Scholes options model, the most powerful economic insight of the 20th century, wasn't accepted as conventional wisdom at most institutions until almost 15 years after the model was published.

At the same time we asked why implementation had taken so long, we both had a strong sense that we knew the answer. In a large bank, insurance company, or investment management company, the derivative product specialists are in a luxurious position even after all of the derivatives-related incidents announced over the past year. Senior management recognizes the derivatives area as one that needs special talents, special software, and special oversight. At the same time, the derivatives specialists are encouraged to be on the leading edge of applied financial mathematics; senior management admits that they don't have the time and often don't have the mathematical training to understand the details, so they delegate the function to people they trust and provide for risk management audits by outside experts to confirm the integrity of the approaches taken. Any analytical finance person worth his or her salt lives for this sort of working arrange-

1

ment, where the standing order is full speed ahead from an analytical point of view.

Life on Stage

The members of the management team responsible for overall risk management, broadly defined, live on stage. Throughout this book, we will use the term *financial institution* in the most general sense to refer to banks, insurance companies, investment management firms, and a wide array of other financial firms. The two of us have worked for British, American, and Japanese institutions and with clients in Australia, Canada, the United States, Japan, and Korea. Overall risk management is done in different places in different organizations: by the asset and liability management committee in banks and by the chief investment officer's organization in many investment management firms and insurance companies. What these managers do is subject to monthly, weekly, or even daily scrutiny by the highest level of management and often by the outside board of directors. It is a rare chief financial officer or chief investment officer who can avoid explaining to the institution's board of directors what financing was done or what securities were purchased since the last meeting and how, *in simple terms*, the conclusion was reached to take that action. We strongly encourage the large amount of senior management attention that's paid to the overall risk management function. In fact, van Deventer's first book, *Financial Risk Management in Banking,* with Dr. Dennis Uyemura, was planned to lay out the nature of the overall risk management discipline for senior management. This senior management attention, however, does have one very important negative side effect: It can unintentionally result in the suppression of incredibly useful but complex analytical techniques for the overall risk management and related treasury functions. Why? Because of the strong sense that if the chairman of the financial institution can't understand a complex technique, then it is either (*a*) no good or (*b*) impractical. Our guess is that this constraint affects management practice for overall risk management in a hundred large financial institutions worldwide at the same time that the derivative products group in these institutions is taking large positions using the same techniques.

Do the Right Thing

The real purpose of *Financial Risk Management in Banking* was to provide a basic comfort level for senior management, to give them a strong sense that the creation of shareholder value was a practical objective, easy to implement, and essential to their job security. To borrow the title of Spike Lee's movie, we wanted senior management to "Do the Right Thing." Part of doing the right thing is to help experts in the overall risk management function gain the kind of freedom that management in the derivative products area has had for some time. What is this freedom? The freedom to crack open this book, look up the Robert Merton formula for pricing risky debt, plug in the right values, and get the best available answer to a tough question. *Financial Risk Management in Banking* was focused on the forest. In this book, we are going to spend a lot of time on the trees and even a few pine needles.

How to Use This Book

This book is intended both for serious students of theoretical and applied finance and for experienced risk management, investment management, and insurance risk management practitioners who need to have at their fingertips an efficient guide to the state of the art with regard to the valuation and risk management of a wide array of financial instruments traded every day by leading financial institutions. In the case of the finance student, we have spent the better part of the last two decades as risk managers ourselves; we want to assure student readers that we use the concepts in this book every day, as do the best firms in Tokyo, London, New York, and other leading financial centers around the world. For the practitioner, we recognize that most readers need to know how to use these techniques yet don't have the resources to spend three weeks of staff time reading old *Journal of Finance* articles to determine what the state of the art is and how to implement it. For this type of reader, we have tried to prepare a volume where the answer to a difficult question can be identified and implemented in the shortest possible time. Lots of the answers to tough questions in finance can be analyzed by anyone with some facility with popular spreadsheet software, a fact we have tried to prove in the disks attached to this volume.

Academic versus the Practical

Both of us are too old and too experienced for someone to claim justifiably that we're too academic. All of the techniques in this book have been implemented for use by many of the world's largest financial institutions. We think the phrase *too academic* can be used justifiably only when a theory is inconsistent with the real world. *Financial Risk Management in Banking* emphasized the 80/20 rule, which explains that often 80 percent of the potential benefits from analysis can be realized with only 20 percent of the total effort required for an analysis that generates 100 percent of the potential benefits. In many cases in overall risk management, it is worth a lot of money to have any answer that is one basis point more precise. That's not a contradiction to the 80/20 rule. We think that it pays to have an answer that's better than 80 percent of perfect in many circumstances. The reader has to determine when perfection is important and when it's not. In this book, we have tried to classify our answers to various problems in a way that gives the reader a menu of choices. The first choice is the quick and dirty answer. The second is usually a complex but directly applicable formula. The third is the perfect answer, often a solution to a complex problem that can only be obtained by numerical methods. We leave it to the reader to determine how asymptotically perfect the answer should be. Most of the institutions we have worked for or worked with vary the quality of their answers with the amount of money involved, spending more for a better answer when the cost of being wrong is high.

Mathematics

Most of us would have enough pride to decline an offer from the London Philharmonic Orchestra to assume the role of concertmaster, the principal violinist. Sometimes it's better not to try things where the qualities for success are qualities we just don't have. Soldiers in the financial trenches are in a similar kind of position. If you are uncomfortable with mathematics, the only way to be comfortable in an overall risk management position is to surround yourself with people who are comfortable with math.

Being a mathematician is no substitute for having good judgment. (The reverse is often true as well!) The techniques in this book are designed to help a chief investment officer or risk manager make the risk and return trade-offs facing the institution clear for senior management. In the end, the institution has to make a judgment call that relies on the best analysis, excellent judgment, and a little good fortune.

When you buy a house, you don't need an explanation of the principal laws of physics before you turn on the lights for the first time. This book is organized in recognition of that fact. We pose the question and we give the answer. No book could be thick enough to present all the derivations of the formulas and techniques summarized in this volume. The same is true of the mathematics used, although we have tried to remind readers like us of things they have probably seen at least once before. No one reading this book who has had a first course in calculus should have a reason to feel uncomfortable, and even those who didn't go beyond algebra shouldn't have too much trouble applying what lies within.

For those readers who want a detailed explanation of the techniques used to derive the approaches summarized here, we have four favorite books. The first is by our good friend and Kamakura Corporation colleague, Robert A. Jarrow. We highly recommend his book *Modelling Fixed Income Securities and Interest Rate Options*, both for its theoretical and expositional elegance. The book is particularly strong on numerical evaluation of fixed-income-related securities. Another excellent starting point for someone with a good tolerance for mathematics is Jonathan Ingersoll's *Theory of Financial Decision Making*. This graduate-level text has already established itself as a challenging but very readable tour de force. The third book we recommend, by David Shimko of J. P. Morgan, is *Finance in Continuous Time: A Primer*. The true power of stochastic processes to solve practical problems in finance is illustrated in great detail in Shimko's book. The final book for the very serious student of finance is a collection of Robert Merton's path-breaking articles called *Continuous Time Finance*. When the Nobel Prize is awarded to Robert Merton, the reasons will be readily apparent in his book.

The Pioneers

The financial world is now widely populated by very talented mathematicians, physicists, and financial economists who have achieved great success using very sophisticated analytical techniques and encouraging others to do the same. Those in the derivative products area have gotten a reasonable amount of attention. We would like to mention a number of others working in more general management or financial functions who have made a lot of money for their institutions using techniques like those in this book. First of all, Eugene Shanks deserves perhaps more credit than he has gotten for the transformation of Bankers Trust into an institution fully committed to risk management and first-class analytics during his tenure as chief executive officer, a post achieved in spite of the "handicap" of a PhD in mathematics. His successor at Bankers Trust, Frank Newman, has sponsored the advancement of analytics in the real world as Undersecretary of the Treasury and as Chief Financial Officer at Bank of America and Wells Fargo & Co. Frank's successor at Wells Fargo, Rod Jacobs, has a PhD in economics and is a former faculty member at UCLA. Early in the 1970s, John A. "Mack" MacQuown led the Wells Fargo Management Science Department, which can claim to have employed two little-known academics as consultants in 1972: Fischer Black and Myron Scholes. Mack continues to make huge contributions to practical banking using leading-edge analytics at KMV Corporation. Wells also had on its management science team Oldrich Vasicek, currently a partner at KMV, whose term structure model remains, 19 years after its 1977 publication, the most popular model for fixed-income derivative valuation. Dan Borge at Bankers Trust and Jon Salmon, first at First Interstate Bancorp and then at Wells Fargo, have also made practical application of advanced analytics a hallmark of their careers. The fact that an analytical tradition has been built over the decades at places like Wells Fargo and Bankers Trust is no accident; we hope this book encourages others to begin or extend their own tradition of analytical excellence.

The two of us have had encouragement from a long line of senior executives in the financial markets. While space doesn't permit the mention of everyone, a number of people stand out.

Don Griffith, John Kooken, Bob Perry, Joe Pinola, Paul Smith, and Gary Updegraft have our thanks and admiration for their contribution to our approach to this subject and the sophistication of the finance function at their institutions. Finally, we thank the team at Kamakura Corporation, which has implemented the techniques in this book for financial institutions around the world. Their support and their critiques have made both of us better at the disciplines within this book.

Kenji Imai and Donald R. van Deventer
Chigasaki, Japan

CHAPTER 1

Fixed-Income
Mathematics

The concept of present value is at the very heart of finance, and yet it can seem like the most mysterious and difficult element of risk management analytics. It is safe to say, though, that no self-respecting finance person in a large financial institution should look forward to a pleasant stay in the finance area if he or she is uncomfortable with the contents of this chapter on the basics of traditional fixed-income mathematics. At the same time, the basic principles of present value have so many applications that a good understanding of them would be very beneficial to a wide variety of finance professionals. In this overview of present value and fixed-income mathematics, we will touch on a wide variety of topics and leave a few to be covered in more detail in later chapters. Yield curve smoothing is covered in Chapter 2, duration and its relatives in Chapters 3 and 4, and more sophisticated models of movements in interest rates are explained in detail in the rest of the book. The present value concept and related issues like yield to maturity and forward interest rates provide the building blocks for these more complex issues.

1.1 PRICE, ACCRUED INTEREST, AND VALUE

The accounting profession and the economics profession have engaged in many wars during their history. Occasionally, there

have been periods of peaceful coexistence and general agreement on what's important in life. There was one important battle
lost by the economics profession that still causes finance professionals pain, however. That battle was fought over three concepts: *price, accrued interest,* and *value.*

   In this chapter we will focus consistently on the concept of
value — what a security is truly worth in the marketplace. In a
rational world, a security's value and the risk-adjusted present
value of future cash flows had better well be close to the same
thing or the reader is wasting a lot of valuable time reading this
book when he or she could be arbitraging the market. For the
purposes of this book, when we say *value,* we really mean *present
value*: what a rational person would pay today for cash flows to
be received in the future.

   Unfortunately, this simple concept has been complicated by
the noble idea that one "earns" interest on a bond even if you buy
it just after the most recent coupon payment was paid and sell it
before the next coupon payment is paid. This idea isn't harmful in
and of itself, but in the form the idea has been implemented in
many markets, nothing could be farther from economic reality.
The person who earns the interest on a bond is the person who is
the owner of record on the record date that determines who receives the interest. For accounting (not economic) purposes, the
accounting profession has decided that the value of a bond has to
be split into two pieces: the "price," which is intended by the
accountants to be relatively stable, and the "accrued interest,"
which is an arbitrary calculation that determines who earned interest on the bond even if that person received no cash from the
issuer of the bond.

   The basic accounting rule for splitting value isn't harmful on
the surface:

Value = Price plus accrued interest

What causes the harm is the formula for accrued interest. In a
calculation left over from the BC (before calculators) era, accrued interest is calculated as a proportion of the next coupon
on a bond. While there are many variations on the calculation
of this proportion, the simplest one divides the actual number
of days between the settlement date and the last bond coupon
payment date by the total number of days between coupon
payments.

Example 1.1.1: Calculation of Accrued Interest
ABC Bank sells a 10-year, 10 percent coupon bond for an amount of money equal to 102 percent of par value, or $1,020.00 per bond. The next semiannual coupon of $50.00 will be paid in 122 days, and it has been 60 days since the last coupon payment.

$$\text{Value} = \$1,020.00$$
$$\text{Accrued interest} = 60 \ (\$50)/[60 + 122] = \$16.48$$
$$\text{Price} = \text{Value} - \text{Accrued interest} = \$1,020.00 - 16.48 = \$1,003.52, \text{ or}$$
$$100.352 \text{ percent of par value}$$

There is one fundamental flaw in these simple rules: In economic terms, the amount of accrued interest is an arbitrary calculation that has no economic meaning.[1] Why? The amount of accrued interest bears no relationship to the current level of interest rates. The "accrued interest" on the bond in Example 1.1.1 is calculated to be the same in an environment when interest rates are 3 percent as in one where interest rates are 30 percent. The amount of accrued interest depends solely on the coupon on the bond, which reflects interest rate levels at the time of issue, not interest rates today. If "price" is calculated as value minus an economically meaningless number, then price is an economically meaningless number as well. Unfortunately, the number referred to most often on a day-to-day basis in the financial industry is price, so those of us who focus on good numbers have to work backward to remain focused on what's important: the value of the transaction, $1,020.00.[2] Market slang labels true present value as *dirty price,* meaning price plus accrued interest. *Clean price* means true present value minus accrued interest, that is, the price quoted in the market. In our minds, the market has applied the words *dirty* and *clean* to the wrong definitions of price.

From now on, when we say *value* we mean true present value, dirty price, price plus accrued interest. To avoid confusion, we will always specify the concept of price we intend to avoid confusion between clean price and dirty price.

---

1. One exception to this comment is the differential tax impact of accrued interest and price. It has long been acknowledged that no group has less influence on government policy than economists, so it is no surprise that the accountants devised the tax code.
2. There are exceptions to this concept of accrued interest. Australia and Korea are two markets where there is no artificial division of value into accrued interest and price.

1.2 PRESENT VALUE

A dollar received in the future is always worth less than a dollar received today. This is more than just a reflection of inflation; it's a recognition that the market requires someone using the resources of others to pay "rent" until those resources are returned. The implications of this simple fact are very important but straightforward.

The Basic Present Value Calculation

If the value of \$1 received at time t_i is written $P(t_i)$, then the present value of an investment that generates n varying cash flows $C(t_i)$ at n times t_i in the future (for i equal to 1 through n) can be written as follows:

$$\text{Present value} = \sum_{i=1}^{n} P(t_i)C(t_i) \tag{1.1}$$

Example 1.2.1

Cash flow 1: \$100.00
Date received: 1 year from now

Cash flow 2: \$200.00
Date received: 10 years from now

Value of \$1 received in the future:
Received in 1 year: \$0.90
Received in 10 years: \$0.50

$$\text{Value} = 100(.9) + 200(.5) = 190.00$$

The simple formula in Equation 1.1 is completely general. It is the heart of most banking calculations and much of finance. Note that the present value formula has the following features:

- It is independent of the number of cash flows.
- It is independent of the method of interest compounding.
- It assumes that cash flows are known with certainty.

The $P(t_i)$ values, the value of \$1 received at time t_i, are called *discount factors*. They provide the basis for all yield curve calculations: bond valuation, forward rates, yield to maturity, forward bond prices, and so on. How they are determined and how they link with other concepts is the topic that makes up the heart of the rest of this book. For the time being, we assume that these discount factors are known. That allows us to write down immediately a number of other formulas for valuation of securities where the contractual cash flows are known with certainty.

Calculating the Value of a Fixed Coupon Bond with Principal Paid at Maturity

If the actual dollar amount of the coupon payment on a fixed coupon bond is C and principal is repaid at time t_n, the value (price plus accrued interest) of the bond is calculated as follows:

$$\text{Value of fixed coupon bond} = C\left[\sum_{i=1}^{n}P(t_i)\right] + P(t_n) * \text{Principal} \qquad (1.2)$$

Note that this formula applies regardless of how often coupon payments are made and regardless of whether the first coupon period is a full period in length.

Example 1.2.2

Principal amount: $1,000.00
Interest paid: Semiannually
Coupon rate: 10 percent
Coupon dollar amount: $50.00
Periods to maturity: 4 semiannual periods
Days to next coupon: 40 days

Value of $1 received in the future:
Received in 40 days: $0.99
Received in 6 months plus 40 days: $0.94
Received in 1 year plus 40 days: $0.89
Received in 1.5 years plus 40 days: $0.83

Value = 50.00 (.99 + .94 + .89 + .83) + .83(1,000) = 1,012.50

Example 1.2.3

Principal amount: $2,000.00
Interest paid: Annually
Coupon rate: 10 percent
Coupon amount: $200.00

Periods to maturity: 3 annual periods
Days to next coupon: 350 days

Value of $1 received in the future:
Received in 350 days: $0.95
Received in 1 year plus 350 days: $0.86
Received in 2 years plus 350 days: $0.76

Value = 200.00 (.95 + .86 + .76) + .76(2,000) = 2,034.00

Calculating the Coupon of a Fixed Coupon Bond with Principal Paid at Maturity When Value Is Known

If the value (price plus accrued interest) of a fixed coupon bond is known and the discount factors are known, the dollar coupon payment that leads a bond to have such a value is calculated by rearranging Equation 1.2:

$$\frac{\text{Dollar coupon amount}}{\text{of fixed coupon bond}} = \frac{\text{Value} - P(t_n) * \text{Principal}}{\sum_{i=1}^{n} P(t_i)} \quad (1.3)$$

Example 1.2.4
Principal amount: $1,000.00
Interest paid: Semiannually
Value: $1,150.00
Periods to maturity: 4 semiannual periods
Days to next coupon: 40 days

Value of $1 received in the future:
Received in 40 days: $0.99
Received in 6 months plus 40 days: $0.94
Received in 1 year plus 40 days: $0.89
Received in 1.5 years plus 40 days: $0.83

Coupon amount = (1,150 − .83 * 1,000)/(.99 + .94 + .89 + .83)
          = 87.67
Coupon rate = (2 payments * Amount)/1,000.00 = 17.53%

Example 1.2.5
Principal amount: $2,000.00
Interest paid: Annually

Periods to maturity: 3 annual periods
Days to next coupon: 350 days
Value: $1,850.00

Value of $1 received in the future:
Received in 350 days: $0.94
Received in 1 year plus 350 days: $0.86
Received in 2 years plus 350 days: $0.76

Coupon amount = $(1{,}850 - .76 * 2{,}000)/(.94 + .86 + .76)$
= 128.91
Coupon rate = (1 payment * Amount)/2,000.00 = 6.45%

The Value of an Amortizing Loan

The value of an amortizing loan is the same calculation as that for a fixed coupon bond except that the variable C represents the constant-level payment received in each period. There is no explicit principal amount at the end since all principal is retired in period-by-period payments included in the amount C. When the periodic payment dollar amount is known, the value of the loan is calculated as follows:

$$\text{Value of amortizing bond} = C\left[\sum_{i=1}^{n} P(t_i)\right] \qquad (1.4)$$

Note again that this formula holds even for a short first period and for any frequency of payments.

Example 1.2.6
Payment frequency: Semiannual
Payment amount: $500.00
Periods to maturity: 4 semiannual periods
Days to next coupon: 40 days

Value of $1 received in the future:
Received in 40 days: $0.99
Received in 6 months plus 40 days: $0.94
Received in 1 year plus 40 days: $0.89
Received in 1.5 years plus 40 days: $0.83

Value = 500.00 (.99 + .94 + .89 + .83) = 1,825.00

Calculating the Payment Amount of an Amortizing Bond When Value Is Known

Like the fixed coupon bond case, the payment amount on an amortizing bond can be calculated using the known amount for value (principal plus accrued interest) and rearranging Equation 1.4.

$$C = \text{Payment amount on amortizing bond} = \frac{\text{Value}}{\sum_{i=1}^{n} P(t_i)} \qquad (1.5)$$

Example 1.2.7

Payment frequency: Annually
Periods to maturity: 3 annual periods
Days to next coupon: 350 days
Value: $1,850.00

Value of $1 received in the future:
Received in 350 days: $0.95
Received in 1 year plus 350 days: $0.86
Received in 2 years plus 350 days: $0.76

Payment amount = $(1,850)/(.95 + .86 + .76) = 719.84$

Up to this point, we have taken the discount functions $P(t_i)$ as given. In the next section, we begin to explore some common assumptions that help determine their value.

Calculating the Value of a Floating-Rate Bond with Principal Paid at Maturity

The calculation of the value of a floating-rate bond is more complicated than the valuation of a fixed-rate bond because future coupon payments are unknown. In order to value floating-rate bonds, we divide the formula for determining the coupon on the bond into two pieces: an index plus a fixed dollar spread over the index. We assume the index is set at a level such that the value of a bond with one period (equal in length to $1/m$ years) to maturity and an interest rate equal to the index would be par value. This is equivalent to assuming that the yield curve (and its movements) that determines future values of the index is the same as the yield curve we should use for valuing the floating-rate security. For example, we assume that the right yield curve for valuing all securities whose rate is reset based on the London interbank offered rate (Libor) should be valued at the Libor yield curve. We will relax this assumption below and in later chapters when we have more powerful tools to analyze more realistic assumptions about the value of a bond whose rate floats at the index plus zero spread. Using our simple assumptions for the time being, the present value of a floating-rate bond priced at the index level plus a fixed dollar amount (the *spread*) per period is equal to par value (the value of all future payments at an interest rate equal to the floating index plus the return of principal) plus the present value of the stream of payments equal to the spread received each period. The value of the stream of payments equal to the spread can be valued using Equation 1.4, the value of an amortizing bond. Therefore the value of a floating-rate bond is

$$P(t_1)\left[\left(1 + \frac{\text{Index}}{m}\right) * \text{Principal}\right] + \text{Spread} * \left[\sum_{i=1}^{n} P(t_i)\right] \quad (1.6)$$

Note that the first term will be equal to the principal value, given our definition of the index, if the time to the first payment t_1 is equal to the normal length of the period between coupons. Note also that the index may not be the interest rate (which we will call the *formula rate* from here on) used as the formula for setting the coupon on the bond. See the examples for valuation of bonds where the index rate and the formula rate are different.

Example 1.2.8

Coupon formula: 6-month Libor (adjusted[3]) + 2 percent

Index value: 6-month Libor + 1 percent

Principal amount: $2,000.00

Spread: $(.02 - .01) * 2,000/2 = 10.00$

Maturity: 2 years

Time to next coupon: Exactly 6 months

---

3. Whenever Libor (the London interbank offered rate) is mentioned in text that follows, we assume the rate has been converted from the market convention of Actual days/360 days per year to Actual days/365 days per year by multiplying nominal Libor by 365/360.

Value of $1 received in the future:

Received in 6 months: $0.96

Received in 1 year: $0.92

Received in 1.5 years: $0.87

Received in 2.0 years: $0.82

$$\text{Value} = .96 * \left[\left(1 + \frac{\text{Libor} + .01}{2} \right) * \text{Principal} \right]$$
$$+ 10.00 * [0.96 + 0.92 + 0.87 + 0.83] = 2{,}035.8$$

Example 1.2.9

Coupon formula: 6-month Libor + 2 percent

Index value: Treasury bill + 1 percent

Rate relationship: Libor = Treasury bill + 1.5 percent

Principal amount: $2,000.00

Spread: (.015 + .02 − .01) * 2,000/2 = 25.00

First coupon rate: 7 percent at Libor = 5 percent

Maturity: 2 years and 91 days

Time to next coupon: 91 days

Value of $1 received in the future:

Received in 91 days: $0.98

Received in 6 months and 91 days: $0.95

Received in 1 year and 91 days: $0.91

Received in 1.5 years and 91 days: $0.86

$$\text{Value} = .98 * \left[\left(1 + \frac{.07}{2} \right) * \text{Principal} \right] + 25.00 * [0.95 + 0.91 + 0.86]$$
$$= 2{,}096.60$$

1.3 COMPOUND INTEREST CONVENTIONS AND FORMULAS

No one who has been in the financial world for long expects interest rates to remain constant. Still, when bankers and treasurers perform compound interest and yield-to-maturity calculations, the constancy of interest rates is a common assumption simply because of the difficulty of making any other choice. Particularly when discussing compound interest, interest rate constancy is a standard assumption. This section discusses those conventions as preparation for the yield-to-maturity discussion later in this chapter.

The Future Value of an Invested Amount Earning at a Simple Interest Rate of y Compounded m Times per Year for n Periods

Almost all discussions of compound interest and future value depend on four factors:

- The constancy of interest rates.
- The nominal annual rate of interest.
- The number of times per year interest is paid.
- The number of periods for which interest is compounded.

$$\text{Future value of invested amount} = (\text{Invested amount}) * \left(1 + \frac{y}{m}\right)^n \quad (1.7)$$

Example 1.3.1
    Invested amount: $100.00
    Simple interest rate: 12 percent
    Interest paid: Monthly
    Investment period: 2 years

$$\text{Future value} = 100.00 * \left(1 + \frac{.12}{12}\right)^{24} = 126.97$$

The Future Value of an Invested Amount Earning at a Simple Interest Rate of y Compounded Continuously for n Years

What happens if the compounding period shrinks smaller and smaller, so that interest is compounded every instant, not every second or every day or every month? If one assumes a simple

interest rate of y invested for n years, the corresponding formula
to Equation 1.7 is

$$\text{Future amount} = \text{Invested amount} * e^{yn} \qquad (1.8)$$

Many financial institutions actually use a continuously compounded interest rate formula for consumer deposits. As we will
see in later chapters, the continuous compounding assumption is
a very convenient mathematical shorthand for compound interest because derivatives of the constant

$$e = 2.7128 \ldots$$

to a power are much simpler (once one gets used to them) than
the derivatives of a discrete compounding formula. The continuous time assumption also allows the use of the powerful mathematical tools called stochastic processes, which we introduce in
Chapter 4.

Example 1.3.2
    Invested amount: $100.00
    Simple interest rate: 12 percent
    Interest paid: Continuously
    Investment period: 2 years and 180 days

$$\text{Future value} = 100.00 * e^{.12 * \left(2 + \frac{180}{365}\right)} = 134.88$$

Equivalent Annual Percentage Rate

In order to easily compare potential investments where compounding assumptions are different, it is common to express the
yield on the investment in terms of an "annual percentage rate."
The annual percentage is the amount an investment would yield if
(1) interest rates were constant and (2) interest is paid only once
per year.

The annual percentage rate formula is a variation on Equation 1.6 where the investment period is regarded to be one year. It
tells how much interest would be earned during the one-year period. If interest is paid m times per year for an investment period
of n periods, the annual percentage rate formula is as follows:

$$\text{Annual percentage rate} = 100 * \left[\left(1 + \frac{y}{m} \right)^m - 1 \right] \quad (1.9)$$

Note that the maturity n does not appear in the formula. For retail financial services like lending and deposit gathering, this U.S.-government-mandated formula helps make apples-to-apples comparisons easier. For derivatives and risk management purposes, it can lead to problems. There is no substitute for the precise specification of the compounding frequency.

Example 1.3.3
Invested amount: $100.00
Simple interest rate: 12 percent
Interest paid: Monthly
Investment period: 2 years

$$\text{Annual percentage rate} = 100 * \left[\left(1 + .12/12 \right)^{12} - 1 \right] = 12.68\%$$

The Present Value of a Future Amount If Funds Are Invested at a Simple Interest Rate of y Compounded m Times per Year for n Periods

A parallel question to the compound interest investment question is this: If one seeks to have 100 dollars n periods in the future and funds had been invested at a constant rate y compounded m periods per year, how much needs to be invested initially? The answer is a rearrangement of Equation 1.7:

$$\text{Invested amount} = \frac{\text{Future value of invested amount}}{\left(1 + \frac{y}{m} \right)^n} \quad (1.10)$$

Example 1.3.4
Future amount: $600.00
Simple interest rate: 10 percent
Interest paid: Monthly
Investment period: 2 years

$$\text{Invested amount} = \frac{600.00}{\left(1 + \frac{.10}{12}\right)^{24}} = 491.65$$

The Present Value of a Future Amount If Funds Are Invested at a Simple Interest Rate of y Compounded Continuously for n Years

When interest is assumed to be paid continuously, the investment amount can be calculated by rearranging Equation 1.8:

$$\frac{\text{Invested}}{\text{amount}} = \frac{\text{Future amount}}{e^{yn}} = \text{Future amount} * e^{-yn} \qquad (1.11)$$

Example 1.3.5
Future amount: $600.00
Simple interest rate: 12 percent
Interest paid: Continuously
Investment period: 2 years and 180 days

$$\text{Invested amount} = 600.00 * e^{-.12 * \left(2 + \frac{180}{365}\right)} = 444.86$$

Calculating the Yield on a Different Compounding Basis

It is often necessary to convert from one compounding basis to another. The formula for doing this is a variation on Equations 1.7 and 1.8.

When converting from an interest rate of y paid m times per year for n periods to an interest rate of y^* paid p times per year for q periods (where n/m years = q/p years), the formula is:

$$\text{Converted yield } y^* = p\left[\left[\left(1 + \frac{y}{m}\right)^n\right]^{\frac{1}{q}} - 1\right] \qquad (1.12)$$

Example 1.3.6
Original compounding basis:
Yield: 10 percent

Interest paid: Monthly
Maturity: 24 months

Desired compounding basis:
Interest paid: Semiannually
Maturity: 4 semiannual periods

(Note that the maturity in each case is two years.)

$$\text{Converted yield } y^* = 2\left[\left[\left(1+\frac{.1}{12}\right)^{24}\right]^{\frac{1}{4}} - 1\right]$$

$$= 10.21\%$$

When converting from an interest rate of y paid m times per year for n periods to an interest rate of y^* paid continuously for n/m years,

$$\text{Converted yield } y^* = \frac{1}{\left(\dfrac{n}{m}\right)}\log\left[\left(1+\frac{y}{m}\right)^n\right] \qquad (1.13)$$

Example 1.3.7
   Original compounding basis:
   Yield: 10 percent
   Interest paid: Monthly
   Maturity: 24 months

   Desired compounding basis:
   Interest paid: Continuously
   Maturity: 2 years

(Note that the maturity in each case is two years.)

$$\text{Converted yield } y^* = \frac{1}{\left(\dfrac{24}{12}\right)}\log\left[\left(1+\frac{.1}{12}\right)^{24}\right]$$

$$= 9.96\%$$

When converting from an interest rate of y paid continuously for p years to an interest rate of $y*$ paid m times per year for n periods (where $p = n/m$),

$$\text{Converted yield } y^* = m\left[\left[e^{yp}\right]^{\frac{1}{n}} - 1\right] \qquad (1.14)$$

Example 1.3.8
Original compounding basis:
Yield: 9 percent
Interest paid: Continuously
Maturity: 2 years

Desired compounding basis:
Interest paid: Quarterly
Maturity: 8 quarters

(Note that the maturity in each case is two years.)

$$\text{Converted yield } y^* = 4\left[\left[e^{.09 \, * \, 2}\right]^{\frac{1}{8}} - 1\right]$$

$$= 9.102\%$$

With these formulas behind us, the yield-to-maturity calculations can be discussed using a combination of the formulas in Sections 1.2 and 1.3.

1.4 YIELDS AND YIELD-TO-MATURITY CALCULATIONS

The concept of yield to maturity is one of the most useful and one of the most deceptive calculations in finance. Take the example of a five-year bond with a current value equal to its par value and coupons paid semiannually. The market is forecasting 10 different forward interest rates (which we discuss in Section 1.5) that have an impact on the pricing of this bond. There are an infinite number of forward rate combinations that are consistent with the bond having a current value equal to its par value. What is the probability that the market is implicitly forecasting all 10 semiannual forward rates to be equal? Except by extraordinary coincidence, the probability is a number only the slightest bit greater than zero. Nonetheless, this is the assumption implied when one asks, "What's the yield to maturity on ABC company's bond?" It's an assumption that is no worse than any other — but no better either, in the absence of any other information.

What if ABC Company has two bonds outstanding — one of 10 years in maturity and another of 5 years of maturity? When an analyst calculates the yield to maturity on both bonds, the result is the implicit assumption that rates are constant at one level when analyzing the first bond and constant at a different level when analyzing the second bond. The implications of this are discussed in detail in Chapter 2. In Chapter 3, we will discuss a number of ways to derive more useful information from a collection of outstanding value information on bonds of a comparable type. As an example, if ABC Company has bonds outstanding at all 10 semiannual maturities, it is both possible and very easy to calculate the implied forward rates, zero coupon bond prices (discount factors), and pricing on all possible combinations of forward bond issues by ABC Company. The calculation of yield to maturity is more complex than these calculations, and it yields less information. Nonetheless, it's still the most often quoted bond statistic other than clean price (present value less accrued interest).

The Formula for Yield to Maturity

For a settlement date (for either a secondary market bond purchase or a new bond issue) that falls exactly one "period" from the next coupon date, the formula for yield to maturity can be written as follows for a bond that matures in n periods and pays a fixed coupon amount C m times per year:

$$\text{Value} = C\left[\sum_{i=1}^{n} P(t_i)\right] + P(t_n) * \text{Principal} \qquad (1.15)$$

$$\text{with } P(t_i) = \frac{1}{\left(1 + \dfrac{y}{m}\right)^i}$$

Yield to maturity is the value of y that makes this equation true. This relationship is the present value equation for a fixed coupon bond, with the addition that the discount factors are all calculated by dividing $1 by the future value (see Equation 1.7) of $1 invested at a constant rate y for i periods with interest compounded m times per year. In other words, y is the internal rate of return on this bond.

Example 1.4.1

Bond principal value: $1,000.00

Interest paid: Semiannually

Semiannual coupon amount: $50.00

Bond value: $1,000.00

One can verify that yield to maturity is 10 percent by showing that the present value of the bond is equal to value, $1,000.00.

$$\text{Value} = 50\left[\sum_{i=1}^{4} P(t_i)\right] + P(t_4) * 1,000$$

with

$$P(t_i) = \frac{1}{\left(1 + \dfrac{.10}{2}\right)^{i}}$$

so

$$\text{Value} = 1,000.00$$

Yield to Maturity for Long or Short First Coupon Payment Periods

For most outstanding bonds or securities, there is a short (or occasionally long) interest payment period remaining until the first coupon payment is received. The length of the short first period is equal to the number of days from settlement to the next coupon, divided by the total number of days from the last coupon (or hypothetical last coupon, if the bond is a new issue with a short coupon date) to the next coupon. The method for counting "days" is specified precisely by the interest accrual method appropriate for that bond. We call this ratio (of "remaining days" to "days between coupons") the fraction x.[4] Then the yield to maturity can be written as follows:

$$\text{Value} = C\left[\sum_{i=1}^{n} P(t_i)\right] + P(t_n) * \text{Principal} \qquad (1.16)$$

$$\text{with } P(t_i) = \frac{1}{\left(1 + \dfrac{y}{m}\right)^{i-1+x}}$$

where, as above, y is the value that makes this equation true.

Example 1.4.2

    Bond maturity: 2 years and 91 days

    Bond principal value: $1,000.00

    Interest paid: Semiannually

    Semiannual coupon amount: $50.00

    Days to next coupon: 91

    Days between coupons: 182

What is the present value if the yield to maturity y is 10 percent?

    Present value = $1,024.695

Calculating Yield to Maturity Using the Newton-Raphson Method

Frankly, if everyone who now uses the term *yield to maturity* had to be able to calculate yield without a specialized bond calculator, the term never would have become popular to begin with. Looking at Equations 1.15 and 1.16 shows that the yield-to-maturity calculation is really an nth degree polynomial equation in y. There is a relatively easy way out for those readers who, like the authors, successfully avoided exposure to solving polynomials other than quadratic functions. The Newton-Raphson method is an iterative approach to solving a nonlinear equation like this one that is very effective for most yield-to-maturity calculations. In brief, the steps in solving for yield to maturity are as follows.

---

4. We reemphasize that the calculation of remaining days to days between coupons will vary depending on which of the common interest accrual methods is used to count the days.

1. Rearrange the appropriate yield-to-maturity equation so the right-hand side, which indicates the difference between the estimated value for a given yield and the actual value (the "difference") is zero. Select the appropriate equation from the following.

     a. For normal length of time to the first coupon payment:

$$\text{Value difference} = C\left[\sum_{i=1}^{n}P(t_i)\right] + P(t_n) * \text{Principal} - \text{Value} = 0$$

$$\text{with } P(t_i) = \frac{1}{\left(1 + \dfrac{y}{m}\right)^{i}}$$

     b. For a long or short period to the first coupon payment:

$$\text{Value difference} = C\left[\sum_{i=1}^{n}P(t_i)\right] + P(t_n) * \text{Principal} - \text{Value} = 0$$

$$\text{with } P(t_i) = \frac{1}{\left(1 + \dfrac{y}{m}\right)^{i-1+x}}$$

2. Guess a starting value for y. The coupon percentage (not the dollar amount of the coupon) is often a good starting point.

3. Calculate the derivative of the value difference equation above with respect to y assuming the guessed value of y is correct. The derivatives of the two relevant equations are as follows.

     a. For normal length of time to the first coupon payment:

$$\text{Derivative of value difference} = C\left[\sum_{i=1}^{n}Q(t_i)\right] + Q(t_n) * \text{Principal}$$

$$\text{with } Q(t_i) = \frac{-i}{m\left(1 + \dfrac{y}{m}\right)^{i+1}}$$

     b. For a long or short period to the first coupon payment:

$$\text{Derivative of value difference} = C\left[\sum_{i=1}^{n}Q(t_i)\right] + Q(t_n) * \text{Principal}$$

$$\text{with } Q(t_i) = \frac{-(i - 1 + x)}{m\left(1 + \dfrac{y}{m}\right)^{i+x}}$$

4. Calculate the new estimated value of *y* from the following equation:

$$\text{New } y = \text{Old } y - \frac{\text{Difference evaluated at Old } y}{\text{Derivative of Difference evaluated at Old } y}$$

5. If the difference between the new estimated value of *y* and the previous guess for y, the old *y*, is less than the maximum allowable error (usually 1 basis point or 0.1 basis point for most applications), then stop. You are done. If the difference is still wider than the maximum allowable error, go back to step 3 and repeat the process until the desired degree of accuracy is achieved.

While it is theoretically possible that this method may not converge, the method has always been effective in the authors' experience for normally structured bonds. If the method does not converge for a given starting value of *y*, try a different starting value of *y*. The Newton-Raphson method provides a very quick and stable solution for almost every conceivable yield-to-maturity problem. Most common spreadsheet packages contain a solution method for nonlinear equations like the yield-to-maturity formula that allow the user to find yield to maturity without going through the steps above. In many cases, the yield to maturity on a bond is itself a function embedded in the software. Note that the yield to maturity on an amortizing instrument where all principal payments are incorporated in the level payment is calculated using exactly the same formula with the ending "principal" set to zero.

Example 1.4.3
Using the fact that the present value in Example 1.4.2 is $1,024.695, we use the Newton-Raphson method to derive yield to maturity. Using an initial guess of 9.5 percent produces an iteration of an estimated value of *y* of 10 percent. The iteration to this solution is shown in Exhibit 1.1.

1.5 CALCULATING FORWARD INTEREST RATES AND BOND PRICES

What is the six-month interest rate that the market expects[5] to prevail two years in the future? Straightforward questions like

---

5. In later chapters, we will discuss "risk-neutral" interest rates and their relationship to the true expected value of future interest rates.

EXHIBIT 1-1

Yield-to-Maturity Estimate for Example 1.4.3 at Each Iteration

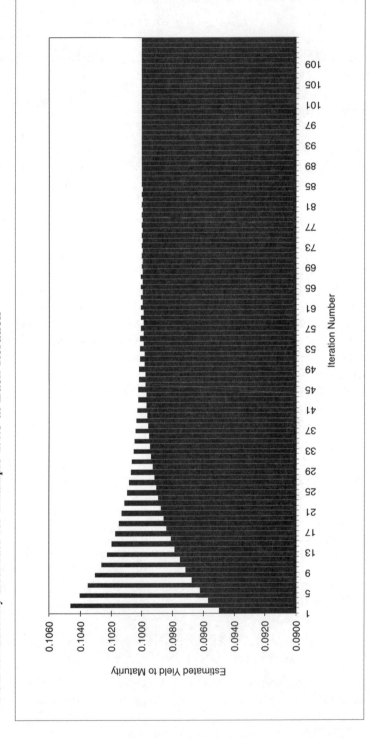

this are the key to funding strategy or investment strategy at many financial institutions. Once discount factors (or, equivalently, zero coupon bond prices) are known, making these calculations is simple.

Implied Forward Interest Rates on Zero Coupon Bonds

The forward interest rate t_i years in the future on a security that pays interest and principal at time t_{i+1} is calculated as follows:

$$\text{Forward interest rate} = \frac{100}{t_{i+1} - t_i}\left[\frac{P(t_i)}{P(t_{i+1})} - 1\right] \qquad (1.17)$$

This forward rate is the simple interest rate consistent with $1/(t_{i+1} - t_i)$ interest payments per year. For example, if t_i is 2 years and t_{i+1} is 2.5 years, then the forward interest rate is expressed on the basis of semiannual interest payments.

Example 1.5.1

Value of $1 received in the future:

Received in 350 days: $0.88

Received in 1 year plus 350 days: $0.80

$$\text{Forward rate} = \frac{100}{1}\left[\frac{.88}{.80} - 1\right]$$
$$= 10.00$$

This is the forward rate the market expects to prevail 350 days in the future on a one-year bond. The forward rate is expressed on the basis of annual compounding of interest.

Example 1.5.2

Value of $1 received in the future:

Received in 2 years: $0.80

Received in 2.5 years: $0.75

$$\text{Forward rate} = \frac{100}{2.5 - 2}\left[\frac{.80}{.75} - 1\right]$$
$$= 13.33\%$$

The forward rate in this case assumes semiannual interest payments consistent with the fact that the underlying instrument has a maturity of 0.5 years.

Implied Forward Zero Coupon Bond Prices

A parallel question to that of the level of forward interest rates is this: What is the forward price of a six-month zero coupon bond two years in the future? The answer is a simple ratio. The price at time t_i of a zero coupon bond with maturity at time t_{i+1} is calculated as follows:

$$\text{Implied forward zero coupon bond price} = \frac{P(t_{i+1})}{P(t_i)} \qquad (1.18)$$

We derive this simple formula using stochastic processes and no arbitrage arguments in a later chapter.

Example 1.5.3
Value of \$1 received in the future:
Received in 3 years: \$0.72
Received in 3.5 years: \$0.64

Implied zero coupon bond price = .64/.72 = .888889

Present Value of a Forward Fixed Coupon Bond

What is the present value of a bond to be issued on known terms at some time in the future? The answer is a straightforward application of Equation 1.2. If the actual dollar amount of the coupon payment on a fixed coupon bond is C and principal is repaid at time t_n, the value (price plus accrued interest) of the bond is

$$C\left[\sum_{i=1}^{n} P(t_i)\right] + P(t_n) * \text{Principal} \qquad (1.19)$$

Example 1.5.4
Principal amount: \$1,000.00
Interest paid: Semiannually
Coupon rate: 10 percent
Coupon amount: \$50.00
Periods to maturity: 4 semiannual periods
Years to next coupon: 3 years

Value of \$1 received in the future:
Received in 3 years: \$0.80
Received in 3.5 years: \$0.75
Received in 4 years and 40 days: \$0.71
Received in 4.5 years: \$0.67

Present value = 50.00 (.80 + .75 + .71 + .67) + .67(1,000) = 816.5

Implied Forward Price on a Fixed Coupon Bond

There is another logical question to ask about a bond to be issued in the future on known terms. What would be the forward price, as of today, of the "when issued" bond if we know its offering date? The answer is again a straightforward application of Equation 1.2. If the actual dollar amount of the coupon payment on a fixed coupon bond is C and principal is repaid at time t_n, the forward value (price plus accrued interest) of the bond at the issuance date t_0 is

$$\frac{C\left[\sum_{i=1}^{n} P(t_i)\right] + P(t_n) * \text{Principal}}{P(t_0)} \qquad (1.20)$$

Example 1.5.5
Principal amount: \$1,000.00
Interest paid: Semiannually
Coupon rate: 10 percent
Coupon amount: \$50.00
Periods to maturity: 4 semiannual periods
Years to next coupon: 3 years

Value of \$1 received in the future:
Received in 2.5 years: \$0.85
Received in 3 years: \$0.80
Received in 3.5 years: \$0.75
Received in 4 years and 40 days: \$0.71
Received in 4.5 years: \$0.67

Present value = 50.00 (.80 + .75 + .71 + .67) + .67(1,000) = 816.5

Forward value = 816.5/0.85 = 960.6

Implied Forward Coupon on a Fixed Coupon Bond

Finally, a treasurer may often be asked the implied forward issue costs (i.e., forward coupon rates) for a bond to be issued at par (or any other value). This question can be answered using a minor modification of Equation 1.3. For a bond to be issued at time t_0 with n interest payments and principal repaid at time t_n, the dollar amount of the coupon is given by the formula

$$\frac{P(t_0) * (\text{Value at issue}) - P(t_n) * \text{Principal}}{\sum_{i=1}^{n} P(t_i)} \qquad (1.21)$$

Example 1.5.6
Principal amount: $1,000.00
Interest paid: Semiannually
Value at issue: $995.00
Periods to maturity: 4 semiannual periods
Years to issuance: 2 years

Value of $1 received in the future:
Received in 2 years: $0.86
Received in 2.5 years: $0.81
Received in 3 years: $0.75
Received in 3.5 years: $0.70
Received in 4.0 years: $0.65

Coupon amount = (.86 × 995 − .65 * 1,000)/(.81 + .75 + .70 + .65)
             = 70.687
Coupon rate = [100 * (2 payments) * Amount]/1,000.00
            = 14.14%

Other Forward Calculations

The same types of calculations can be performed for a very wide variety of other instruments and statistics. For instance, the forward yield to maturity can be calculated on a fixed coupon bond. Forward amortizing bond prices and payment amounts can be calculated as well. The present values and forward prices for literally any form of cash flow can be analyzed using the formulas presented in this chapter.

1.6 SUMMARY

This chapter has summarized the building blocks of all financial market calculations: the concepts of present value, compound interest, yield to maturity, and forward bond yields and prices. All of these concepts can be expressed using algebra and nothing else. There are no mysteries here, yet the power of these simple concepts is great. Risk managers who make full use of present value and its implications truly do have a leg up on the competition. Those who don't bear a heavy burden in a very competitive world.

At this point, there are probably more than a few readers thinking, Yes, these concepts aren't so difficult as long as someone gives you the discount factors — but where am I supposed to get them? We give the answers to that question in Chapter 2. There are so many potential ways to calculate the "correct" discount factors that we purposely have chosen to speak about them generally in this chapter so that no one technique would obscure the importance of the present value calculations.

EXERCISES

Assume for purposes of the following exercises that today is January 15, 2000, and that the prevailing market prices in the government bond market for the following zero coupon bonds are as follows:

April 15, 2000	.974
October 15, 2000	.949
April 15, 2001	.921
October 15, 2001	.892
April 15, 2002	.862
October 15, 2002	.831
April 15, 2003	.798
October 14, 2003	.763
April 15, 2004	.725

Also, assume that all government bonds pay interest semiannually, including both fixed- and floating-rate instruments.

Accrued interest is calculated according to the ratio of the actual days from the last interest payment to the total days between interest payments. Assume the par value of all government bonds is $1,000.

1.1 What is the present value of the 6 percent government bond maturing October 15, 2002?

1.2 What is the amount of accrued interest on the bond in Exercise 1.1? What would be the quoted "price" in the U.S. market and other markets using similar accrued interest conventions?

1.3 Assuming there is no arbitrage in the market, what is the coupon that would prevail in the forward market if the government plans to issue a four-year bond at par on April 15, 2000, with a four-year maturity?

1.4 What would be the forward price on the bond in Exercise 1.1 if the government has announced in advance that the annual coupon rate will be 9 percent?

1.5 What are the semiannual forward rates prevailing in the government bond market for six-month periods beginning April 15, 2000?

1.6 If the government decided to issue today an amortizing bond with present value of $1,000 and equal payments on each April 15 and October 15 until maturity April 15, 2004, what would the semiannual payment have to be?

1.7 What is the yield to maturity on the amortizing bond in Exercise 1.6?

1.8 What is the yield to maturity on the 6 percent bond in Exercise 1.1?

1.9 What are the annual forward rates prevailing in the government bond market from each April 15 in the years 2000, 2001, 2002, and 2003?

1.10 What are the continuously compounding yields to maturity for each of the discount government bonds whose prices are given above?

1.11 What is the quarterly compounded rate of interest on the government discount bond maturing on October 15, 2003?

1.12 What is the present value of a government bond that pays the prevailing six-month government bond rate plus 0.50 percent semiannually on each April 15 and October 15, maturing April 15, 2004? Assume the coupon payment to be received April 15, 2000, is an annual rate of 6 percent.

1.13 How much will the present value of the 6 percent bond in Exercise 1.1 change if its yield to maturity goes up by 0.50 percent?

1.14 How much will the present value of the 6 percent bond in Exercise 1.1 change if the continuously compounded yields to maturity on each of the zero coupon bonds given above increase by 0.50 percent?

1.15 Assume that you hold a $1,000 principal amount of the 6 percent bond maturing October 15, 2002. Assume also that you can only hedge this position by taking a "short" position in 7 percent government bonds maturing April 15, 2001. If the continuous yields to maturity on all the discount bonds given above will increase by 0.50 percent, how much of the April 15, 2001, bonds should be shorted to offset the risk?

1.16 The ABC Life Insurance Company's liabilities include policies on Ms. Jones and Mr. Smith. Ms. Jones's insurance policy results in payments of $500 to ABC every April 15 and October 15 until she passes away. Mr. Smith's policy pays $750 to ABC on each April 15 and October 15. Ms. Jones's and Mr. Smith's probabilities of passing away have been determined from actuarial tables and adjustments to reflect (a) Ms. Jones's high-risk lifestyle as a professor of finance at a well-known university and (b) Mr. Smith's bungee-jumping hobby. The probabilities of passing away are as follows:

	Ms. Jones	Mr. Smith
April 15, 2002	10%	20%
October 15, 2002	20%	30%
April 15, 2003	30%	40%
October 15, 2003	20%	10%
April 15, 2004	20%	0%

Both Ms. Jones's and Mr. Smith's policies pay $10,000 upon their death.

a. What is the net present value, discounted at the government securities yield curve, of ABC's cash flows on each policy? Assume that ABC is "risk neutral" with regard to the probabilities of death, so no risk premium has to be reflected in the net present value calculation.

b. Assume that the only bonds available for purchase in the government bond market are the following bonds, whose present values are consistent with the zero coupon bond prices quoted above. How much, in terms of both principal amount and present value, of each bond does ABC have to buy to perfectly match the expected cash flows on these policies?

Coupons Prevailing in the Government Bond Market

Maturity Date	Coupon
April 15, 2002	10%
October 15, 2002	9%
April 15, 2003	8%
October 15, 2003	7.5%
April 15, 2004	7%

ABC Company has decided not to follow the perfectly matched cash flow strategy in 1.16 (b). Instead, the company owns $10,000 principal amount of the 7.5

percent bonds due October 15, 2003, and $15,000 of the 7 percent bonds due April 15, 2004.

c. What is the mark-to-market value of ABC Company (market value of assets minus market value of liabilities), assuming that the government yield curve is the appropriate yield curve for discounting all of the company's assets and liabilities?

d. By what percent does the market value change if the continuous yield to maturity on each of the zero coupon bond prices quoted above shifts (1) up by 1 percent, (2) down by 1 percent?

REFERENCES

The First Boston Corporation. *Handbook of Securities of the United States Government and Federal Agencies and Related Money Market Instruments.* New York: The First Boston Corporation, 1984.

Lynch, John J., Jr., and Jan H. Mayle. *Standard Securities Calculation Methods: Fixed Income Securities Formulas.* New York: Securities Industry Association, 1986.

Stigum, Marcia. *Money Market Calculations: Yields, Break-evens, and Arbitrage.* Homewood, IL: Dow Jones–Irwin, 1981.

CHAPTER 2

Yield Curve Smoothing[1]

In Chapter 1, the basics of present value, forward rates, and interest rate compounding were discussed on the assumption that the present value of $1 to be paid at various times in the future was known with certainty. The examples and exercises provided these "discount factors," or zero coupon bond prices. Chapter 2 is devoted to yield curve smoothing, the technique used for extracting discount factors, forward rates, and zero coupon bond yields from observable market data with different maturities than the maturities needed for analysis. In a recent article, Adams and van Deventer (1994) introduced a mathematical measure of smoothness, often used in engineering applications, as an objective criterion for choosing among various yield curve smoothing techniques. In that article the authors show that the yield curve with the smoothest possible forward rate function, consistent with observable data, is closely related to, but significantly different from, the popular cubic spline approach to the smoothing of both yields and discount bond prices. The yield curve that produces the smoothest possible forward rates consistent with given zero coupon bond prices has a quartic forward rate function that spans each time interval between observable data points. This contrasts

1. We are grateful for the enormously helpful comments and insights of Oldrich Vasicek, Robert Jarrow, Volf Frishling, and Kenneth Adams on this chapter.

with the cubic polynomial used to fit either yields or discount bond prices in the cubic spline approach. In this chapter, we show how to apply the maximum smoothness forward rate approach to coupon-bearing bond price data and illustrate its use on a sample set of data. We compare the solution process to that for cubic splines, noting that cubic spline smoothing produces forward rate curves that are not "smooth" in that they have discontinuous second derivatives when using the conventional implementation of the spline approach. We also present a restated proof of the maximum smoothness forward rate formula.

We begin by reviewing the cubic spline approach to yield curve smoothing in Sections 2.1 and 2.2. In Section 2.3, we introduce the maximum smoothness forward rate approach and discuss the alternative implementations of this technique. We then go on to show how the maximum smoothness forward rate technique is applied to coupon-bearing bond data in Section 2.4. Section 2.5 concludes the chapter. Appendix A contains a restated proof of the maximum smoothness forward rate approach.

2.1 CUBIC SPLINE YIELD SMOOTHING

Cubic splines have historically been the method preferred for yield curve smoothing. In spite of the popularity of the cubic spline approach, market participants have often relied on linear yield curve smoothing as a technique that is especially easy to implement; its limitations, however, are well known:

- Linear yield curves are continuous but not smooth; at each knot point there is a kink in the yield curve.
- Forward rate curves associated with linear yield curves are linear and discontinuous at the knot points. This means that linear yield curve smoothing sometimes cannot be used with the Heath, Jarrow, and Morton (1992) term structure model (which we cover in later chapters), since it usually assumes the existence of a continuous forward rate curve.
- Estimates for the parameters associated with popular term structure models like the extended Vasicek (1977) or Cox, Ingersoll, and Ross (1985) models are unreliable because the structure of the yield curve is unrealistic. The shape of the yield curve, because of its linearity, is

fundamentally incompatible with an academically sound term structure model, so resulting parameter estimates are often implausible.

The cubic spline approach, first applied to yield curve smoothing by McCulloch (1975), was designed to address the first of these concerns.

In the following sections, we show how to use the smoothing methods mentioned above in an example where we are given data at time zero, one year, and two years on either (*a*) the simple interest yield on zero coupon bonds, (*b*) the continuous yield on zero coupon bonds, or (*c*) the zero coupon bond price. We assume that simple interest yields are the following:

Instantaneous interest rate	6.00%
One-year interest rate	5.25%
Two-year interest rate (annually compounded)	4.00%

Exhibit 2–1 summarizes the equivalent continuously compounded yields and zero coupon bond prices that are consistent with this data and that are used in subsequent sections. In Section 2.4, we use the same data to calculate the maximum smoothness forward rate curve on the alternative assumption that the input data in Exhibit 2–1 represent the coupons on semiannual payment bonds trading at par. Exhibit 2–2 gives the results of the calculations for linear yield curve smoothing when we model the yield *y* as the following linear function:

$$y(t) = a_i + b_i t \text{ for } i = 1,2 \text{ with } t_{i-1} \le t \le t_i.$$

E X H I B I T   2-1

Examples of Various Smoothing Calculations
Base Case Assumptions

Period	Simple Interest	Continuous Yield	Discount Bond Price
0	6	0.060000	1.000000
1	5.25	0.051168	0.950119
2	4	0.039221	0.924556

EXHIBIT 2-2

Linear Smoothing

General form: $y = a + b\,t$

		Coefficients in Equation				
Constraint	Time	a1	b1	a2	b2	Constant
Time 0: Must equal actual	0	1	0	0	0	0.06
Time 1: Must equal actual	1	1	1	0	0	0.051168
Time 1: Must equal actual	1	0	0	1	1	0.051168
Time 2: Must equal actual	2	0	0	1	2	0.039221

Inverse Matrix

				Answers
1	0	0	0	0.06
−1	1	0	0	−0.00883
0	0	2	−1	0.063116
0	0	−1	1	−0.01195

	a1	b1	a2	b2
Calculated coefficients	0.06	−0.00883	0.063116	−0.01195

Check on Constraints

	Constraint Value	Calculated Value	Difference
Time 0: Must equal actual	0.06	0.06	0
Time 1: Must equal actual	0.051168	0.051168	0
Time 1: Must equal actual	0.051168	0.051168	0
Time 2: Must equal actual	0.039221	0.039221	0

In the linear smoothing case, there are four constraints that must be met. The yield curve is broken into segment 1 and segment 2. Segment 1 spans maturities from time 0 to year 1. Segment 2 spans the maturities from time 1 to time 2. The four constraints require that the two segments equal the actual data. The results produce a yield curve such that $y = .06 - .00883t$ during the first segment and $y = .063116 - .01195t$ during the second segment. These results are produced by solving the four equations in four unknowns using matrix inversion. This can be done in simple spreadsheet software.

The Mathematical Rationale for the Cubic Polynomial

The choice of the cubic polynomial for smoothing is not arbitrary. It can be proved mathematically that there is no smoother function (see Schwartz, 1989), of any functional form, that fits the observable data points and is continuous and twice differential at the knot points than a cubic spline. Smoothness is defined mathematically as the value Z given by the formula

$$Z = \int_0^T [f''(s)]^2 ds$$

where the function f is the function used to smooth the observable data. If Z is 0, then the line is perfectly smooth. Function 1 is more smooth than function 2 if Z is less for function 1 than it is for function 2. If the objective of the analyst is the smoothest possible yield curve, then the cubic spline of yields produces the smoothest yield curve. If the objective of the analyst is the smoothest possible discount bond price function, then a cubic spline of zero coupon bond prices produces the smoothest curve. Any other functional form, given these objectives, is inferior to cubic splines by the smoothness criterion. For more on smoothness, see Adams and van Deventer (1994).

Using Cubic Spline Smoothing to Smooth Yields: A Review

Assume that we are given zero coupon bond yields $y_0, y_1, y_2, \ldots,$ y_n consistent with maturities $t_0, t_1, t_2, \ldots, t_n$. We assume without loss of generality that t_0 is 0. We fit the function

$$y_i(t) = a_i + b_i t + c_i t^2 + d_i t^3$$

to the interval between t_i and t_{i-1}. Therefore, we have $4n$ unknowns to solve for, since we need to know a, b, c, and d for all n intervals between the $n + 1$ data points. In order to solve for all of these a, b, c, and d values, we make use of the fact that these equations must fit the observable data points, that the first derivatives be equal at the $n - 1$ knot points t_1, t_2, t_3, . . . , t_{n-1}, and that the second derivatives must also be equal at the knot points. We have the following equations, which constrain the values of a, b, c, and d:

n equations requiring that the cubic polynomials fit the n data points t_1, t_2, . . . , t_n

$$y(t_i) = a_i + b_i t_i + c_i t_i^2 + d_i t_i^3$$

for i from 1 to n.

n equations requring that the cubic polynomials fit the n data points t_0, t_1, t_2, . . . , t_{n-1}

$$y(t_{i-1}) = a_i + b_i t_{t-1} + c_i t_{t-1}^2 + d_i t_{i-1}^3$$

for i from 1 to n.

$n - 1$ equations requiring that the first derivatives of the cubic polynomials on each side of the knot points be equal

$$b_i + 2c_i t_i + 3d_i t_i^2 - b_{i+1} - 2c_{i+1} t_i - 3d_{i+1} t_i^2 = 0$$

for i from 1 to $n - 1$.

$n - 1$ equations requiring that the second derivatives of the cubic polynomials on each side of the knot points be equal

$$2c_i + 6d_i t_i - 2c_{i+1} - 6d_{i+1} t_i = 0$$

for i from 1 to $n - 1$.

This gives us $4n - 2$ equations to solve for $4n$ unknowns. We need two more equations to complete the system. The first equation is usually chosen such that the yield curve is instantaneously straight $[(y''(0) = 0)]$ at the left-hand side of the yield curve:

$$2c_1 + 6d_1t_0 = 0$$

The right-hand side, or long end, of the yield curve offers the opportunity to impose another constraint. There are two common choices: Either the yield curve can be set to be flat $(y' = 0)$ or the yield curve can be set to be instantaneously straight $(y'' = 0)$ at the longest maturity. We select one of the following equations to complete the system: Either

$$b_n + 2c_nt_n + 3d_nt_n^2 = 0$$

or

$$2c_n + 6d_nt_n = 0$$

This gives us $4n$ equations and $4n$ unknowns, and all of the equations are linear in the unknowns. We can solve this set of linear equations simply by using matrix inversion, which can be done in spreadsheet software or more complex software implementations.

Problems with Cubic Splines of Yields

To summarize the problems with the cubic splines of yields, we need to recall that at each knot point we have set yields and the first two derivatives with respect to yields equal for each polynomial meeting at a given knot point:

$$y_i(t_i) = y_{i+1}(t_i)$$
$$y'_i(t_i) = y'_{i+1}(t_i)$$
$$y''_i(t_i) = y''_{i+1}(t_i)$$

In continuous time, the continuous forward rate $f(t)$ can be written as

$$f(t) = y(t) + ty'(t)$$

We can write the derivatives of f in terms of the derivatives of y as follows:

$$f'(t) = 2y' + ty''$$
$$f''(t) = 3y'' + ty'''$$

At the knot points, this means that

$$f_i(t_i) = f_{i+1}(t_i)$$
$$f'_i(t_i) = f'_{i+1}(t_i)$$
$$f''_i(t_i) \neq f''_{i+1}(t_i)$$

The second derivative of the forward rate curve will *not* be equal at the knot points since we have not constrained y''', the third derivative of the yield curve, to be equal at the knot points. This leads to the two principal problems associated with the use of cubic yield (or price) splines:

- The forward rate curve is not twice differentiable at the knot points, so it is not "smooth." The first derivative of the forward rate curve will have a kink in it at each knot point.
- In addition, the forward rate curves associated with a cubic spline–based yield curve tend to be volatile, particularly on the right-hand side of the yield curve, to such a degree that their use can lead to implausible forward rate curves.

For these reasons, the maximum smoothness forward rate approach offers a number of advantages.

Examples of the Use of the Cubic Yield Spline

In order to make use of the results of any yield curve smoothing method, we have to be familiar with the continuous time links between zero coupon bond prices, continuously compounded yields on zero coupon bond prices (i.e., continuous yields), and continuous forward rates.

In Chapter 1, we showed that a zero coupon bond price can be calculated from its maturity and its continuously compounded yield to maturity from the equation

$$P(\tau) = e^{-\tau y(\tau)}$$

The definition of a continuous forward rate is minus the percentage change in zero coupon bond prices for an infinitely small change in years to maturity, as given by the following formula:

$$f[\tau] = -\frac{\dfrac{\partial P[\tau]}{\partial \tau}}{P[\tau]}$$

Since P can be written as a function of time to maturity, so can the forward rate:

$$f[\tau] = -\frac{\dfrac{\partial P[\tau]}{\partial \tau}}{P[\tau]}$$

$$= -\frac{\dfrac{\partial (e^{-\tau y[\tau]})}{\partial \tau}}{P[\tau]}$$

$$= y[\tau] + \tau y'[\tau]$$

Finally, it can be shown that P can be written as a function of forward rates alone:

$$P[\tau] = e^{-\int_0^\tau f[s]ds}$$

We can use these relationships to derive useful information from a cubic spline of yields. If a cubic spline of yields has been calculated, then the continuous yield at any point in time is given by a cubic polynomial:

$$y[\tau] = a + b\tau + c\tau^2 + d\tau^3$$

That means zero coupon bond prices can be calculated using the formulas above:

$$P[\tau] = e^{-a\tau - b\tau^2 - c\tau^3 - d\tau^4}$$

Finally, continuous forward rates can be written as follows:

$$f[\tau] = y + \tau y'$$

$$= a + b\tau + c\tau^2 + d\tau^3 + \tau(b + 2c\tau + 3d\tau^2)$$

$$= a + 2b\tau + 3c\tau^2 + 4d\tau^3$$

We can apply these formulas to a concrete example.

Example 2.1.1
Assume that a cubic yield spline has been fitted to real data and that the cubic polynomial for the continuous yield y is such that $y(t) = .05 + .001t + .0002t^2 + .00001t^3$. Solving for the continuous yields at annual maturities gives the following values:

Maturity	Continuous Yield
5	6.1250%
6	6.5360%
7	7.0230%
8	7.5920%
9	8.2490%
10	9.0000%

Example 2.1.2
Using the same cubic polynomial for the continuous yield y in Example 2.1.1, we can derive zero coupon bond prices as follows:

Maturity	Zero Coupon Bond Price
5	0.73620
6	0.67560
7	0.61164
8	0.54479
9	0.47597
10	0.40657

Note that, from the zero coupon bond prices that are derived from the cubic yield spline, all of the calculations given in Chapter 1 can be done successfully.

Example 2.1.3
Using the cubic polynomial for the continuous yield y from Example 2.1.1, the continuous forward rates at each annual maturity are derived by substituting the appropriate time to maturity in the formula for continuous forward rates given above:

Maturity	Continuous Forward Rates
5	8.0000%
6	9.2240%
7	10.7120%
8	12.4880%
9	14.5760%
10	17.0000%

Example 2.1.4
As on p. 43, assume that we are given the following interest rates as input:

Instantaneous interest rate	6.00%
One-year interest rate	5.25%
Two-year interest rate (annually compounded)	4.00%

Fit a cubic yield spline to this data.

Exhibit 2–3 provides the coefficients a, b, c, and d, using cubic yield smoothing with the yield curve held flat at the right-hand side of the curve.

Solving the eight equations in eight unknowns in Exhibit 2–3 results in the two cubic polynomials with the coefficients $a1$, $b1$, $c1$, and $d1$ for segment 1, from time 0 to time 1, and with coefficients $a2$, $b2$, $c2$, and $d2$ for segment 2, from year 1 to year 2.

Exhibit 2–4 shows that if we try to force the second derivative of the forward rate function f'' to be equal at each knot point, cubic yield smoothing reduces to a simple cubic function where a, b, c, and d are equal for each line segment.

Exhibit 2–5 shows the parameters for the case when the right-hand side of the yield curve is held instantaneously straight, $y'' = 0$.

EXHIBIT 2-3

Cubic Yield Spline Smoothing
Right-Hand Side Contraint: $y' = 0$

		Coefficients of Equations								Equation Value
	Time	a1	b1	c1	d1	a2	b2	c2	d2	
Time 0: Must equal actual	0	1	0	0	0	0	0	0	0	0.06
Time 1: Must equal actual	1	1	1	1	1	0	0	0	0	0.051168
Time 1: Must equal actual	1	0	0	0	0	1	1	1	1	0.051168
Time 2: Must equal actual	2	0	0	0	0	1	2	4	8	0.039221
Equal first derivatives at T1	1	0	1	2	3	0	-1	-2	-3	0
Equal second derivatives at T1	1	0	0	2	6	0	0	-2	-6	0
Left-hand side constraint: $y'' = 0$	0	0	0	2	0	0	0	0	0	0
Right-hand side constraint: $y' = 0$	2	0	0	0	0	0	1	4	12	0

Inverse of Matrix										Answer
	1	1	0	0	0	0	0	0	0	0.06
	2	-1.28571	1.285714	0.428571	-0.42857	-0.28571	-0.07143	-0.28571	0.142857	-0.00623
	3	0	0	0	0	0	0	0.5	0	0
	4	0.285714	-0.28571	-0.42857	0.428571	0.285714	0.071429	-0.21429	-0.14286	-0.0026
	5	1.714286	-1.71429	-0.57143	1.571429	1.714286	-0.57143	-0.28571	-0.85714	0.047534
	6	-3.42857	3.428571	5.142857	-5.14286	-3.42857	1.142857	0.571429	2.714286	0.031165
	7	2.142857	-2.14286	-4.71429	4.714286	2.142857	-0.71429	-0.35714	-2.57143	-0.0374
	8	-0.42857	0.428571	1.142857	-1.14286	-0.42857	0.142857	0.071429	0.714286	0.009869

EXHIBIT 2-3

(continued)

Coefficient	a1	b1	c1	d1	a2	b2	c2	d2
Calculated Value	0.060000	−0.006235	0.000000	−0.002597	0.047534	0.031165	−0.037399	0.009869

Constraint	Constraint Value	Calculated Value	Difference
Time 0: Must equal actual	0.06	0.060000	0.00
Time 1: Must equal actual	0.051168	0.051168	0.00
Time 1: Must equal actual	0.051168	0.051168	0.00
Time 2: Must equal actual	0.039221	0.039221	0.00
Equal first derivatives at T1	0	0.000000	0.00
Equal second derivatives at T1	0	0.000000	0.00
Left-hand side constraint: $y'' = 0$	0	0.000000	0.00
Right-hand side constraint: $y' = 0$	0	0.000000	0.00

EXHIBIT 2-4

Cubic Yield Spline Smoothing
Right-Hand Side Constraint: $y' = 0$ and f'' equal

					Coefficients of Equations					Equation Value
Time	a1	b1	c1	d1	a2	b2	c2	d2		
Time 0: Must equal actual — 0	1	0	0	0	0	0	0	0		0.06
Time 1: Must equal actual — 1	1	1	1	1	0	0	0	0		0.051168
Time 1: Must equal actual — 1	0	0	0	0	1	1	1	1		0.051168
Time 2: Must equal actual — 2	0	0	0	0	1	2	4	8		0.039221
Equal first derivatives at T1 — 1	0	1	2	3	0	-1	-2	-3		0
Equal second derivatives at T1 — 1	0	0	2	6	0	0	-2	-6		0
Equal f'' at T1 — 1	0	0	6	24	0	0	-6	-24		0
Right-hand side constraint: $y' = 0$ — 2	0	0	0	0	0	1	4	12		0

Inverse of Matrix

	a1	b1	c1	d1	a2	b2	c2	d2	Answer
1	1	0	0	0	0	0	0	0	0.06
2	-2	2	2	-2	-1	-0.5	0.166667	1	0.006232
3	1.25	-1.25	-2.75	2.75	1.25	0.75	-0.29167	-1.5	-0.02182
4	-0.25	0.25	0.75	-0.75	-0.25	-0.25	0.125	0.5	0.006753
5	1	-1	1	0	1	-1	0.166667	0	0.06
6	-2	2	2	-2	-2	2	-0.33333	1	0.006232
7	1.25	-1.25	-2.75	2.75	1.25	-1.25	0.208333	-1.5	-0.02182
8	-0.25	0.25	0.75	-0.75	-0.25	0.25	-0.04167	0.5	0.006753

EXHIBIT 2-4

(continued)

Coefficient	a1	b1	c1	d1	a2	b2	c2	d2
Calculated Value	0.060000	0.006232	-0.021816	0.006753	0.060000	0.006232	-0.021816	0.006753

Constraint	Constraint Value	Calculated Value	Difference
Time 0: Must equal actual	0.06	0.060000	0.00
Time 1: Must equal actual	0.051168	0.051168	0.00
Time 1: Must equal actual	0.051168	0.051168	0.00
Time 2: Must equal actual	0.039221	0.039221	0.00
Equal first derivatives at T_1	0	0.000000	0.00
Equal second derivatives at T_1	0	0.000000	0.00
Equal f'' at T_1	0	0.000000	0.00
Right-hand side constraint: $y' = 0$	0	0.000000	0.00

EXHIBIT 2-5

Cubic Yield Spline Smoothing
Right-Hand Side Constraint: $y'' = 0$

Coefficients of Equations

	Time	a1	b1	c1	d1	a2	b2	c2	d2	Equation Value
Time 0: Must equal actual	0	1	0	0	0	0	0	0	0	0.06
Time 1: Must equal actual	1	1	1	1	1	0	0	0	0	0.051168
Time 1: Must equal actual	1	0	0	0	0	1	1	1	1	0.051168
Time 2: Must equal actual	2	0	0	0	0	1	2	4	8	0.039221
Equal first derivatives at T1	1	0	1	2	3	0	-1	-2	-3	0
Equal second derivatives at T1	1	0	0	2	6	0	0	-2	-6	0
Left-hand side constraint: $y'' = 0$	0	0	0	2	0	0	0	0	0	0
Right-hand side constraint: $y'' = 0$	2	0	0	0	0	0	0	2	12	0

Inverse of Matrix

	a1	b1	c1	d1	a2	b2	c2	d2	Answer
1	1	0	0	0	0	0	0	0	0.06
2	-1.25	1.25	0.25	-0.25	-0.25	-0.08333	-0.29167	0.041667	-0.00805
3	0	0	0	0	0	0	0.5	0	0
4	0.25	-0.25	-0.25	0.25	0.25	0.083333	-0.20833	-0.04167	-0.00078
5	1.5	-1.5	0.5	0.5	1.5	-0.5	-0.25	-0.25	0.058442
6	-2.75	2.75	1.75	-1.75	-2.75	0.916667	0.458333	0.791667	-0.00338
7	1.5	-1.5	-1.5	1.5	1.5	-0.5	-0.25	-0.75	-0.00467
8	-0.25	0.25	0.25	-0.25	-0.25	0.083333	0.041667	0.208333	0.000779

EXHIBIT 2-5

(continued)

Coefficient	a_1	b_1	c_1	d_1	a_2	b_2	c_2	d_2
Calculated Value	0.060000	-0.008053	0.000000	-0.000779	0.058442	-0.003379	-0.004674	0.000779

Constraint	Constraint Value	Calculated Value	Difference
Time 0: Must equal actual	0.06	0.060000	0.00
Time 1: Must equal actual	0.051168	0.051168	0.00
Time 1: Must equal actual	0.051168	0.051168	0.00
Time 2: Must equal actual	0.039221	0.039221	0.00
Equal first derivatives at T_1	0	0.000000	0.00
Equal second derivatives at T_1	0	0.000000	0.00
Left-hand side constraint: $y'' = 0$	0	0.000000	0.00
Right-hand side constraint: $y'' = 0$	0	0.000000	0.00

2.2 CUBIC SPLINE PRICE SMOOTHING

The same basic approach to the smoothing of yield curves applies to the smoothing of zero coupon bond prices, from which
smooth yield curves can be derived. The basic steps follow in
parallel fashion from the yield smoothing case.

Using Cubic Spline Smoothing to Smooth
Zero Coupon Bond Prices

Assume that we are given zero coupon bond prices $P[t_0]$, $P[t_1]$,
$P[t_2]$, . . . , $P[t_n]$ consistent with maturities t_0, t_1, t_2, . . . , t_n. We assume without loss of generality that t_0 is 0. We fit the function

$$P_i(t) = a_i + b_i t + c_i t^2 + d_i t^3$$

to the interval between t_i and t_{i-1}. Therefore we have $4n$ unknowns
to solve for, since we need to know a, b, c, and d for all n intervals
between the $n + 1$ data points, as in the yield curve smoothing
case. In order to solve for all of these a, b, c, and d values, we make
use of the fact that these equations must fit the observable data
points, that the first derivatives be equal at the $n - 1$ knot points
t_1, t_2, t_3, . . . , t_{n-1}, and that the second derivatives also be equal at
the knot points. We have the following equations that constrain
the values of a, b, c, and d:

n equations requiring that the cubic polynomials fit the
n data points t_1, t_2, . . . , t_n

$$P(t_i) = a_i + b_i t_i + c_i t_i^2 + d_i t_i^3$$

for i from 1 to n.

n equations requiring that the cubic polynomials fit the
n data points t_0, t_1, t_2, . . . , t_{n-1}

$$P(t_{i-1}) = a_i + b_i t_{t-1} + c_i t_{t-1}^2 + d_i t_{i-1}^3$$

for i from 1 to n.

$n - 1$ equations requiring that the first derivatives of the cubic
polynomials on each side of the knot points be equal

$$b_i + 2c_i t_i + 3d_i t_i^2 - b_{i+1} - 2c_{i+1} t_i - 3d_{i+1} t_i^2 = 0$$

for i from 1 to $n - 1$.

$n - 1$ equations requiring that the second derivatives of the cubic polynomials on each side of the knot points be equal

$$2c_i + 6d_i t_i - 2c_{i+1} - 6d_{i+1}t_i = 0$$

for i from 1 to $n - 1$.

This gives us $4n - 2$ equations to solve for $4n$ unknowns as in the yield smoothing case. We again need two more equations to complete the system. Unlike the yield case, however, constraining the right-hand side of the zero coupon price curve has to be examined with great care to make sure that the assumptions have economic meaning. For example, in the yield case, we constrained the first derivative of the smoothed curve such that $y' = 0$ at the far right-hand side of the yield curve. The parallel constraint, requiring $P' = 0$ at the right-hand side of the curve, has some powerful and harmful implications. The continuous forward rate consistent with the smoothed price curve can be written

$$f(t) = \frac{-\dfrac{\partial P(t)}{\partial t}}{P(t)}$$

Therefore, an assumption that P' is 0 is equivalent to assuming that the forward rate is 0 at that point on the curve. We have to reject this assumption as a candidate for one of our two remaining constraints.

As in the yield smoothing case, the first equation is usually chosen such that the yield at time 0 equals an observable short rate $y(0)$. In order to do so, we note that

$$f(t) = \frac{-P'(t)}{P(t)} = -\frac{b + 2ct + 3dt^2}{P(t)}$$

At time zero, $P = 1$ and $f(0) = y(0)$, so this constraint becomes

$$-b_1 = y(0)$$

There are two common choices for the constraint affecting the right-hand side of the yield curve; either the yield curve can be set to be flat ($y' = 0$) or the price curve can be set to be instantaneously straight ($P'' = 0$) at the longest maturity. The first of these two possible constraints can be derived from the fact that

$$y(t) = \frac{-1}{t}\ln[P(t)]$$

and

$$y'(t) = \frac{1}{t^2}\ln[P] - \frac{1}{tP}\left(b + 2ct + 3dt^2\right)$$

If y' is set to zero at the right-hand side of the yield curve, then this constraint can be written as

$$\ln[P(t_n)] = -\frac{t_n}{P(t_n)}\left(b + 2ct_n + 3dt_n^2\right)$$

after multiplying both sides by t to the second power. P is a constant at the right-hand side of the yield curve, so this equation remains a linear equation in the parameters a, b, c, and d.

The other candidate for selection is the following equation, which constrains the second derivative $P'' = 0$ at the right-hand side of the curve:

$$2c_n + 6d_nt_n = 0$$

As in the yield smoothing case, we can solve this system of $4n$ equations in $4n$ unknowns using matrix inversion and spreadsheet software.

Problems with Cubic Splines of Prices

The problems with cubic splines of the zero coupon price curve are the same as those resulting from the cubic spline of yield curves:

- The forward rate curve is not twice differentiable; the second derivative of the forward rate is discontinuous at the knot points, since we did not constrain the third derivative of the price functions to be continuous and the second derivative of the forward rate function depends on the third derivative of the price function:

$$f(t) = \frac{-P'(t)}{P(t)}$$

$$f'(t) = \frac{-P''(t)}{P(t)} + \frac{P'(t)^2}{P(t)^2}$$

$$f''(t) = \frac{-P'''(t)}{P(t)} + \frac{3P'(t)P''(t)}{P(t)^2} - \frac{2P'(t)^3}{P(t)^3}$$

- Forward rate curves can be implausibly volatile, particularly on the right-hand side of the yield curve.

Examples of the Use of the Cubic Price Spline

We can use the continuous time linkages between zero coupon bond prices, continuous yields, and continuous forward rates just as we did in Section 2.1 to derive practical calculations from the cubic price splines above. Assume that for the cubic polynomial that spans years 5 to 10, the zero coupon bond price is given by the polynomial $P(t) = 1.00 - .03t - .00001t^2 - .00001t^3$. We also need to make use of the fact that

$$f[\tau] = -\frac{\frac{\partial P[\tau]}{\partial \tau}}{P[\tau]}$$

so f can be calculated from the cubic price spline using the following relationship:

$$f[\tau] = \frac{-b - 2c\tau - 3d\tau^2}{a + b\tau + c\tau^2 + d\tau^3}$$

The continuous yield can be derived from the fact that

$$y[\tau] = -\frac{1}{\tau}\ln[P(\tau)]$$

Example 2.2.1
What are the zero coupon prices for maturities at 5, 6, 7, 8, 9, and 10 years? We get the answer by substituting the proper value for t in the equation for $P(t)$ above.

Maturity	Zero Coupon Bond Price
5	0.84850
6	0.81748
7	0.78608
8	0.75424
9	0.72190
10	0.68900

Example 2.2.2

What are the continuous zero coupon bond yields for the same maturities as in Example 2.2.1? We make use of the equation on page 61, linking continuous yields and zero coupon bond prices to derive the following:

Maturity	Continuous Yield
5	3.2857%
6	3.3588%
7	3.4385%
8	3.5256%
9	3.6208%
10	3.7251%

Example 2.2.3

What are the continuous forward rates at points 5, 6, 7, 8, 9, and 10 years on the yield curve? The answer is determined by the relationship given above between forward rates and zero coupon bond prices.

Maturity	Continuous Forward Rates
5	3.6358%
6	3.8166%
7	4.0212%
8	4.2533%
9	4.5172%
10	4.8186%

Example 2.2.4

As in Section 2.1, assume that we are given the following interest rates as input:

Instantaneous interest rate	6.00%
One-year interest rate	5.25%
Two-year interest rate (annually compounded)	4.00%

Fit a cubic price spline to this data.

Exhibit 2–6 gives a, b, c, and d for the cubic price smoothing case where the price curve is held instantaneously straight ($P'' = 0$) at the right-hand side of the yield curve.

Exhibit 2–7 shows the results for the cubic price spline calculated such that yields on the far right-hand side of the curve are held flat ($y' = 0$).

2.3 MAXIMUM SMOOTHNESS FORWARD RATES

Adams and van Deventer (1994) attempt to remedy the two problems of cubic spline smoothing with a new approach that addresses both problems directly:

- They seek to derive a forward rate curve that is continuous and twice differentiable.
- They derive the curve in such a way that the forward rate curve is the smoothest curve of any of the family of curves that are continuous, twice differentiable, and consistent with the observable data.

Again, we assume that there are n observable data points t_1, t_2, t_3, . . . , t_n and n observable zero coupon bond prices $P[t_1]$, . . . , $P[t_n]$.

Deriving Maximum Smoothness Forward Rates

Adams and van Deventer (1994) show that the smoothest possible forward rate curve consists of a quartic forward rate function that is fitted between each knot point. The conclusions regarding the maximum smoothness forward rate curve can be summarized in the following theorem:[2]

---

2. This theorem, contributed by Oldrich Vasicek, is a restated version of the theorem in Adams and van Deventer (1994).

EXHIBIT 2–6

Cubic Price Spline Smoothing
Right-Hand Side Constraint: $p'' = 0$

Coefficients of Equations

	Time	a1	b1	c1	d1	a2	b2	c2	d2	Equation Value
Time 0: Must equal actual	0	1	0	0	0	0	0	0	0	1
Time 1: Must equal actual	1	1	1	1	1	0	0	0	0	0.950119
Time 1: Must equal actual	1	0	0	0	0	1	1	1	1	0.950119
Time 2: Must equal actual	2	0	0	0	0	1	2	4	8	0.924556
Equal first derivatives at T1	1	0	1	2	3	0	-1	-2	-3	0
Equal second derivatives at T1	1	0	0	2	6	0	0	-2	-6	0
Left-hand side constraint: $f = y(0)$	0	0	-1	0	0	0	0	0	0	0.06
Right-hand side constraint: $p'' = 0$	2	0	0	0	0	0	0	2	12	0

Inverse of Matrix

									Answer
1	1	0	0	0	0	0	0	0	1
2	0	0	0	0	0	0	-1	0	-0.06
3	-2.14286	2.142857	0.428571	-0.42857	-0.42857	-0.14286	1.714286	0.071429	0.006924
4	1.142857	-1.14286	-0.42857	0.428571	0.428571	0.142857	-0.71429	-0.07143	0.003195
5	2.571429	-2.57143	0.285714	0.714286	1.714286	-0.42857	-0.85714	-0.28571	1.008697
6	-4.71429	4.714286	2.142857	-2.14286	-3.14286	0.785714	1.571429	0.857143	-0.08609
7	2.571429	-2.57143	-1.71429	1.714286	1.714286	-0.42857	-0.85714	-0.78571	0.033016
8	-0.42857	0.428571	0.285714	-0.28571	-0.28571	0.071429	0.142857	0.214286	-0.0055

(continued)

Coefficient	a1	b1	c1	d1	a2	b2	c2	d2
Calculated Value	1.000000	−0.060000	0.006924	0.003195	1.008697	−0.086092	0.033016	−0.005503

Constraint	Constraint Value	Calculated Value	Difference
Time 0: Must equal actual	1	1.000000	0.00
Time 1: Must equal actual	0.950119	0.950119	0.00
Time 1: Must equal actual	0.950119	0.950119	0.00
Time 2: Must equal actual	0.924556	0.924556	0.00
Equal first derivatives at T1	0	0.000000	0.00
Equal second derivatives at T1	0	0.000000	0.00
Left-hand side constraint: $y = y(0)$	0.06	0.060000	0.00
Right-hand side constraint: $p'' = 0$	0	0.000000	0.00

EXHIBIT 2-7

Cubic Price Spline Smoothing
Right-Hand Side Constraint: $y' = 0$

		Coefficients of Equations								Equation Value
	Time	a1	b1	c1	d1	a2	b2	c2	d2	
Time 0: Must equal actual	0	1	0	0	0	0	0	0	0	1
Time 1: Must equal actual	1	1	1	1	1	0	0	0	0	0.950119
Time 1: Must equal actual	1	0	0	0	0	1	1	1	1	0.950119
Time 2: Must equal actual	2	0	0	0	0	1	2	4	8	0.924556
Equal first derivatives at T1	1	0	1	2	3	0	−1	−2	−3	0
Equal second derivatives at T1	1	0	0	2	6	0	0	−2	−6	0
Left-hand side constraint: $f = y(0)$	0	0	−1	0	0	0	0	0	0	0.06
Right-hand side constraint: $y' = 0$	2	0	0	0	0	0	−2.1632	−8.6528	−25.9584	0.078441

Inverse of Matrix

	a1	b1	c1	d1	a2	b2	c2	d2	Answer
1	1	0	0	0	0	0	0	0	1
2	0	0	0	0	0	0	−1	0	−0.06
3	−2.25	2.25	0.75	−0.75	−0.5	−0.125	1.75	−0.11557	0.002874
4	1.25	−1.25	−0.75	0.75	0.5	0.125	−0.75	0.11557	0.007245
5	3	−3	−1	2	2	−0.5	−1	0.462278	1.024899
6	−6	6	6	−6	−4	1	2	−1.38683	−0.1347
7	3.75	−3.75	−5.25	5.25	2.5	−0.625	−1.25	1.271265	0.077571
8	−0.75	0.75	1.25	−1.25	−0.5	0.125	0.25	−0.34671	−0.01765

EXHIBIT 2-7

(continued)

Coefficient	a1	b1	c1	d1	a2	b2	c2	d2
Calculated Value	1.000000	-0.060000	0.002874	0.007245	1.024899	-0.134697	0.077571	-0.017654

Constraint	Constraint Value	Calculated Value	Difference
Time 0: Must equal actual	1	1.000000	0.00
Time 1: Must equal actual	0.950119	0.950119	0.00
Time 1: Must equal actual	0.950119	0.950119	0.00
Time 2: Must equal actual	0.924556	0.924556	0.00
Equal first derivatives at T1	0	0.000000	0.00
Equal second derivatives at T1	0	0.000000	0.00
Left-hand side constraint: $y = y(0)$	0.06	0.060000	0.00
Right-hand side constraint: $y' = 0$	0.078441	0.078441	0.00

Theorem. The term structure $f(t)$, $0 \leq t \leq T$, of forward rates that satisfies the maximum smoothness criterion

$$\min \int_0^T [f''(s)]^2 ds$$

while fitting the observed prices P_1, P_2, ..., P_m of zero coupon bonds with maturities t_1, t_2, ..., t_m is a fourth-order spline given by

$$f(t) = e_i t^4 + d_i t^3 + c_i t^2 + b_i t + a_i \quad \text{for } t_{i-1} < t \leq t_i, \; i = 1, 2, \ldots, m+1$$

where $\quad 0 = t_0 < t_1 < t_2 < \ldots < t_m < t_{m+1} = T$

The coefficients a_i, b_i, c_i, d_i, and e_i where $i = 1, 2, \ldots, m + 1$ satisfy the following equations

$$e_i t_i^4 + d_i t_i^3 + c_i t_i^2 + b_i t_i + a_i = e_{i+1} t_i^4 + d_{i+1} t_i^3 + c_{i+1} t_i^2 + b_{i+1} t_i + a_{i+1} \quad \text{for } i = 1,2,\ldots,m$$

$$4 e_i t_i^3 + 3 d_i t_i^2 + 2 c_i t_i + b_i = 4 e_{i+1} t_i^3 + 3 d_{i+1} t_i^2 + 2 c_{i+1} t_i + b_{i+1} \quad \text{for } i = 1,2,\ldots,m$$

$$12 e_i t_i^2 + 6 d_i t_i + 2 c_i = 12 e_{i+1} t_i^2 + 6 d_{i+1} t_i + 2 c_{i+1} \quad \text{for } i = 1,2,\ldots,m$$

$$24 e_i t_i + 6 d_i = 24 e_{i+1} t_i + 6 d_{i+1} \quad \text{for } i = 1,2,\ldots,m$$

$$\frac{1}{5} e_i \left(t_i^5 - t_{i-1}^5 \right) + \frac{1}{4} d_i \left(t_i^4 - t_{i-1}^4 \right) + \frac{1}{3} c_i \left(t_i^3 - t_{i-1}^3 \right) + \frac{1}{2} b_i \left(t_i^2 - t_{i-1}^2 \right) + a_i \left(t_i - t_{i-1} \right)$$

$$= -\log \left(\frac{P_i}{P_{i-1}} \right) \quad \text{for } i = 1,2,\ldots,m$$

The proof of this theorem is given in the appendix to this chapter.

Using the Maximum Smoothness Forward Rate Function in Practice

The use of the maximum smoothness forward rate function in practice is somewhat more complex than the use of the cubic spline approach because there is a larger number of parameters to be determined. In the case where we have n observable data points, we have $5n$ unknowns since we need to find a, b, c, d, and e for each of the n segments of the forward rate curve. We have the following constraints that are essential to ensure the reasonableness of the resulting forward rate, yield, and price curves:

$n - 1$ equations requiring that the forward rates be equal at each knot point

$$a_i + b_i t_i + c_i t_i^2 + d_i t_i^3 + e_i t_i^4 - a_{i+1} - b_{i+1} t_i - c_{i+1} t_i^2 - d_{i+1} t_i^3 - e_{i+1} t_i^4 = 0$$

at knot points for i from 1 to $n - 1$. We also have

$n - 1$ equations requiring that the first derivative of the forward rates be equal at each knot point

$$b_i + 2c_i t_i + 3d_i t_i^2 + 4e_i t_i^3 - b_{i+1} - 2c_{i+1} t_i - 3d_{i+1} t_i^2 - 4d_{i+1} t_i^3 = 0$$

at knot points for i from 1 to $n - 1$. Unlike the cubic yield smoothing case and the cubic price smoothing approach, we specifically require that the second derivatives of the forward rate curve be equal at each knot point to ensure that the curve is everywhere twice differentiable:

$n - 1$ equations requiring that the second derivative of the forward rate curve be equal at each knot point

$$2c_i + 6d_i t_i + 12e_i t_i^2 - 2c_{i+1} - 6d_{i+1} t_i - 12e_{i+1} t_i^2 = 0$$

$n - 1$ equations requiring that the third derivative of the forward rate curve be equal at each knot point

$$6d_i + 24e_i t_i - 6d_{i+1} - 24e_{i+1} t_i = 0$$

The next set of constraints comes from the fact that

$$P[t] = e^{-\int_0^t f(s)ds}$$

Since we are using a forward rate function broken into quartic segments and we have observable data, we can write

$$P[t_i] = P[t_{i-1}]e^{-\int_{t_{i-1}}^{t_i} f(s)\,ds}$$

Rearranging this equation and expressing it as a linear function of the parameters a, b, c, d, and e gives the next set of constraints:

n constraints that the forward rate curves be consistent with observable data

$$a_i(t_i - t_{i-1}) + \frac{b_i}{2}\left(t_i^2 - t_{i-1}^2\right) + \frac{c_i}{3}\left(t_i^3 - t_{i-1}^3\right) + \frac{d_i}{4}\left(t_i^4 - t_{i-1}^4\right) + \frac{e_i}{5}\left(t_i^5 - t_{i-1}^5\right)$$

$$= -\ln\left[\frac{P(t_i)}{P(t_{i-1})}\right]$$

for the n observable data points from $i = 1$ to n, noting that P for $t = t_0$ is 1.

So far, these constraints give us $4(n - 1) + n$ or $5n - 4$ equations. We require two other constraints of economic significance:

- That the forward rate curve be consistent with an observable short rate $y(0)$, or

$$a_1 = y(0) = f(0)$$

- That the slope[3] of the forward rate curve at the righthand side of the yield curve be zero (i.e., $f' = 0$):

$$b_n + 2c_n t_n + 3d_n t_n^2 + 4e_n t_n^3 = 0$$

We can complete the system of $5n$ equations in $5n$ unknowns by imposing the additional constraints that the forward rate curve be instantaneously straight at both the left-hand and right-hand side of the curve, so that

$$f''(t_0) = 2c_1 + 6d_1 t_0 + 12e_1 t_0^2 = 0$$

$$f''(t_n) = 2c_n + 6d_n t_n + 12e_n t_n^2 = 0$$

We can then solve for each of the n sets of a, b, c, d, and e using matrix inversion.

---

3. An imposition on the forward rate curve like the constraint that follows does have an impact on the level of smoothness. The resulting forward curve will be less smooth than one for which such a constraint had not been imposed.

Example of the Use of the Maximum Forward Rate Smoothing Approach

Adams and van Deventer (1994) report on the relative performance of maximum smoothness forward rate smoothing as a predictor of true market yields. Adams and van Deventer performed this test of the accuracy of the maximum smoothness approach in comparison with five other smoothing methods; they collected observable market data, left out one observable data point, and then estimated the missing data point using each smoothing method. This calculation was repeated over a large number of daily observations and the mean absolute error associated with each smoothing method was calculated. Over 660 days of data in the U.S. dollar swap market, Adams and van Deventer found the mean absolute pricing errors in estimating the true seven-year U.S. dollar swap rate as follows:

Maximum smoothness forward rate smoothing	0.0573%
Cubic price spline, $y'(10 \text{ years}) = 0$	0.0640%
Linear yield curve smoothing	0.0691%
Cubic price spline, $p''(10 \text{ years}) = 0$	0.0790%
Cubic yield spline, $y'(10 \text{ years}) = 0$	0.0851%
Cubic yield spline, $y''(10 \text{ years}) = 0$	0.0898%

In results for the yen market over 848 daily observations, the maximum smoothness forward rate approach again was the most successful:

Maximum smoothness forward rate smoothing	0.0111%
Linear yield curve smoothing	0.0166%
Cubic yield spline, $y''(10 \text{ years}) = 0$	0.0192%
Cubic yield spline, $y'(10 \text{ years}) = 0$	0.0198%
Cubic price spline, $p''(10 \text{ years}) = 0$	0.0208%
Cubic price spline, $y'(10 \text{ years}) = 0$	0.0418%

In general, the technique considerably outperforms spline and linear smoothing techniques in all of the varieties outlined above. For this reason, it remains the most appropriate technique for most practical applications.

For purposes of the next three examples, we will assume that the maximum smoothness forward rate curve has been fitted to observable data and that the forward rate curve has the form

$$f(t) = 0.04 + 0.0001t + 0.0001t^2 + 0.000005t^3 + 0.000001t^4$$

We also assume that the zero coupon bond price in year 5 is 0.79. When using the maximum smoothness forward rate approach, we need to express the zero coupon bond price as a function of the forward rate quartic polynomial

$$f(t) = a + bt + ct^2 + dt^3 + et^4$$

Since we fit a different forward rate quartic polynomial over each time interval between knot points, we have a different zero coupon price function between each set of knot points. For the interval between t_i and t_{i-1}, the zero coupon bond price function is

$$P[t] = P[t_{i-1}]e^{-\left[a_i(t-t_{i-1}) + \frac{b_i}{2}\left(t^2 - t_i^2\right) + \frac{c_i}{3}\left(t^3 - t_{i-1}^3\right)\right.}$$
$$\left. + \frac{d_i}{4}\left(t^4 - t_{i-1}^4\right) + \frac{e_i}{5}\left(t^5 - t_{i-1}^5\right)\right]$$

since

$$P[t] = P[t_{i-1}]\, e^{-\int_{t_{i-1}}^{t} f(s)ds}$$

The continuous yield y is written as a function of forward rates in the following manner:

$$y[t] = -\frac{1}{t}\left[\ln P[t_{i-1}] - \left(\begin{array}{c} a_i(t - t_i) + \frac{b_i}{2}\left(t^2 - t_{i-1}^2\right) + \frac{c_i}{3}\left(t^3 - t_{i-1}^3\right) \\ + \frac{d_i}{4}\left(t^4 - t_{i-1}^4\right) + \frac{e_i}{5}\left(t^5 - t_{i-1}^5\right) \end{array}\right)\right]$$

as shown in the appendix to this chapter.

Given these facts, we can derive the results in the three examples below and do any of the calculations in Chapter 1.

Example 2.3.1: Continuous Yields

The continuous yield at the points at 5, 6, 7, 8, 9, and 10 years is calculated using the expression above, inserting the proper values for a, b, c, d, and e for the 5- to 10-year interval on the yield curve.

Maturity	Continuous Yield
5	4.7144%
6	4.5988%
7	4.5291%
8	4.4996%
9	4.5114%
10	4.5697%

Example 2.3.2: Zero Coupon Bond Prices

Zero coupon bond prices can be calculated from the integral of the forward rate curve and the zero coupon bond price prevailing at the beginning of the relevant time interval.[4]

Maturity	Zero Coupon Bond Price
5	0.79000
6	0.75887
7	0.72831
8	0.69770
9	0.66629
10	0.63320

Example 2.3.3: Continuous Forward Rates

The continuous forward rates themselves are obtained directly from the quartic polynomial.

Maturity	Continuous Forward Rates
5	4.4250%
6	4.6576%
7	4.9716%
8	5.3856%
9	5.9206%
10	6.6000%

Note that all the calculations of Chapter 1 can be derived from a maximum smoothness forward rate function in a manner similar to the equations given above.

---

4. The zero coupon bond price prevailing at the beginning of the time interval is in turn calculated from the prior segments of the continuous forward rate curve.

Example 2.3.4
The advantages of the maximum smoothness approach are fairly apparent even using the simple example given above. Exhibit 2–8 shows how a, b, c, d, and e are calculated for the maximum smoothness forward rate method.

Exhibit 2–9 graphs the continuous yields for each of the smoothing methods, and Exhibit 2–10 graphs the forward rates.

The graph of forward rates highlights the differences between the various methods most clearly, showing the discontinuity of the linear forward rate curve at year 1 and the tendency of the cubic splines to bend sharply up or down at the right-hand side of the yield curve.

2.4 SMOOTHING COUPON-BEARING BOND DATA OR OTHER DATA

It is logical but incorrect to reach the conclusion that the techniques discussed above apply only to the smoothing of zero coupon bond yields or prices, since they are at the heart of the constraints imposed by each smoothing method. In reality, however, the same techniques can be used to create a smooth yield curve from almost any market data. In general, the process used in smoothing is as follows:

1. From observable market data (such as bond prices), select key maturity points.
2. Guess zero coupon bond prices for these key maturity points.
3. Smooth the yield curve by the desired method.
4. Calculate the implied values of the observable market data (i.e., a bond price).
5. If the implied price is within the desired tolerance of the actual price, then the yield curve smoothing process is completed.
6. If the implied price is not within the desired tolerance, then improve the guess of zero coupon bond prices and return to step 3. Repeat until within tolerance.

EXHIBIT 2-8

Maximum Smoothness Forward Rate Smoothing
Right-Hand Side Constraint: $f' = 0$

	Time					Coefficients of Equations						Equation Value
		a1	b1	c1	d1	e1	a2	b2	c2	d2	e2	
Time 0: Must equal actual $y(0)$	0	1	0	0	0	0	0	0	0	0	0	0.06
Time 1: Must equal actual $\ln[P(t1)/P(t0)]$	1	-1	-0.5	-0.33333	-0.25	-0.2	0	0	0	0	0	-0.05117
Time 2: Must equal actual $\ln[P(t2)/P(t1)]$	2	0	0	0	0	0	-1	-1.5	-2.33333	-3.75	-6.2	-0.02727
Equal first derivatives at T1	1	0	1	2	3	4	0	-1	-2	-3	-4	0
Equal second derivatives at T1	1	0	0	2	6	12	0	0	-2	-6	-12	0
Equal third derivatives at T1	1	0	0	0	6	24	0	0	0	-6	-24	0
Right-hand side constraint: $f' = 0$	2	0	0	0	0	0	0	1	4	12	32	0
Right-hand side constraint: $f'' = 0$	2	0	0	0	0	0	0	0	2	12	48	0
Left-hand side constraint: $f'' = 0$	0	0	1	0	0	0	0	0	0	0	0	0
Equal f at t1	1	1	1	1	1	1	-1	-1	-1	-1	-1	0

Inverse of Matrix

	a1	b1	c1	d1	e1	a2	b2	c2	d2	e2	Answer
1	1	0	0	0	0	0	0	0	0	0	0.060000
2	0	0	0	0	0	0	0	0	0	0	0.000000
3	-9.76744	-11.8605	2.093023	-0.48837	0.05814	0.040698	0.55814	-0.15116	-3.34884	-2.09302	-0.036250
4	12.32558	16.39535	-4.06977	0.866279	-0.1686	-0.09302	-1.1686	0.321705	3.261628	4.069767	0.011608
5	-4.12791	-5.72674	1.598837	-0.2689	0.113857	0.04845	0.530523	-0.15019	-0.99564	-1.59884	0.001748
6	6.813953	8.488372	-2.67442	1.290698	-0.71318	0.142442	-1.04651	0.387597	1.27907	1.674419	0.047442

EXHIBIT 2-8

(continued)

Inverse of Matrix

	a1	b1	c1	d1	e1	a2	b2	c2	d2	e2	Answer
7	−23.2558	−33.9535	10.69767	−2.16279	1.852713	−0.4031	4.186047	−1.55039	−4.11628	−10.6977	0.050234
8	25.11628	39.06977	−13.9535	1.255814	−1.72093	0.395349	−5.72093	2.174419	4.325581	13.95349	−0.111601
9	−10.9302	−17.5581	6.627907	−0.29651	0.684109	−0.16279	3.017442	−1.22868	−1.85465	−6.62791	0.061842
10	1.686047	2.761628	−1.07558	0.021802	−0.09932	0.024225	−0.51599	0.237403	0.28343	1.075581	−0.010810

Coefficient	a1	b1	c1	d1	e1	a2	b2	c2	d2	e2
Calculated Value	0.060000	0.000000	−0.036250	0.011608	0.001748	0.047442	0.050234	−0.111601	0.061842	−0.010810

Constraint	Constraint Value	Calculated Value	Difference
Time 0: Must equal actual $y(0)$	0.06	0.060000	0.00
Time 1: Must equal actual $\ln[P(t1)/P(t0)]$	−0.05117	−0.051168	0.00
Time 2: Must equal actual $\ln[P(t2)/P(t1)]$	−0.02727	−0.027273	0.00
Equal first derivatives at T1	0	0.000000	0.00
Equal second derivatives at T1	0	0.000000	0.00
Equal third derivatives at T1	0	0.000000	0.00
Right-hand side constraint: $f' = 0$	0	0.000000	0.00
Right-hand side constraint: $f'' = 0$	0	0.000000	0.00
Left-hand side constraint: $f'' = 0$	0	0.000000	0.00
Equal f at $t1$	0	0.000000	0.00

EXHIBIT 2–9

Continuous Yield Curves for Various Smoothing Methods

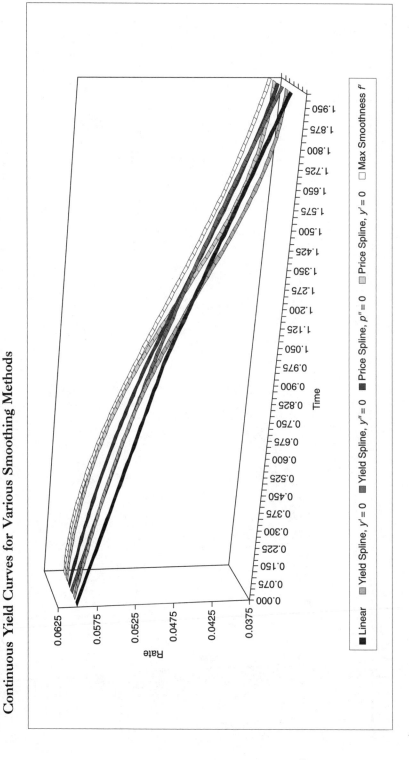

■ Linear ■ Yield Spline, $y' = 0$ ■ Yield Spline, $y'' = 0$ ■ Price Spline, $p'' = 0$ ■ Price Spline, $y' = 0$ □ Max Smoothness f'

EXHIBIT 2-10

Continuous Forward Rates for Various Yield Curve Smoothing Methods

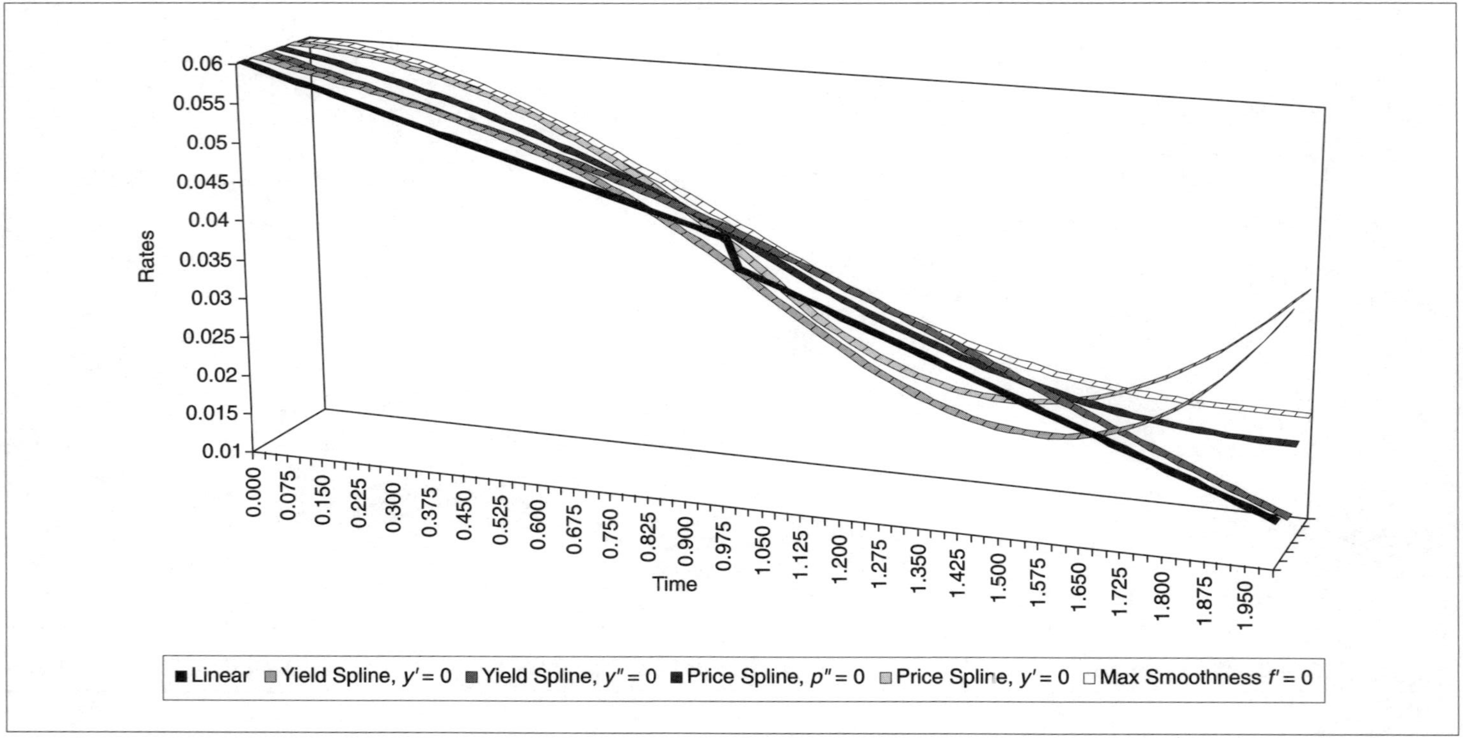

■ Linear ■ Yield Spline, $y' = 0$ ■ Yield Spline, $y'' = 0$ ■ Price Spline, $p'' = 0$ ■ Price Spline, $y' = 0$ □ Max Smoothness $f' = 0$

The heart of this iterative method is the step 6 improvement in the guess of zero coupon bond prices. Normally, the successive substitution method is very effective in providing an efficient convergence to actual market prices.[5]

The successive substitution method requires that the unknown parameters which need to be identified by iteration be expressed in a form as follows:

$$x_n = h(x_1, x_2, ..., x_n)$$

In this formula, x_n is the variable to be obtained by iteration. The initial guess for x_n is input to the function h and a new value of x_n is produced. If this new x_n differs by less than the desired tolerance from the old x_n, the process is complete. If not, the process is repeated.

We can change our assumptions about the example above to show how the maximum smoothness forward rate approach can be used on coupon-bearing bond data. Assume that the input data on yields (6 percent short rate, 5.25 percent one-year rate, and 4 percent two-year rate) represented coupon rates on new issue bonds issued at par with semiannual payments. The parameters of the forward rate function are not the directly targeted variables of the iteration process. It is more efficient to iterate on key zero coupon bond prices and smooth the results, iterating until we have a maximum smoothness forward rate curve for which bonds with the assumed coupons have a present value of par. Therefore, the direct inputs to the iteration process are the one-year and two-year zero coupon bond prices $P(1)$ and $P(2)$. There are many choices for possible specifications for the two equations necessary to use the successive substitution method. One such set of equations uses the present value of each bond

---

5. In practice, the successive substitution method provides difficulties in only one case: the use of the cubic yield spline on data with observations with a long time gap (say from 10 to 30-years), a long maturity (like 30 years), and high interest rates. As part of the iteration, negative 30 year zero coupon bond prices may result as part of an interim step in the calculation. With yields calculated as the log of prices, the iteration comes to a premature halt. This problem can be avoided in a number of ways.

$$V_i = \sum_{j=1}^{n_i} \frac{P(t_j)C_i}{2} + P(t_{n_i})100$$

which is simply the present value of the semiannual coupon payments $C_i/2$ and the ending principal, which we arbitrarily set at 100. Equations that produce fairly efficient solutions from the successive substitution method take the following form in this example:

$$P(1) = (100 - V_1)/100 + P(1)$$

$$P(2) = (100 - V_2)/100 + P(2)$$

Both equations are derived by adding the appropriate present value factor to both sides of the equation, which specifies that the present value of each bond should be 100. This completes step 1 of the smoothing process.

In step 2, we need a guess for the initial values of $P(1)$ and $P(2)$. A guess of high quality is the guess that $P(1)$ and $P(2)$ have the values that they would have if the 5.25 percent and 4 percent coupons were zero coupon bond yields. From our prior examples, this leads to initial guesses for $P(1)$ of .950119 and $P(2)$ of .924556.

Using these data as inputs, we smooth the yield curve, getting the a, b, c, d, and e parameters of Exhibit 2–8. We then calculate zero coupon bond prices for .5 years and 1.5 years and use them to calculate the V_i values: 100.0567 for the one-year bond and 100.0198 for the two-year bond. We input the $P(1)$ and $P(2)$ values and the V_i values into the right-hand side of the equations above to obtain new values for $P(1)$ and $P(2)$ of .950686 and .924358. We repeat this process for 5 iterations until the prices of the zero coupon bonds change by less than 0.0000001, leaving us with a smooth forward rate curve and present values for the one- and two-year bonds of 100.0000.

The same iterative approach can be used for all of the other yield curve smoothing techniques as well.

2.5 CONCLUSION

The maximum smoothness forward rate approach is a powerful technique for smoothing yield curves when the smoothness and continuity of the forward rate curve that results are important to the user. For most practical applications, these considerations are essential to obtaining a high-quality estimate of term structure model parameters for any of the popular term structure models. We have demonstrated the practical implementation of the maximum smoothness forward rate technique in comparison with four variations on the cubic spline approach and the linear smoothing technique that have been popular for years. The linear approach is often unusable since the forward rate curves are discontinuous, a violation of one of the often-used assumptions of the Heath, Jarrow, and Morton (1992) term structure model. The cubic spline approaches produce discontinuous second derivatives of the forward rate curve. While this is not a technical violation of the Heath, Jarrow, and Morton model, most market participants would prefer the smoothness of a forward rate curve that is continuous and twice differentiable. As shown in Adams and van Deventer (1994), using 848 daily observations from the yen swap market and 660 daily observations from the U.S. dollar swap market, the maximum smoothness forward rate approach is also more accurate in modeling true market yields.

EXERCISES

The exercises in this chapter are all based on the assumption that the following rates are observable in the market:

Instantaneous interest rate	4.00%
3-year continuous yield	5.00%
10-year continuous yield	6.50%

2.1 What are the coefficients of a yield curve that is linear in time to maturity for continuously compounded yields and that is consistent with this observable market data?

2.2 Using this linear yield curve, what is the quarterly payment on an amortizing bond with 12 quarters to maturity and a present value of 100?

2.3 What are the semiannual forward rates out to 10 years associated with this yield curve?

2.4 What are the coefficients of a cubic yield spline calculated such that the continuous yield curve is flat ($y' = 0$) at the 10-year maturity?

2.5   Using this cubic yield spline, what would the coupon be on a new bond issue with semiannual coupons, all principal due in 10 years, and a present value equal to 99?

2.6   What are the coefficients of a cubic yield spline calculated such that the continuous yield curve is instantaneously straight ($y'' = 0$) at the 10-year maturity?

2.7   Using this yield curve, how would your answer to Exercise 2.5 differ?

2.8   What are the coefficients of a cubic price spline calculated such that the continuous yield at the 10-year point (not the zero coupon price curve) is flat ($y' = 0$) at the 10-year maturity?

2.9   What are the semiannual "par coupons" for bonds associated with the yield curve in Exercise 2.8 such that they all have present values of 100?

2.10 What are the coefficients of the maximum smoothness forward rate curve consistent with the observable data?

2.11 Using spreadsheet software, graph the forward rates associated with all five yield curves at quarterly intervals. Which forward rate curve would you select as the most realistic?

2.12 Using the maximum smoothness curve, what would be the par coupon (i.e., the coupon such that on the issue date the present value would be 100) for a semiannual bond with a maturity of five years that will be issued in 18 months?

2.13 Using the maximum smoothness yield curve, what is the semiannual payment on a level payment lease that will settle in one year and have a present value of $125,000 at that time?

2.14 Using the maximum smoothness yield curve, what semiannual premium produces a life insurance policy with a net present value of zero if the amount paid out upon death of the insured is $100,000 and there is a 50 percent probability of death in year 9 and a 50 percent probability in year 10?

2.15 Ms. Jones, the finance professor who lives dangerously, has borrowed $100,000 from an extremely unpleasant relative. She is due to repay it via a lump sum payment of $120,000 in two years, but she is tired of being nagged about it by the relative. Assume she doesn't care if she ever sees this relative again. What is the very best offer she should make the relative, using the maximum smoothness yield curve, for immediate repayment? What is Ms. Jones's gain if the relative will settle for $75,000 cash today?

2.16 Assume that there are three securities observable in the market: an instantaneous interest rate of 4 percent, a one-year zero coupon bond with an instantaneous yield of 4.5 percent, and a two-year bond with semiannual interest payments that has a present value of 100 and a coupon of 4.75 percent. Find the cubic yield spline that is flat at two-year ($y' = 0$) and that is consistent with the observable data. (Hint: Use the "solver" tool in common sheet software to find the two-year continuous yield, which when combined with the other two data points and a cubic yield spline, makes the bond's four payments have a present value of 100.)

REFERENCES

Adams, Kenneth J., and Donald R. van Deventer. "Fitting Yield Curves and Forward Rate Curves with Maximum Smoothness." *The Journal of Fixed Income*, June 1994, pp. 52–62.

Buono, Mark; Russell B. Gregory-Allen; and Uzi Yaari. "The Efficacy of Term Structure Estimation Techniques: A Monte Carlo Study." *The Journal of Fixed Income* 1, March 1992, pp. 52–59.

Cox, John C.; Jonathan E. Ingersoll, Jr.; and Stephen A. Ross. "A Theory of the Term Structure of Interest Rates." *Econometrica* 53, March 1985, pp. 385–407.

Dothan, L. Uri. "On the Term Structure of Interest Rates." *Journal of Financial Economics* 6, March 1978, pp. 59–69.

Heath, D.; R. Jarrow; and A. Morton. "Bond Pricing and the Term Structure of Interest Rates: A New Methodology for Contingent Claims Valuation." *Econometrica* 60, January 1992, pp. 77–105.

Hildebrand, F. B. *Introduction to Numerical Analysis.* New York: Dover Publications Inc., 1987.

Ho, Thomas S. Y., and Sang-Bin Lee. "Term Structure Movements and Pricing Interest Rate Contingent Claims." *Journal of Finance* 41, December 1986, pp. 1011–29.

Hull, John, and Alan White. "One-Factor Interest-Rate Models and the Valuation of Interest-Rate Derivative Securities." *Journal of Financial and Quantitative Analysis* 28, June 1993, pp. 235–54.

McCulloch, J. Huston. "The Tax Adjusted Yield Curve." *Journal of Finance* 30, June 1975, pp. 811–29.

Mitsubishi Finance Risk Directory 1990/1991. London: Researched and compiled by *Risk* Magazine, 1990.

Penter, P. M. *Splines and Variational Methods.* New York: John Wiley & Sons, 1989.

Schwartz, H. R. *Numerical Methods: A Comprehensive Introduction.* New York: John Wiley & Sons, 1989.

Shea, Gary S. "Term Structure Estimation with Exponential Splines." *Journal of Finance* 40, March 1985, pp. 319–25.

Vasicek, Oldrich A. "An Equilibrium Characterization of the Term Structure." *Journal of Financial Economics* 5, 1977, pp. 177–88.

Vasicek, Oldrich A., and H. Gifford Fong. "Term Structure Modeling Using Exponential Splines." *Journal of Finance* 37, November 1982, pp. 339–56.

A P P E N D I X

Proof of the Theorem[6]

Schwartz (1989) demonstrates that cubic splines produce the maximum smoothness discount functions or yield curves if the spline is applied to discount bond prices or yields, respectively. In this appendix, we derive by a similar argument the functional form that produces the forward rate curve with maximum smoothness. Let $f(t)$ be the current forward rate function, so that

$$P(t) = \exp\left(-\int_0^t f(s)ds\right) \quad \text{(A1)}$$

is the price of a discount bond maturing at time t. The maximum smoothness term structure is a function f with a continuous derivative that satisfies the optimization problem

$$\textbf{min} \quad \int_0^T f''^2(s)ds \quad \text{(A2)}$$

subject to the constraints

$$\int_0^{t_i} f(s)ds = -\textbf{log } P_i \quad \text{for } i = 1,2,...,m. \quad \text{(A3)}$$

Here the $P_i = P(t_i)$, for $i = 1,2, \ldots , m$ are given prices of discount bonds with maturities $0 < t_1 < t_2 < \ldots < t_m < T$.
Integrating twice by parts we get the following identity:

$$\int_0^t f(s)ds = \frac{1}{2}\int_0^t (t-s)^2 f''(s)ds + tf(0) + \frac{1}{2}t^2 f'(0) \quad \text{(A4)}$$

Put

$$g(t) = f''(t), \quad 0 \le t \le T \quad \text{(A5)}$$

---

6. This proof was kindly provided by Oldrich Vasicek. We also appreciate the comments of Volf Frishling, who pointed out an error in the proof in Adams and van Deventer (1994).

and define the step function

$$u(t) = 1 \quad \text{for } t \geq 0$$
$$= 0 \quad \text{for } t < 0$$

The optimization problem can then be written as

$$\min \int_0^T g^2(s)\,ds \qquad (A6)$$

subject to

$$\frac{1}{2}\int_0^T (t_i - s)^2 u(t_i - s) g(s)\,ds = -\log P_i - t_i f(0) - \frac{1}{2}t_i^2 f'(0) \qquad (A7)$$

for $i = 1, 2, \ldots, m$. Let λ_i for $i = 1, 2, \ldots, m$ be the Lagrange multipliers corresponding to the constraints in Equation A7. The objective then becomes

$$\min \quad Z[g] = \int_0^T g^2(s)\,ds \qquad (A8)$$

$$+ \sum_{i=1}^m \lambda_i \left(\frac{1}{2}\int_0^T (t_i - s)^2 u(t_i - s) g(s)\,ds + \log P_i + t_i f(0) + \frac{1}{2}t_i^2 f'(0) \right)$$

According to the calculus of variations, if the function g is a solution to Equation A8, then

$$\frac{d}{d\varepsilon} Z[g + \varepsilon h]_{\varepsilon=0} = 0 \qquad (A9)$$

for any function $h(t)$ identically equal to $w''(t)$ where $w(t)$ is any twice differentiable function defined on $(0,T)$ with $w'(0) = w(0) = 0$.[7] We get

$$\frac{d}{d\varepsilon} Z[g + \varepsilon h]_{\varepsilon=0} = 2\int_0^T \left[g(s) + \frac{1}{4}\sum_{i=1}^m \lambda_i (t_i - s)^2 u(t_i - s) \right] h(s)\,ds$$

7. We are grateful to Robert Jarrow for his assistance on this point.

In order that this integral is zero for any function h, we must have

$$g(t) + \frac{1}{4}\sum_{i=1}^{m}\lambda_i(t_i - t)^2 u(t_i - t) = 0 \tag{A10}$$

for all t between 0 and T. This means that

$$g(t) = 12e_i t^2 + 6d_i t + 2c_i \tag{A11}$$

$$\text{for } t_{i-1} < t \le t_i, \; i = 1,2, \ldots, m + 1$$

where

$$e_i = -\frac{1}{48}\sum_{j=i}^{m}\lambda_j \tag{A12}$$

$$d_i = \frac{1}{12}\sum_{j=i}^{m}\lambda_j t_j$$

$$c_i = -\frac{1}{8}\sum_{j=i}^{m}\lambda_j t_j^2$$

and we define $t_0 = 0$, $t_{m+1} = T$. Moreover Equation A10 implies that g and g' (and therefore f'' and f''') are continuous. From Equation A4 we get

$$f(t) = e_i t^4 + d_i t^3 + c_i t^2 + b_i t + a_i \tag{A13}$$

for $t_{i-1} < t \le t_i$, $i = 1,2, \ldots, m + 1$. Continuity of f, f', f'' and f''' then implies that

$$e_i t_i^4 + d_i t_i^3 + c_i t_i^2 + b_i t_i + a_i \tag{A14}$$
$$= e_{i+1} t_i^4 + d_{i+1} t_i^3 + c_{i+1} t_i^2 + b_{i+1} t_i + a_{i+1}$$

$$4e_i t_i^3 + 3d_i t_i^2 + 2c_i t_i + b_i = 4e_{i+1} t_i^3 + 3d_{i+1} t_i^2 + 2c_{i+1} t_i + b_{i+1}$$

$$12e_i t_i^2 + 6d_i t_i + 2c_i = 12e_{i+1} t_i^2 + 6d_{i+1} t_i + 2c_{i+1} \tag{A15}$$

$$24e_i t_i + 6d_i = 24e_{i+1} t_i + 6d_{i+1}$$

for $i = 1,2, \ldots, m$.

The constraints in Equation A3 become

$$\frac{1}{5}e_i(t_i^5 - t_{i-1}^5) + \frac{1}{4}d_i(t_i^4 - t_{i-1}^4) + \frac{1}{3}c_i(t_i^3 - t_{i-1}^3) + \frac{1}{2}b_i(t_i^2 - t_{i-1}^2) \quad \text{(A16)}$$

$$+ a_i(t_i - t_{i-1}) = -\log\left[\frac{P_i}{P_{i-1}}\right] \text{ for } i = 1,2,\ldots,m$$

where we define $P_0 = 1$. This proves the theorem.

CHAPTER 3

Duration and Convexity: The Traditional Risk Management Tools

The use of duration has become standard practice for interest rate hedging and risk analysis in financial markets. In 1978, Jonathan Ingersoll, Jeffrey Skelton, and Roman Weil published an appreciation of Frederick R. Macaulay's 1938 work on duration, entitled "Duration Forty Years Later." In that work, the authors pointed out a number of key aspects of duration and potential pitfalls of duration that we want to emphasize in this chapter, which introduces the concepts of duration and convexity and relates them to Macaulay's 1938 work. "Standard practice" in financial markets has gradually drifted away from Macaulay's original concept of duration. In the 16 years since Ingersoll, Skelton, and Weil published their article, the standard practice has become even more entrenched. Our purpose is to reemphasize the point made about duration by Ingersoll, Skelton, and Weil and to highlight the errors that can result from deviating from Macaulay's original formulation of duration. Most of the vocabulary of financial markets still stems from the use of the traditional fixed-income mathematics used in this chapter, but the underlying meanings have evolved as financial instruments and financial mathematics have become more complex.

3.1 MACAULAY'S DURATION: THE ORIGINAL FORMULA

As in Chapters 1 and 2, we define the price of a zero coupon bond with maturity of t years as $P(t)$. We let its continuously compounded yield be $y(t)$, and we label the cash flow in period t as $X(t)$. As we discussed in Chapter 2, the present value of these cash flows is

$$\text{Present value} = \sum_{i=1}^{n} P(t_i) X(t_i)$$

$$= \sum_{i=1}^{n} e^{-y(t_i)t_i} X(t_i)$$

The last line substitutes the relationship between $y(t)$ and $P(t)$ when yields $y(t)$ are continuously compounded. Macaulay investigated the change in present value as each yield $y(t)$ makes a parallel shift of amount x, so the new yield at any maturity $y(t)* = y(t) + x$. The change in present value that results is

$$\frac{\partial \text{ Present value}}{\partial x} = \sum_{i=1}^{n} - t_i e^{-y(t_i)t_i} X(t_i)$$

$$= \sum_{i=1}^{n} - t_i P(t_i) X(t_i)$$

Macaulay defined duration as the percentage change (expressed as a positive number, which requires changing the sign in the equation above) in present value that results from this parallel shift in rates:

$$\text{Duration} = - \frac{\dfrac{\partial \text{Present value}}{\partial x}}{\text{Present value}}$$

$$= \frac{\displaystyle\sum_{i=1}^{n} t_i P(t_i) X(t_i)}{\displaystyle\sum_{i=1}^{n} P(t_i) X(t_i)}$$

From this formula, one can see the reason that duration is often called the present value–weighted average time to maturity of a given security. The time to maturity of each cash flow t_i is weighted by the share of the present value of the cash flow at that time in total present value.

In the case of a bond with n coupon payments of C dollars (note that C is not the annual percentage interest payment unless payments are made only once per year) and a principal amount of $100, this duration formula can be rewritten as

$$\text{Duration} = -\frac{\dfrac{\partial \text{Present value}}{\partial x}}{\text{Present value}}$$

$$= \frac{C\left[\displaystyle\sum_{i=1}^{n} t_i P(t_i)\right] + t_n P(t_n)100}{C\left[\displaystyle\sum_{i=1}^{n} P(t_i)\right] + P(t_n)100}$$

This form of duration, the form its inventor intended, has come to be known as Fisher-Weil duration. All discounting in the present value calculations is done at a different continuous yield to maturity $y(t_i)$ for each maturity.

3.2 USING DURATION FOR HEDGING

How is the duration concept used for hedging? Let's examine the case where an institution owns one unit of a security with present value B_1 and wants to form a no-risk portfolio that includes the hedging security (which has present value B_2). Let the amount of the hedging security be w. Then the total value of this portfolio W is

$$B_1 + w B_2$$

We want the change in the value of this hedged portfolio to be zero for infinitely small parallel shifts in the term structure of interest rates. We can call the amount of this shift x. For the hedge to be successful, we must have

$$\frac{\partial W}{\partial x} = \frac{\partial B_1}{\partial x} + w\frac{\partial B_2}{\partial x} = 0$$

From this equation, we can calculate the right amount of B_2 to hold for a perfect hedge as

$$w = -\frac{\dfrac{\partial B_1}{\partial x}}{\dfrac{\partial B_2}{\partial x}}$$

Notice that this formula doesn't directly include duration. We can incorporate the duration calculation by modifying the original equation for a perfect hedge as follows:

$$\frac{\partial W}{\partial x} = B_1 \frac{\dfrac{\partial B_1}{\partial x}}{B_1} + w B_2 \frac{\dfrac{\partial B_2}{\partial x}}{B_2}$$

$$= -B_1 \text{ Duration}[B_1] - w B_2 \text{ Duration}[B_2] = 0$$

Therefore, the hedge amount w can be rewritten

$$w = \frac{-B_1 \text{ Duration}[B_1]}{B_2 \text{ Duration}[B_2]}$$

Using either formula for w, we can establish the "correct" hedge for the portfolio. This hedge has the following characteristics:

- It is correct only for infinitely small parallel shifts in interest rates.
- It has to be "rebalanced" like a Black-Scholes options delta hedge whenever (1) rates change or (2) time passes.

The hedge will not be correct if there are large parallel jumps in interest rates, nor will it be correct for nonparallel shifts in interest rates.

3.3 DURATION: THE MARKET CONVENTION

The conventional wisdom has drifted over time from Macaulay's original formulation of the duration concept. The reason for the change from Macaulay's original formulation is a simple one: Until recently, it has been difficult for market participants to easily take the $P(t)$ values from the current yield curve using the techniques that were outlined in Chapter 2. Now that yield curve smoothing has become easier, this problem has declined in importance, but the market's simpler formulation persists. The best way to explain the market convention is to review the formula for yield to maturity.

The Formula for Yield to Maturity

For a settlement date (for either a secondary market bond purchase or a new bond issue) that falls exactly one period from the next coupon date, the formula for yield to maturity can be written as follows for a bond that matures in n periods and pays a fixed dollar coupon amount C m times per year, as shown in Chapter 1:

$$\text{Price} = \text{Present value} = C\left[\sum_{i=1}^{n} P(t_i)\right] + P(t_n) * \text{Principal}$$

$$\text{where} \qquad P(t_i) = \frac{1}{\left(1 + \dfrac{y}{m}\right)^i}$$

Yield to maturity is the value of y that makes this equation true. This relationship is the present value equation for a fixed coupon bond, with the addition that the discount factors are all calculated by dividing $1 by the future value of $1 invested at y for i periods, with interest compounded m times per year. In other words, y is the internal rate of return on this bond. Note also that, using these discount factors, the present value of the bond and the "price" of the bond are equal since there is no accrued interest.

Yield to Maturity for Long or Short First Coupon Payment Periods

For most outstanding bonds or securities, the number of periods remaining usually contains a short (or occasionally a long) first period. The length of the short first period is equal to the number of days from settlement to the next coupon, divided by the total number of days from the last coupon (or hypothetical last coupon, if the bond is a new issue with a short coupon date) to the next coupon. The exact method of counting days for purpose of this calculation depends on the interest accrual method associated with the bond. (Examples are actual/actual, the National Association of Securities Dealers 30/360 method in the United States, and the Euro market implementation of the 30/360 accrual method.) We call the ratio of remaining days (as appropriately calculated) to days between coupons (as appropriately calculated) x. Then the yield to maturity can be written

$$\text{Present value} = C\left[\sum_{i=1}^{n} P(t_i)\right] + P(t_n) * \text{Principal}$$

where
$$P(t_i) = \frac{1}{\left(1 + \dfrac{y}{m}\right)^{i-1+x}}$$

As in the case of even first coupon periods, y is the yield to maturity that makes this relationship true, the internal rate of return on the bond. Note that when x is 1, this reduces to the formula above for even-length first periods. For a review of the use of the Newton-Raphson method for calculating y, see Chapter 1.

Applying the Yield-to-Maturity Formula to Duration

The conventional definition of duration is calculated by applying the implications of the yield-to-maturity formula to the original Macaulay duration formula, which is given below:

$$\text{True duration} = -\frac{\dfrac{\partial \text{Present value}}{\partial x}}{\text{Present value}}$$

$$= \frac{\displaystyle\sum_{i=1}^{n} t_i P(t_i) X(t_i)}{\displaystyle\sum_{i=1}^{n} P(t_i) X(t_i)}$$

We can rewrite this formula for a conventional bond by substituting directly into this formula on the assumptions that market interest rates are equal for all maturities at the yield to maturity y and that interest rates are compounded at discrete, instead of continuous, intervals. This results in the following changes:

- The discount factors $P(t_i)$, taken from the smoothed yield curve by Macaulay, are replaced by a simpler formulation that uses the same interest rate (the yield to maturity) at each maturity:

$$P(t_i) = \frac{1}{\left(1 + \dfrac{y}{m}\right)^{i-1+x}}$$

- The time t_i is directly calculated as

$$t_i = \frac{i-1+x}{m}$$

Using this formulation, the "conventional" definition of duration for a bond with dollar coupon C and principal of $100 is

Conventional duration

$$= \frac{C\left[\displaystyle\sum_{i=1}^{n} t_i P(t_i)\right] + t_n P(t_n)100}{\text{Present value}}$$

$$= \frac{C\left[\displaystyle\sum_{i=1}^{n} \frac{i-1+x}{m}\left(\frac{1}{\left(1+\dfrac{y}{m}\right)^{i-1+x}}\right) + \frac{n-1+x}{m}\left(\frac{1}{\left(1+\dfrac{y}{m}\right)^{n-1+x}}\right)100\right]}{\text{Present value}}$$

This is just a discrete time transformation of Macaulay's formula. As shown below, however, it doesn't measure the percentage change in present value for a small change in the discrete yield to maturity.

Modified Duration

In the case of Macaulay duration, the formula was based on the calculation of

$$\text{Duration} = -\frac{\dfrac{\partial \text{Present value}}{\partial x}}{\text{Present value}}$$

$$= \frac{\displaystyle\sum_{i=1}^{n} t_i P(t_i) X(t_i)}{\displaystyle\sum_{i=1}^{n} P(t_i) X(t_i)}$$

The second line of the above equation results from the fact that the yield to maturity of a zero coupon bond with maturity t_i, written as $y(t_i)$, is continuously compounded. It is a little appreciated fact that the conventional measure of duration, given on p. 95, is not consistent with Macaulay's derivation of duration when interest payments are discrete instead of continuous. What happens to the percentage change in present value when the discrete yield to maturity (instead of the continuous yield to maturity analyzed by Macaulay) shifts from y to $y + z$ for infinitely small changes in z? Using the yield-to-maturity formula as a starting point and differentiating with respect to z, we get the following formula, which is called *modified duration*:

$$\text{Modified duration} = \frac{C\left[\displaystyle\sum_{i=1}^{n} \frac{i-1+x}{m}\left(\frac{1}{\left(1+\dfrac{y}{m}\right)^{i+x}}\right)\right] + \frac{n-1+x}{m}\left(\frac{1}{\left(1+\dfrac{y}{m}\right)^{n+x}}\right)100}{\text{Present value}}$$

$$= \frac{\text{Conventional duration}}{1 + \dfrac{y}{m}}$$

This modified duration measures the same thing that Macaulay's original formula was intended to measure: the percentage change in present value for an infinitely small change in yields. The Macaulay formulation and the conventional duration are different for the following reasons:

- The Macaulay measure (most often called Fisher-Weil duration) is based on continuous compounding and correctly measures the percentage change in present value for small parallel changes in these continuous yields. The conventional duration measure, a literal translation to discrete compounding of the Macaulay formula, does *not* measure the percentage change in price for small changes in discrete yield to maturity. The percentage change in present value is measured by conventional modified duration. When using continuous compounding, *duration* and *modified duration* are the same.
- The Macaulay measure uses a different yield for each payment date instead of using the yield to maturity as the appropriate discount rate for each payment date.

The impact on hedging of these differences in assumptions is outlined in Section 3.4.

3.4 THE PERFECT HEDGE: THE DIFFERENCE BETWEEN THE ORIGINAL MACAULAY AND CONVENTIONAL DURATIONS

Both the original Macaulay (Fisher-Weil) and conventional formulation of duration are intended to measure the percentage change in "value" for a parallel shift in yields. The percentage change is measured as the percentage change in present value; it is important to note that it is *not* the percentage change in *price* (Present value − Accrued interest) that is measured. The difference between a hedge calculated based on the percentage change in present value (the correct way) versus a hedge based on the percentage change in price (the incorrect way) can be significant if the bond to be hedged and the instrument used as the hedging instrument have different amounts of accrued interest. The impact of this "accrued interest" effect varies with the level of interest rates and the amount of accrued interest on the underlying instrument and the instrument used as a hedge. If payment dates on the two bonds are different and the relative amounts of accrued interest are different, the hedge ratio error can exceed 5 percent.

The second source of error when using modified duration to calculate hedge ratios is the error induced by using the yield to maturity as the discount rate at every payment date instead of using a different discount rate for every maturity. The hedging error (relative to Fisher-Weil duration) from this source can easily vary from −2 percent to +2 percent as a linear yield curve takes on different slopes. The hedge ratio error is obviously most significant when the yield curve has a significant slope.

3.5 CONVEXITY AND ITS USES

The word *convexity* can be heard every day on trading floors around the world, and yet it's a controversial subject. Usually ignored by leading financial academics, it's an important topic to two diverse groups of financial market participants: (1) adherents to the historical yield-to-maturity bond mathematics that predates the derivatives world and the use of term structure models that is the central topic of this book, and (2) modern "rocket scientists" who must translate the latest in derivatives mathematics to hedges that work. This section is dedicated to bridging the gap between these constituencies.

Convexity: A General Definition

The duration concept, reduced to its most basic nature, involves the ratio of the first derivative of a valuation formula f to the underlying security's value:

$$\text{Duration} = \frac{-f'(y)}{f(y)}$$

The variable y could be any stochastic variable that determines present value according to the function f. It may be yield to maturity, it may be the short rate in a term structure model, and so on. It is closely related to the delta hedge concept, which has become a standard hedging tool for options-related securities. The underlying idea is exactly the same as that discussed in Section 3.2: For infinitely small changes in the random variable, the first derivative (whether called duration or delta) results in a perfect hedge if the model incorporated in the function f is "true." So far in our discussion, the constituencies mentioned above are all in agreement.

As we showed in Section 3.4, the duration and modified duration concepts are *not* "true" whenever the yield curve is not flat. The academic community and the derivatives hedgers agree on this point, and neither group would be satisfied with a hedge ratio based on the discrete yield-to-maturity formulas presented in this chapter, despite their long and glorious place in the history of fixed-income markets. All three constituencies agree, however, that when the random variable in a valuation formula "jumps" by more than an infinitely small amount, a hedging challenge results.

Leading academics solve this problem either by assuming it away or by breaking a complex security into more liquid "primitive" securities and assembling a perfect hedge that exactly replicates the value of the complex security. In the case of a noncallable bond, the perfect hedge is the portfolio of zero coupon bonds that exactly offsets the cash flows of the underlying bond portfolio. Traditional practitioners of "bond math" and derivatives experts often are forced to deal with the fact that no perfect hedge exists or that the required rebalancing of a hedge can only be done at discrete, rather than continuous, intervals.

The fundamental essence of the convexity concept involves the second derivative of a security's value with respect to a random input variable y. It is usually expressed as a ratio to the value of the security, as calculated using the formula f:

$$\text{Convexity} = \frac{f''(y)}{f(y)}$$

It is very closely linked with the "gamma" calculation (the second derivative of an option's value with respect to the price of the underlying security).

When a security's value makes a discrete jump because of a discrete jump in the input variable y, the new value can be calculated to any desired degree of precision using a Taylor expansion, which gives the value of the security at the new input variable level, say $y + z$, relative to the old value at input variable level y:

$$f(y+z) = f(y) + f'(y)z + f''(y)\frac{z^2}{2!} + \ldots + f^{[n]}(y)\frac{z^n}{n!} + \ldots$$

Rearranging these terms and dividing by the security's original value $f(y)$ gives us the percentage change in value that results from the shift z:

$$\frac{f(y+z)-f(y)}{f(y)} = \frac{f'(y)}{f(y)}z + \frac{f''(y)}{f(y)}\frac{z^2}{2!} + \ldots + \frac{f^{[n]}(y)}{f(y)}\frac{z^2}{n!} + \ldots$$

$$= (\text{Duration})z + (\text{Convexity})\frac{z^2}{2!} + \text{Error}$$

The percentage change can be expressed in terms of duration and convexity and an error term. Note that modified duration should replace duration in this expression if the random factor is the discrete yield to maturity. We will see in Chapter 4 that this Taylor expansion is very closely related to Ito's lemma, the heart of the stochastic mathematics we introduce in Chapter 4.

Convexity for the Present Value Formula

For the case of the present value of a security with cash flows of X_i per period, payments m times per year, and a short first coupon of x periods, the convexity formula can be derived by differentiating the present value formula twice with respect to the yield to maturity y and then dividing by present value:

$$\text{Convexity} = \frac{\left[\sum_{i=1}^{n} X(t_i)\left(\frac{-(i-1+x)}{m}\right)\left(\frac{-(i-1+x)-1}{m}\right)\left(\frac{1}{1+\frac{y}{m}}\right)^{-(i-1+x)-2}\right]}{\text{Present value}}$$

When present value is calculated using the continuous time approach,

$$\text{Present value} = \sum_{i=1}^{n} e^{-t_i y(t_i)} X(t_i)$$

then the continuous compounding or Fisher-Weil version of convexity is

$$\text{Convexity} = \frac{\left[\sum_{i=1}^{n} t_i^2 P(t_i)X(t_i)\right]}{\text{Present value}}$$

Hedging Implications of the Convexity Concept

To the extent that rebalancing a hedge is costly or to the extent that the underlying random variable jumps rather than moving in a continuous way, the continuous rebalancing of a duration (or delta) hedge will be either expensive or impossible. In either case, the best hedge is the hedge that comes closest to a "buy-and-hold" hedge, a hedge that can be put in place and left there with no need to rebalance until the portfolio being hedged has matured or been sold. A hedge that matches both the duration (or modified duration in the case of a hedger using a present-value-based valuation formula) and the convexity of the underlying portfolio will come closer to this objective than most simple duration hedges. Consider the case of a portfolio with value P and two securities with values S_1 and S_2. Denoting first and second derivatives of value with respect to the random factor and duration by D and convexity by C, the best hedge ratios w_1 and w_2 for a hedge using both securities S_1 and S_2 can be obtained by solving either

$$P' = w_1 S'_1 + w_2 S'_2$$
$$P'' = w_1 S''_1 + w_2 S''_2$$

or

$$P D_P = w_1 S_1 D_1 + w_2 S_2 D_2$$
$$P C_P = w_1 S_1 C_1 + w_2 S_2 C_2$$

for the hedge ratios w_1 and w_2.

Consider the following examples of duration and convexity on both a Fisher-Weil basis and on a discrete basis. Assume that the yield curve smoothing process has generated zero coupon bond yields on a continuously compounded basis as follows:

Maturity	Continuous Yield
0.5	5.00%
1.0	5.75%
1.5	6.25%
2.0	6.50%

We want to analyze the duration and convexity of a bond with two years to maturity, semiannual payments, and a coupon of 12 percent. The present value of the bond can be calculated as 110.05777 using the techniques of Chapter 1. The Fisher-Weil duration is 1.84395.

Example 3.5.1: Fisher-Weil Duration

Coupon	12.00%
Principal	100
Payments per year	2

Years to Maturity	Zero Yield	Discount Factor	Cash Flow	Present Value	Time-Weighted Present Value
0.5	5.00%	0.97531	6.00	5.85186	2.92593
1	5.75%	0.94412	6.00	5.66473	5.66473
1.5	6.25%	0.91051	6.00	5.46306	8.19459
2	6.50%	0.87810	106.00	93.07812	186.15623
Total				110.05777	202.94149
Fisher-Weil duration					**1.84395**

The Fisher-Weil convexity can be calculated in a similar way to be 3.5593.

Example 3.5.2: Fisher-Weil Convexity

Coupon	12.00%
Principal	100
Payments per year	2

Years to Maturity	Zero Yield	Discount Factor	Cash Flow	Present Value	Time-Squared-Weighted Present Value
0.5	5.00%	0.97531	6.00	5.8519	1.4630
1	5.75%	0.94412	6.00	5.6647	5.6647
1.5	6.25%	0.91051	6.00	5.4631	12.2919
2	6.50%	0.87810	106.00	93.0781	372.3125
Total				110.0578	391.7320
Fisher-Weil convexity					**3.5593**

The same calculation can be done on a discrete basis. Step 1 is to use the Newton-Raphson method to solve for the yield to maturity on the bond that gives its present value of 110.05777. This yield is 6.5526 percent. We then use this constant yield of 6.5526 percent to calculate new discount factors, multiply them by cash flow and years to maturity for each payment, and divide the sum of these calculations by present value to get a traditional duration of 1.8450. This is quite close to Fisher-Weil duration, but as noted above the traditional duration number does not measure the percentage change in price for small changes in yield to maturity, which is our objective. This is measured by modified duration, which can be calculated as 1.7864, a dramatically different number from Fisher-Weil duration.

Example 3.5.3: Duration and Modified Duration

Yield to maturity	6.5526%
Coupon	12.00%
Principal	100
Payments per year	2

Years to Maturity	Yield to Maturity	Discount Factor	Cash Flow	Present Value	Time-Weighted Present Value
0.5	6.5526%	0.96828	6.00	5.8097	2.9048
1	6.5526%	0.93756	6.00	5.6254	5.6254
1.5	6.5526%	0.90782	6.00	5.4469	8.1703
2	6.5526%	0.87902	106.00	93.1759	186.3517
Total				110.0578	203.0522
Duration					**1.8450**
Modified duration					**1.7864**

Convexity can be calculated in a similar way. We arrive at a figure of 4.2046, again significantly different from the Fisher-Weil version of convexity.

Example 3.5.4: Convexity

Yield to maturity	6.5526%
Coupon	12.00%
Principal	100
Payments per year	2

Years to Maturity	Yield to Maturity	$(i - 1 + x)/m$	$(i + x)/m$	Cash Flow	Convexity Discount Factor	Time-Weighted Total
0.5	6.5526%	0.5	1.0	6.00	0.9078	2.7234
1	6.5526%	1.0	1.5	6.00	0.8790	7.9112
1.5	6.5526%	1.5	2.0	6.00	0.8511	15.3204
2	6.5526%	2.0	2.5	106.00	0.8241	436.7895
Total						462.7444
Convexity						4.2046

3.6 CONCLUSION

Over the last 56 years, the market's conventional definition has drifted from Macaulay's original concept to a measure that appears similar but that can be very misleading if used inappropriately. As Ingersoll, Skelton, and Weil (1978) point out, the Macaulay formulation offers considerable value as a guide to the correct hedge if one takes a back-to-basics approach: The measure should focus on the percentage change in present value, not price, and the discount rate at each maturity should reflect its actual continuous yield to maturity as obtained using the techniques in Chapter 2. Assuming the yield to maturity is the same for each cash flow or coupon payment on a bond can result in serious hedging errors. The duration (or modified duration) approach to hedging is a strong foundation on which to build a hedging program, if properly modified to recognize the expense of rebalancing the hedge or the likelihood of discrete jumps in the underlying random variable that prevent an economical, continuous rebalancing of the hedge. The convexity approach provides a useful guide to maximizing hedging efficiency, but the term *convexity* has outlasted the simple convexity formula commonly used for bonds. The formula itself has been supplanted by the concepts we will introduce in subsequent chapters.

EXERCISES

Use the following zero coupon bond prices to derive continuous yields to maturities that will allow you to answer the following questions. Assume that the zero coupon bond prices have been obtained from one of the yield curve smoothing techniques in Chapter 2 and that you believe the technique to be the appropriate one in today's market. Assume today is January 15, 2000.

April 15, 2000	.974
October 15, 2000	.949
April 15, 2001	.921
October 15, 2001	.892
April 15, 2002	.862
October 15, 2002	.831
April 15, 2003	.798
October 14, 2003	.763
April 15, 2004	.725

3.1 Using the Fisher-Weil duration formula, what is the duration of the 6 percent semiannual payment bond that matures April 15, 2003?

3.2 You own a $2,000 principal amount of the bond in Exercise 3.1. The only hedging instrument you can use to hedge your position, because of liquidity considerations, is the zero coupon bond maturing October 15, 2001. Assuming infinitely small parallel shifts in zero coupon bond yields, how much (in terms of principal amount) of the October 15, 2001, zero coupon bond should you sell short to perfectly hedge your position in the 6 percent bonds due April 25, 2003?

3.3 Assume that the accrued interest calculation method appropriate for the 6 percent bonds in Exercise 3.1 shows that the short first period to the April 15, 2000, coupon is exactly half a period in length. What is the yield to maturity on this bond? Using the yield-to-maturity formula, what is the traditional duration on this bond? What is the modified duration?

3.4 Calculate the modified duration of the October 15, 2001, zero coupon bond after calculating its yield to maturity on a semiannual basis. (Use the techniques in Chapter 1 to make this adjustment.)

3.5   Using the modified duration concept, how much of the October 15, 2001, zero coupon bonds should you sell short to hedge the $2,000 of 6 percent bonds due 2003 based on your answers in Exercises 3.3 and 3.4? How much does this answer deviate from the answer to Exercise 3.2?

3.6   Which hedge ratio will generally get you the best hedge, the ratio in Exercise 3.2 or the ratio in Exercise 3.5?

3.7   Using the continuously compounded Fisher-Weil approach, what is the continuous convexity of the 6 percent bonds maturing 2003?

3.8   Using the discrete yield-to-maturity approach to convexity, what is the convexity of the 6 percent bonds maturing 2003?

3.9   Assume you can use both the October 15, 2001, zero coupon bond and the October 15, 2003, zero coupon bond to hedge your $2,000 position in the 6 percent bonds due 2003. Using the Fisher-Weil duration and convexity calculations, what should your position be in the two zero coupon bonds for the hedge that perfectly matches both the Fisher-Weil duration and convexity of the 6 percent bonds due 2003?

3.10 Continuing the assumptions of Exercise 3.9 but using the discrete yield-to-maturity formula-based modified duration and convexity formulas, what should your position be in the two zero coupon bonds for the hedge that perfectly matches both the modified duration and the discrete convexity of the 6 percent bonds due 2003?

3.11 What are the Fisher-Weil convexity and duration of the two life insurance policies described in Exercise 1.16 (p. 37)? Using the Fisher-Weil duration and convexity formulas, how much of the zero coupon bonds due October 15, 2001, and October 15, 2003, should you own to match the Fisher-Weil duration and convexity of the life policies?

REFERENCES

Ingersoll, Jonathan E., Jr.; Jeffrey Skelton; and Roman L. Weil. "Duration Forty Years Later." *Journal of Financial and Quantitative Analysis*, November 1978, pp. 627–48.

Lynch, John J., Jr., and Jan H. Mayle. *Standard Securities Calculation Methods: Fixed Income Securities Formulas*. New York: Securities Industry Association, 1986.

Macaulay, Frederick R. *Some Theoretical Problems Suggested by Movements of Interest Rates, Bond Yields, and Stock Prices in the United States since 1856*. New York: Columbia University Press, 1938.

CHAPTER 4

Duration as a Term Structure Model

In Chapter 3, we were introduced to Frederick Macaulay's duration concept. At the heart of the duration concept is the implicit assumption that "rates" at all maturities move at the same time in the same direction by the same absolute amount. For example, one might assume that the amount of change for the yield to maturity of all bonds observable in the market at all maturities is 3 basis points. This assumption about how rates move can be labeled a *term structure model*. The purpose of this chapter is to introduce the concept of term structure models and the procedure for evaluating the reasonableness of a given term structure model. We then apply this procedure to the "duration" term structure model in Section 4.6.

4.1 WHAT IS A TERM STRUCTURE MODEL AND WHY DO WE NEED ONE?

When analyzing a fixed-income portfolio, the value of a balance sheet, or a fixed-income option, it is not enough to know where interest rates currently are. It's not possible to know where rates will be in the future with any certainty. Instead, we can analyze a portfolio or a specific security by making an assumption about the random process by which rates will move in the future. Once we have made an assumption about the random (or stochastic) process by which rates move, we can then derive the probability distribution of interest rates at any point in the future. Without this kind of assumption, we can't analyze interest rate risk effectively.

4.2 THE VOCABULARY OF TERM STRUCTURE MODELS

The mathematics for analyzing something whose value changes continuously but in a random process is heavily used in physics. In this stochastic process mathematics, the change in a random variable x over the next instant is written dx. The most common assumption about the random jumps in the size of a variable x is that they are normally distributed. The "noise" or shock to the random variable is assumed to come from a random number generator called a Wiener process. It is a random variable, say z, whose value changes from instant to instant but that has a normal distribution with mean 0 and standard deviation of 1. For example, if we want to assume that the zero coupon bond yield y for a given maturity jumps continuously with mean 0 and standard deviation of 1, we would write

$$dy = dz$$

In stochastic process mathematics, all interest rates are written as decimals like .03 instead of 3, so the assumption that rates jump each instant by 1 (which means 100 percent) is too extreme. We can scale the jumps of interest rates by multiplying the noise-generating Wiener process by a scale factor. In the case of interest rates, this scale factor is the "volatility" of the stochastic process driving interest rate movements. We label this volatility σ. In that case, the stochastic process for the movement in yields is

$$dy = \sigma dz$$

We can set this interest rate volatility scale factor to any level we want, although normally it would be set to levels that most realistically reflect the movements of interest rates. We can calculate this implied interest rate volatility from the prices of observable securities like interest rate caps, interest rate floors, or callable bonds. Note that this volatility is not the volatility of the well-known Black-Scholes option pricing model. We will show the relationship between interest rate volatility and the volatility of the Black-Scholes model in Chapter 9.

The yield that we have modeled above is a random walk, a stochastic process where the random variable drifts randomly with no trend. As time passes, ultimately the yield will rise to infinity or fall to negative infinity. This isn't a very realistic assumption about interest rates, which usually move in cycles of three to five years. How can we introduce interest rate cycles to our model? We need to introduce some form of drift in interest rates over time. One form of drift is to assume that interest rates change by some formula as time passes:

$$dy = \alpha(t)dt + \sigma dz$$

The formula above assumes that on average, the change in interest rates over a given instant will be the change given by the function $\alpha(t)$, with random shocks in the amount of σdz. This formula is closely linked to the term structure models proposed by Ho and Lee (1986) and Heath, Jarrow, and Morton (1992). Both of these models make it easy to fit actual yield curve data exactly with a simple assumption about how interest rates move, since the function $\alpha(t)$ can be chosen to fit a yield curve smoothed using the techniques of Chapter 2 exactly. We go into more detail on both of these term structure models in Chapters 5 and 18.

The assumption about yield movements above isn't satisfactory in the sense that it is still a random walk of interest rates, although there is the drift term $\alpha(t)$ built into the random walk. The best way to build the interest rate cycle into the random movement of interest rates is to assume that the interest rate drifts back to some long-run level, except for the random shocks from the dz term. One process that does this is

$$dy = \alpha(\gamma - y)dt + \sigma dz$$

This is the Ornstein-Uhlenbeck process, which is at the heart of the Vasicek (1977) model introduced in Chapter 5. The term α is called the speed of mean reversion. It is assumed to be a positive number. The larger it is, the faster y drifts back toward its long-run mean γ and the shorter and more violent interest rate cycles will be. Since α is positive, when y is above γ, it will be pulled down except for the impact of the shocks that emanate from the dz term. When y is less than γ, it will be pulled up.

In almost every term structure model, the speed of mean reversion and the volatility of interest rates will play a key role in determining the value of securities that either are interest options or have interest rate options embedded in them.

4.3 ITO'S LEMMA

Once a term structure model has been chosen, we need to be able to draw conclusions about how prices of securities whose values depend on interest rates move around. For instance, if a given interest rate y is assumed to be the random factor that determines the price of a zero coupon bond P, it is logical to ask how the zero coupon bond price moves as time passes and y varies. The formula used to do this is called Ito's lemma.[1] Ito's lemma puts the movement in the bond price P in stochastic process terms like this:

$$dP = P_y dy + \frac{1}{2} P_{yy}(dy)^2 + P_t$$

where the subscripts denote partial derivatives. The terms dy and $(dy)^2$ depend on the stochastic process chosen for y. If the stochastic process is the Ornstein-Uhlenbeck process given above, then movements in P can be rewritten as follows:

$$dP = P_y[\alpha(\gamma - y)dt + \sigma dz] + \frac{1}{2} P_{yy}\sigma^2 dt + P_t dt$$

$$= \left[P_y \alpha(\gamma - y) + \frac{1}{2} P_{yy}\sigma^2 + P_t \right]dt + P_y \sigma dz$$

$$= g(y,t)dt + h(y,t)dz$$

For any stochastic process, the dy term is the stochastic process itself. The term $(dy)^2$ is the instantaneous variance of y. In the case of the Ornstein-Uhlenbeck process, it is the square of the coefficient of dz, σ^2. The term $g(y,t)$, which depends on the level of rates y and time t, is the "drift" in the bond price. The term $h(y,t)$

---

1. For more on Ito's lemma, see Shimko (1992).

is the bond price volatility in the term structure model sense, not the Black-Scholes sense.[2]

4.4. ITO'S LEMMA FOR MORE THAN ONE RANDOM VARIABLE

What if the zero coupon bond price depended on two random variables, x and y? The formula for the movement in the bond's price is given by Ito's lemma as follows:

$$dP = P_x dx + P_y dy + \frac{1}{2} P_{xx}(dx)^2 + \frac{1}{2} P_{yy}(dy)^2 + P_{xy}(dxdy) + P_t$$

where $(dxdy) = \rho \sigma_x \sigma_y$

The instantaneous correlation between the two Wiener processes Z_x and Z_y, which provide the random shocks to x and y, is reflected in the formula for the random movement of P by the instantaneous correlation coefficient ρ. See Shimko (1992) for a more detailed discussion of Ito's lemma.

4.5 USING ITO'S LEMMA TO BUILD A TERM STRUCTURE MODEL

The steps involved in building a term structure model are almost always as follows:

1. Make an assumption about the random (stochastic) process that interest rates follow.
2. Use Ito's lemma to specify how zero coupon bond prices move.
3. Impose the constraint that there not be riskless arbitrage in the bond market via the following steps:
   a. Use a bond of one maturity (in the case of a "one-factor" model) to hedge the risk of a bond that has another maturity.[3]

---

2. See Chapter 5 for the relationship between volatility in the Black-Scholes sense and the term structure model sense.
3. If there are two random factors driving movements in interest rates, two bonds would be necessary to eliminate the risk of these random factors. N bonds would be necessary for an N factor model.

   b. After eliminating the risk of this "portfolio," impose
   the constraint that this hedged portfolio earn the
   instantaneous (short-term) risk-free rate of interest.
4. Solve the resulting partial differential equation for zero
   coupon bond prices.
5. Examine whether this implies reasonable or
   unreasonable conditions on the market.
6. If the economic implications are reasonable, proceed to
   value other securities with the model. If they are
   unreasonable, reject the assumption about how rates
   move as a reasonable basis for a term structure model.

We will illustrate this process by analyzing the economic implications of the assumption of parallel yield curve shifts underlying
the traditional duration analysis.

4.6 DURATION AS A TERM STRUCTURE MODEL

In this section, we assume that the continuous yield to maturity y_i
on a zero coupon bond with maturity t_i has the relationship we
outlined in Chapter 1 with zero coupon bond prices:

$$P(t_i) = e^{-y_i t_i}$$

We want to examine what happens when all yields at time zero, y_0,
shift by a parallel amount x, with x being the same for all maturities.
After the shift of x, the price of a zero coupon bond with maturity τ
$= T - t$ (t is the current time in years, and T is the maturity date of
the bond in years, for a maturity of $T - t$) will be

$$P(\tau) = e^{-(y_0 + x)\tau}$$

where $y = y_0 + x$. We assume that x is initially zero and that we are
given today's yield curve and know the values of y for all maturities.

   We now make our assumption about the term structure of
interest rates. We assume that the movements in x follow a random walk; that is, we assume changes in x have no drift term and
that the change in x is normally distributed as follows:

$$dx = \sigma dz$$

The scale factor σ controls the volatility of the parallel shifts x. We now proceed to step 2 of Section 4.5 by using Ito's lemma to specify how the zero coupon bond price for a bond with time to maturity $T - t$ moves. Ito's lemma says

$$dP = P_x dx + \frac{1}{2} P_{xx}(dx)^2 + P_t$$

$$= -\tau P \sigma dz + \frac{1}{2}\tau^2 P \sigma^2 dt + yP dt$$

$$= \left[\frac{1}{2}\tau^2 P \sigma^2 + yP\right] dt - \tau P \sigma dz$$

$$= g(y,t)P dt + h(y,t)P dz$$

because

$$y = y_0 + x$$

$$\tau = T - t$$

$$P = \exp^{-y\tau}$$

$$P_x = -\tau P$$

$$P_{xx} = \tau^2 P$$

$$P_t = yP$$

$$g(y,t) = \frac{1}{2}\tau^2 \sigma^2 + y$$

$$h(y,t) = -\tau\sigma$$

We now go to step 3 of the process outlined in Section 4.5. We want to form a portfolio of one unit of bond 1 with maturity τ_1 and w units of the bond 2 with maturity τ_2. The value of this portfolio is

$$W = P_1 + w P_2$$

We then apply Ito's lemma to analyze how the value of this portfolio moves as the parallel shift amount x moves:

$$dW = dP_1 + w dP_2$$

$$= g_1 P_1 dt + h_1 P_1 dz + w[g_2 P_2 dt + h_2 P_2 dz]$$

$$= [g_1 P_1 + w g_2 P_2] dt + [h_1 P_1 + w h_2 P_2] dz$$

As in step 3b of the process, we want to eliminate the interest rate risk in this portfolio. Since all interest rate risk comes from the random shock term dz, eliminating the interest rate risk means choosing w such that the coefficient of dz is 0. This means that the proper hedge ratio w for zero interest rate risk is

$$w = \frac{-h_1 P_1}{h_2 P_2} = \frac{-\tau_1 P_1}{\tau_2 P_2}$$

Substituting this into the equation above means

$$dW = \left[g_1 P_1 - \frac{\tau_1 P_1}{\tau_2 P_2} g_2 P_2 \right] dt$$

Now we impose the no-arbitrage condition. Since the interest rate risk has been eliminated from this portfolio, the instantaneous return on the portfolio dW should equal the riskless short-term rate r [the rate y with maturity 0, $y(0)$] times the value of the portfolio W:

$$dW = r(P_1 + w P_2)dt$$

$$= \left[g_1 P_1 + w g_2 P_2 \right] dt$$

Rewritten, this means that

$$\frac{r P_1 - \left(\frac{1}{2} \tau_1^2 \sigma^2 + y_1 \right) P_1}{\tau_1 P_1} = \frac{r P_2 - \left(\frac{1}{2} \tau_2^2 \sigma^2 + y_2 \right) P_2}{\tau_2 P_2} = k$$

This ratio has to be equal for any two maturities or there will be riskless arbitrage opportunities in this bond market. We define this ratio k as the "market price of risk." Choosing bond 1 and dropping the subscript 1, this means that the yield y must satisfy the following relationship:

$$r P - \frac{1}{2} t^2 \sigma^2 P - y P = k \tau P$$

Rearranging means that the yield y for any maturity must adhere to the following relationship:

$$y(\tau) = r - k\tau - \frac{1}{2} \tau^2 \sigma^2$$

This equation comes from Step 4 of the process described in Section 4.5. For a no-arbitrage equilibrium in the bond market under a parallel shift in the yield curve, the yield y must be a quadratic function of time to maturity τ. If the function is not quadratic, there would be riskless arbitrage in the market.

4.7 CONCLUSIONS ABOUT THE USE OF DURATION'S PARALLEL SHIFT ASSUMPTIONS

Unfortunately, the assumption that yields move in parallel fashion results in a number of conclusions that don't make sense if we impose the no-riskless-arbitrage conditions: First, interest rates can have only one "hump" in the yield curve. This hump will occur at the maturity

$$\tau = -\frac{k}{\sigma^2}$$

Also, beyond a certain maturity, yields will turn negative since σ is positive. Yields will zero for two values of T defined by setting y equal to zero and solving for the maturities consistent with zero yield:

$$T = -\frac{k}{\sigma^2} \pm \sqrt{\frac{2r}{\sigma^2} + \frac{k^2}{\sigma^4}}$$

For normal values of k, these values of T define a range over which y will be positive. Outside of that range, yields to maturity will be negative. Forward rates are also quadratic and have the form

$$f(\tau) = r - 2k\tau - \frac{3}{2}\tau^2\sigma^2$$

because forward rates are related to yields by the formula

$$f(\tau) = y(\tau) + \tau y'(\tau)$$

as shown in Chapter 2. Zero coupon bond prices are given by

$$P(\tau) = e^{-y(\tau)\tau} = e^{-r\tau + k\tau^2 + \frac{1}{2}\sigma^2\tau^3}$$

These features of a parallel shift-based term structure model pose very serious problems. If the parallel yield curve shift assumption is used, as it is when one uses the traditional duration approach to hedging, the resulting bond market is either (a) inconsistent with the real world because of negative yields, if we impose the no-arbitrage conditions, or (b) allowing of riskless arbitrage if we let yields have a shape that is not quadratic in the term to maturity. In either case, the model is unacceptable for use by market participants because its flaws are so serious. In Chapter 5, we use the same sort of analysis to identify some more attractive alternative models.

Example 4.7.1

The Wall Street Journal reported closing prices for U.S. Treasury strips (zero coupon bonds) at the following levels on March 25, 1996:

Maturity	Price	Years to Maturity	Yield
5/15/96	99.28	0.14	5.163%
11/15/96	96.70	0.64	5.207%
11/15/97	91.30	1.64	5.539%
11/15/98	86.03	2.64	5.691%
11/15/99	80.89	3.64	5.820%
11/15/00	76.02	4.65	5.902%
11/15/01	71.22	5.65	6.011%
11/15/02	66.78	6.65	6.075%
11/15/03	62.36	7.65	6.176%
11/15/04	58.16	8.65	6.267%
11/15/05	54.20	9.65	6.347%
11/15/06	50.42	10.65	6.430%
11/15/07	46.92	11.65	6.496%
11/15/08	43.64	12.65	6.554%
11/15/09	40.05	13.65	6.703%
11/15/10	37.61	14.65	6.674%
11/15/11	34.89	15.65	6.727%
11/15/12	32.42	16.65	6.763%
11/15/13	30.11	17.65	6.799%
11/15/14	27.97	18.65	6.830%
11/15/15	26.00	19.65	6.854%
11/15/16	24.17	20.66	6.874%
11/15/17	22.53	21.66	6.881%
11/15/18	21.02	22.66	6.885%
11/15/19	19.66	23.66	6.876%
11/15/20	18.34	24.66	6.877%
11/15/21	17.22	25.66	6.856%

Maturity	Price	Years to Maturity	Yield
11/15/22	16.22	26.66	6.823%
11/15/23	15.38	27.66	6.769%
11/15/24	14.56	28.66	6.722%

The yield shown above is the continuously compounded yield to maturity. What values of r, k, and σ provide the best fit to this actual data?

Using spreadsheet software to find the best-fitting parameters (minimizing the sum of the squared error versus the actual continuous yields) gives the following results:

$$k = -0.00149839$$
$$\sigma = 0.00825377$$
$$r = 5.234\%$$

The fit to the observed zero coupon yield curve using these parameters is actually quite good, as shown in Exhibit 4–1.

E X H I B I T   4-1

Actual U.S. Treasury Strip Yields versus Best-Fitting Duration Model March 25, 1996

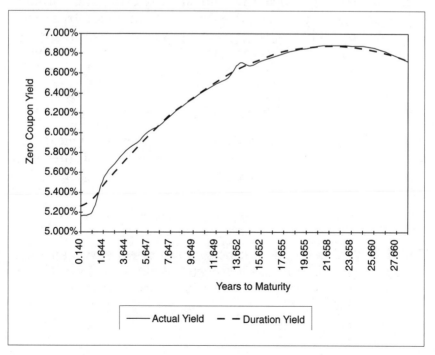

The fitted yield curve is not a bad match for the actual yield curve, with errors beyond six years in maturity of generally less than two basis points. Nonetheless, there are many problems using this approach in practice, as illustrated in the following examples.

Example 4.7.2
At what maturity will there be a peak in the yield curve?

Using the values for k, r, and σ above, the formula at the beginning of this section indicates a peak at 21.99 years. Beyond that point, the yield curve steadily declines and will reach negative infinity when the maturity gets long enough.

Example 4.7.3
At what maturities will yields turn negative?

Using the formulas above, yields turn negative in two places since the yield curve is a quadratic function of time to maturity. Yields reach zero for maturities of −22.95 years (which isn't relevant) and 66.94 years (which is relevant). Outside of these points, yields will be negative.

Examples 4.7.2 and 4.7.3 indicate the dangers of the assumptions behind the duration approach: Either the yield curve is locally no-arbitrage with the undesirable quadratic form, or arbitrage will be possible. Even in the local no-arbitrage yield curve environment, arbitrage will be possible once it is admitted that consumers will hold cash rather than invest at negative interest rates. We turn to more attractive solutions in Chapter 5.

EXERCISES

Assume for Exercises 4.1–4.4 that zero coupon bond yields prevailing in the market are such that r is 6.00 percent, the 3-year continuous yield is 8.00 percent, and the 20-year yield is 8.25 percent.

4.1 What values of k and σ are consistent with this yield curve?

4.2 What is the highest point on the yield curve, and at what maturity does it occur? What is the lowest point on the yield curve, and at what maturity does it occur?

4.3 At what maturities will the yield curve reach zero?

4.4 Would you buy a 99-year bond in this market? Why or why not?

Assume for Exercises 4.5–4.8 that the yield curve has the following features: r is 7 percent, the 5-year yield is 6.25 percent, and the 20-year yield is 8.00 percent.

4.5 What values of k and σ are consistent with this yield curve?

4.6 What is the highest point on the yield curve, and at what maturity does it occur? What is the lowest point on the yield curve, and at what maturity does it occur?

4.7 At what maturities will the yield curve reach zero?

4.8 Would you buy a 99-year bond in this market? Why or why not?

REFERENCES

Ingersoll, Jonathan E. *Theory of Financial Decision Making.* Savage, MD: Rowman & Littlefield, 1987.

Merton, Robert C. "A Dynamic General Equilibrium Model of the Asset Market and Its Application to the Pricing of the Capital Structure of the Firm." Working Paper No. 497-70. Cambridge, MA: A. P. Sloan School of Management, Massachusetts Institute of Technology, 1970. Reproduced as Chapter 11 in Robert C. Merton, *Continuous Time Finance* (Cambridge, MA: Blackwell, 1993).

Shimko, David C. *Finance in Continuous Time: A Primer.* Miami: Kolb, 1992.

Vasicek, Oldrich A. "An Equilibrium Characterization of the Term Structure," *Journal of Financial Economics* 5, November 1977, pp. 177–88.

CHAPTER 5

The Vasicek and Extended Vasicek Models

In this chapter, we introduce four term structure models based on increasingly realistic assumptions about the random movement of interest rates. As we saw in Chapter 4, the historically popular assumption that the yield curve shifts in a parallel fashion can be consistent with a no-arbitrage economy, but only if the yield curve is quadratic and only if yields become negative beyond a given point on the yield curve. For this reason, we need a new set of assumptions about yield curve movements, rich enough to allow us to derive a theoretical yield curve whose shape is as close as possible, if not identical, to observable market yields and whose other properties are realistic.

We start with the simplest possible model, assuming bond prices in all four models depend solely on a single random factor: the short rate of interest. We then go through the same steps as in Chapter 4 to derive the form that zero coupon bond prices and yields must have for the bond market to be a no-arbitrage market:

- We specify the stochastic process for the movements in interest rates.
- We use Ito's lemma to derive the stochastic movements in zero coupon bond prices.

- We impose no-arbitrage restrictions to generate the partial differential equation that determines zero coupon bond prices.
- We solve this equation for bond prices, subject to the boundary condition that the price of a zero coupon bond with zero years to maturity must be 1.

The four models we will discuss all assume that changes in the short-term rate of interest are normally distributed:

1. Changes in r are a random walk with zero drift over time (the Merton model).
2. Changes in r are a random walk with nonzero drift, allowing a perfect fit to an observable yield curve (the "extended" Merton model).
3. Changes in r follow the Ornstein-Uhlenbeck process with a drift term reverting to a constant long-term value plus normally distributed shocks (the Vasicek model).
4. Changes in r follow the Ornstein-Uhlenbeck process with a drift term reverting to a time-dependent long-term value plus normally distributed shocks (the "extended" Vasicek or Hull and White model).

Each of these models has its strengths and weaknesses. We discuss them, in turn, in Sections 5.1 through 5.4.

5.1 THE MERTON MODEL

One simple assumption about interest rates is that they follow a simple random walk[1] with a zero drift. In stochastic process terms, we would write the change in r as

$$dr = \sigma dZ$$

The change in the short rate of interest r equals a constant sigma (σ) times a random shock term, where Z represents a standard Wiener process with a mean of 0 and standard deviation of 1. The constant σ is the instantaneous volatility of interest rates. We will be careful to distinguish between interest rate volatility and the

---

1. To be precise, a Gaussian random walk.

volatility of zero coupon bond prices throughout the rest of this book. From Chapter 4, we know that Ito's lemma can be used to write the stochastic process for the random changes in the price of a zero coupon bond price as of time t with maturity T:

$$dP = P_r dr + \frac{1}{2} P_{rr} (dr)^2 + P_t$$

In the simple random walk model, $(dr)^2 = \sigma^2$, so the expression can be expanded to read

$$dP = P_r \sigma dZ + \frac{1}{2} P_{rr} \sigma^2 + P_t$$

Our goal is to find the formula for P as a function of the short rate r.

The next step in doing this is to impose the condition that no arbitrage is possible in the bond market. Since we have only one random factor in the economy, we know that we can eliminate this risk factor by hedging with only one instrument. If we had n independent risk factors, we would need n instruments to eliminate the n risks. Let's assume that an investor holds one unit of a zero coupon bond, bond 1, with maturity T_1. The investor forms a portfolio of amount W that consists of the one unit of bond 1 and w units of bond 2, which has a maturity T_2. The value of the portfolio is

$$P_1 + w P_2$$

What is the proper hedge ratio w, and what are the implications of a perfect hedge for bond pricing? We know from Ito's lemma that the change in the value of this hedged portfolio is

$$dW = dP_1 + w dP_2$$

$$P_{1_r} \sigma dZ + \left(\frac{1}{2} P_{1_{rr}} \sigma^2 + P_{1_t} \right) dt + w \left[P_{2_r} \sigma dZ + \left(\frac{1}{2} P_{2_{rr}} \sigma^2 + P_{2_t} \right) dt \right]$$

Gathering together the coefficients of the random shock term dZ gives

$$dW = \left(\frac{1}{2} P_{1_{rr}} \sigma^2 + P_{1_t} \right) dt + w \left(\frac{1}{2} P_{2_{rr}} \sigma^2 + P_{2_t} \right) dt + \left[P_{1_r} + w P_{2_r} \right] \sigma dZ$$

If we choose w, the hedge amount of bond 2, such that the coefficient of the random shock term dZ is 0, then we have a perfect hedge and a riskless portfolio. The value of w for which this is true is

$$w = \frac{-P_{1r}}{P_{2r}}$$

Note that this is identical to the hedge ratio we found for the duration-based parallel shift model in Chapter 4. If we use this hedge ratio, then the instantaneous return on the portfolio should exactly equal the short-term rate of interest times the value of the portfolio:

$$dW = rWdt = (rP_1 + rwP_2)dt$$

If this is not true, then riskless arbitrage will be possible. Imposing this condition and rearranging the equation above gives us the following relationship:

$$dW = (rP_1 + rwP_2)dt = \left(\frac{1}{2}P_{1rr}\sigma^2 + P_{1t}\right)dt + w\left(\frac{1}{2}P_{2rr}\sigma^2 + P_{2t}\right)dt$$

We then substitute the expression for w above into this equation, eliminate the dt coefficient from both sides, rearrange, and divide by interest rate volatility σ to get the following relationship:

$$-\lambda = \frac{\frac{1}{2}P_{1rr}\sigma^2 + P_{1t} - rP_1}{\sigma P_{1r}} = \frac{\frac{1}{2}P_{2rr}\sigma^2 + P_{2t} - rP_2}{\sigma P_{2r}}$$

For any two maturities T_1 and T_2, the no-arbitrage condition requires that this ratio be equal. We call the negative of this ratio λ,[2] the market price of risk. For normal risk aversion, the market price of risk should be positive (1) because in a risk-averse market, riskier (longer-maturity) bonds should have a higher expected return than the short rate r and (2) because the rate sensitivity of all bonds P_r is negative. Since the choice of T_1 and T_2

---

2. In subsequent chapters, we insert the minus sign in front of λ to be consistent with other authors' notation.

is arbitrary, the market price of risk ratio must be constant for all maturities. It is the fixed-income equivalent of the Sharpe ratio, which measures "excess return" per unit of risk with the following statistic:

$$\text{Sharpe ratio} = \frac{\text{Expected return} - \text{Risk free return}}{\text{Standard deviation of return}}$$

In our case, the numerator is made up of the drift in the bond's price:

$$\text{Drift} = \text{Expected return} = \frac{1}{2}P_{rr}\sigma^2 + P_t$$

which also equals the expected return since the shock term or stochastic component of the bond's price change on average has zero expected value.

We now solve the equation above for any given bond with maturity T and remaining time to maturity $T - t = \tau$ as of time t, under the assumption that λ is constant over time. Rearranging the equation gives the following partial differential equation:

$$\lambda\sigma P_r + \frac{1}{2}P_{rr}\sigma^2 + P_t - rP = 0$$

which must be solved subject to the boundary condition that the price of the zero coupon bond upon maturity T must equal its principal amount 1:

$$P(r,T,T) = 1$$

We use a common method of solving partial differential equations: the educated guess. We guess that P has the solution

$$P(r,t,T) = P(r,\tau) = e^{rF(\tau)+G(\tau)}$$

where $T - t = \tau$ and we need to solve for the forms of the functions F and G. We know that

$$P_r = F(\tau)P$$

$$P_{rr} = F(\tau)^2 P$$

$$P_t = -P_\tau = (-rF' - G')P$$

Substituting these values into the partial differential equation and dividing by the bond price P gives the following:

$$\lambda\sigma F + \frac{1}{2}\sigma^2 F^2 - rF' - G' - r = 0$$

We know from Merton (1970) and the similar equation in Chapter 4 that the solution to this equation is

$$F(\tau) = -\tau$$

$$G(\tau) = -\frac{\lambda\sigma\tau^2}{2} + \frac{1}{6}\sigma^2\tau^3$$

and therefore the formula for the price of a zero coupon bond is given by

$$P(r,t,T) = P(r,\tau) = e^{-r\tau - \frac{\lambda\sigma\tau^2}{2} + \frac{1}{6}\sigma^2\tau^3}$$

This is nearly the same bond pricing equation as the one we obtained in Chapter 4 under the assumption of parallel shifts in bond prices. It has the same virtues and the same liabilities of the duration approach:

- It is a simple analytical formula.
- Zero coupon bond prices are a quadratic function of time to maturity.
- Yields turn negative (and zero coupon bond prices rise above 1) beyond a certain point.
- If interest rate volatility σ is zero, zero coupon bond yields are constant for all maturities and equal to r.

From the Chapter 1 formula

$$P(r,\tau) = e^{-y(\tau)\tau}$$

the zero coupon bond yield formula can be calculated as

$$y(\tau) = r + \frac{1}{2}\lambda\sigma\tau - \frac{1}{6}\sigma^2\tau^2$$

The last term in this formula ultimately becomes so large as time to maturity increases that yields become negative. Setting $y' = 0$

and solving for the maximum level of y (the "hump" in the yield curve) shows that this occurs at a time to maturity of

$$\tau* = \frac{3\lambda}{2\sigma}$$

and that the yield to maturity at that point is

$$y(\tau*) = r + \frac{3}{8}\lambda^2$$

Note that the peak in the yield curve is independent of interest rate volatility, although the location of this hump is affected by rate volatility. As volatility increases, the hump moves to shorter and shorter maturity points on the yield curve. Using the quadratic formula, we can also determine the point at which the zero coupon bond yield equals 0. This occurs when the yield curve reaches a time to maturity of

$$\tau* = \frac{3\lambda}{2\sigma} + \frac{3}{\sigma}\sqrt{\frac{\lambda^2}{4} + \frac{2r}{3}}$$

The market price of risk is normally expected to be positive, so this formula shows rates will turn negative at a positive term to maturity τ^*.

The price volatility of zero coupon bonds is given by

$$-\sigma P_r = \tau\sigma P$$

The percentage change in price of zero coupon bonds for small changes in the short rate r under the Merton model is

$$r\text{-duration} = -\frac{P_r}{P} = -\frac{-\tau P}{P} = \tau$$

so the rate sensitivity of a zero coupon bond in this model is its time to maturity in years. We label this percentage change "r-duration" to contrast it with Macaulay's measure of price sensitivity discussed in Chapter 3, where price is differentiated with respect to its continuous yield to maturity. The hedge ratio w given above for hedging of a bond with maturity T_1 with a bond maturing at T_2 is

$$w = \frac{-P_{1_r}}{P_{2_r}} = -\frac{\tau_1 P_1}{\tau_2 P_2}$$

The Merton model gives us very important insights into the process of deriving a term structure model. Its simple formulas make it a useful expository tool, but the negative yields that result from the formula are a major concern. It leads to a logical question: Can we "extend" the Merton model to fit the actual yield curve perfectly? If so, this superficially at least would allow us to avoid the negative yield problems associated with the model.

5.2 THE EXTENDED MERTON MODEL

Ho and Lee (1986) extended the Merton model to fit a given initial yield curve perfectly in a discrete time framework. In this section, we derive the equivalent model using continuous time and the no-arbitrage approach of Chapter 4 and Section 5.1. In the extended Merton case, we assume that the short rate of interest is again the single stochastic factor driving movements in the yield curve. Instead of assuming that the short rate r is a random walk, however, we assume that it has a time-dependent drift term $a(t)$:

$$dr = a(t)dt + \sigma dZ$$

As before, Z represents a standard Wiener process with a mean of 0 and standard deviation of 1. The instantaneous standard deviation of interest rates is again the constant σ. Ito's lemma gives us the same formula for changes in the value of a zero coupon bond P, except for substitution of the slightly more complex expression for dr:

$$dP = P_r dr + \frac{1}{2} P_{rr} (dr)^2 + P_t$$

$$P_r[a(t) + \sigma dZ] + \frac{1}{2} P_{rr} \sigma^2 + P_t$$

We form a no-arbitrage portfolio with value W, as in Section 5.1, so that the coefficient of the dZ term is 0. We get the same hedge ratio as given in the original Merton model:

$$w = \frac{-P_{1_r}}{P_{2_r}}$$

By applying the no-arbitrage condition that $dW = rW$, we are led to a no-arbitrage condition closely related to that of the original Merton model:

$$-\lambda = \frac{P_{1r}a(t) + \frac{1}{2}P_{1rr}\sigma^2 + P_{1t} - rP_1}{\sigma P_{1r}}$$

$$= \frac{P_{2r}a(t) + \frac{1}{2}P_{2rr}\sigma^2 + P_{2t} - rP_2}{\sigma P_{2r}}$$

In the Ho and Lee model, the market price of risk must be equal for any two zero coupon bonds with arbitrary maturities T_1 and T_2. In the Ho and Lee case, the market price of risk again is the fixed-income counterpart of the Sharpe ratio, with expected return on each bond equal to

$$\text{Drift} = \text{Expected return} = P_r a(t) + \frac{1}{2}P_{rr}\sigma^2 + P_t$$

Now the value of the zero coupon bond price P for any given maturity is fixed by the shape of the yield curve which Ho and Lee seek to match perfectly. Our mission in solving the partial differential equation in the Ho and Lee model is to find the relationship between the drift term $a(t)$ and the bond price P. The partial differential equation that must be solved comes from rearranging the no-arbitrage condition above, and our continued assumption that λ is constant:

$$P_r[a(t) + \lambda\sigma] + \frac{1}{2}P_{rr}\sigma^2 + P_t - rP = 0$$

which must hold subject to the fact that the value of a zero coupon bond must equal 1 at maturity.

$$P(r,T,T) = 1$$

We use an educated guess to postulate a solution and then see what must be true for our guess to be correct (if it is possible to make it correct). We guess that the solution P is closely related to the Merton model:

$$P(r,t,T) = e^{-rt+G(t,T)}$$

We seek to find the function G that satisfies the partial differential equation. We take the partial derivatives of P and substitute them into the partial differential equation:

$$P_r = -\tau P$$

$$P_{rr} = \tau^2 P$$

$$P_t = (r + G')P$$

When we substitute these partial derivatives into the partial differential equation and simplify, we get the following relationship:

$$-[a(t) + \lambda\sigma]\tau + \frac{1}{2}\sigma^2\tau^2 + G' = 0$$

We solve this differential equation in G by translating the derivative of G with respect to the current time t (not τ) into this expression:

$$G(t,T) = -\frac{\lambda\sigma\tau^2}{2} + \frac{1}{6}\sigma^2\tau^3 - \int_t^T a(s)(T - s)ds$$

Therefore, the value of a zero coupon bond in the extended Merton/Ho and Lee model is given by the equation

$$P(r,t,T) = e^{-r\tau - \frac{\lambda\sigma\tau^2}{2} + \frac{1}{6}\sigma^2\tau^3 - \int_t^T a(s)(T - s)ds}$$

Note that this is identical to the formula for the zero coupon bond price in the Merton model with the exception of the last term. The value of the zero coupon bond is 1 when $t = T$ as the boundary condition demands.

Like the Merton model, the price volatility of zero coupon bonds is given by[3]

$$-\sigma P_r = \tau\sigma P$$

---

[3]. We could change the sign of this expression to make it positive, since the sign of the Wiener process dZ is arbitrary.

and the percentage change in price of zero coupon bonds for small changes in the short rate r is

$$r\text{-duration} = -\frac{P_r}{P} = -\frac{-\tau P}{P} = \tau$$

The behavior of the yield to maturity on a zero coupon bond in the extended Merton/Ho and Lee model is always consistent with the observable yield curve, since the expression for yield to maturity

$$y(\tau) = r + \frac{\lambda\sigma\tau}{2} - \frac{1}{6}\sigma^2\tau^2 + \frac{1}{\tau}\int_t^T a(s)(T-s)ds$$

contains the "extension term"

$$\text{extension}(\tau) = \frac{1}{\tau}\int_t^T a(s)(T-s)ds$$

The function $a(s)$ is chosen such that the theoretical zero coupon yield to maturity y and the actual zero coupon yield are exactly the same. The function $a(s)$ is the "plug" that makes the model fit and corrects for "model error" that would otherwise cause the model to give implausible results. Since any functional form for yields can be adapted to fit a yield curve precisely,[4] it is critical in examining any model for plausibility to minimize the impact of this extension term. Why? Because the extension term itself contains no economic content.

In the case of the Ho and Lee model, the underlying model would otherwise cause interest rates to sink to negative infinity, just as in the Merton model. The extension term's magnitude, therefore, must offset the negative-interest zero coupon bond yields that would otherwise be predicted by the model. As maturities get infinitely long, the magnitude of the extension term will become infinite. This is a significant cause for concern, even in the extended form of the model.

---

4. For example, consider this term structure model: $y(\tau) = .05 + .01\tau$. It is clearly a ridiculous model, but it can be made to fit the yield curve exactly in a manner similar to the Ho and Lee model.

5.3 THE VASICEK MODEL

Both the Merton model and its extended counterpart, the Ho and Lee model, are based on an assumption about random interest rate movements that implies that for any positive interest rate volatility, zero coupon bond yields will be negative at every single instant in time for long maturities beyond a critical maturity τ. The extended version of the Merton model, the Ho and Lee model, offsets the negative yields with an extension factor that must grow larger and larger as maturities lengthen. Vasicek (1977) proposed a model that avoids the certainty of negative yields and eliminates the need for a potentially infinitely large extension factor. Vasicek accomplishes this by assuming that the short rate r has a constant volatility σ like the models above, with an important twist — the short rate exhibits "mean reversion":

$$dr = \alpha(\mu - r)dt + \sigma dZ$$

where

r = The instantaneous short rate of interest
α = The speed of mean reversion
μ = The long-run expected value for r
σ = The instantaneous standard deviation of r

Z is the standard Wiener process with a mean of 0 and standard deviation of 1. The stochastic process used by Vasicek is known as the Ornstein-Uhlenbeck process. The first term in the stochastic process proposed by Vasicek pulls the short rate r back toward μ, so μ can be thought of as the long-run level of the short rate. When the short rate r is above μ, the first term tends to pull r downward since α is assumed to be positive. When the short rate r is below μ, r tends to drift upward. The second term of the stochastic process, of course, applies random shocks to the short rate that may temporarily offset the tendencies toward mean reversion of the underlying stochastic process. The impact of mean reversion is to create realistic interest rate cycles, with the level of α determining the length and violence of rises and falls in interest rates. What are the implications of this model for the pricing of bonds?

We use the notation of Chen (1992) to answer this question using the same process as in the Merton and Ho and Lee models. By Ito's lemma, the movement in the price of a zero coupon bond is

$$dP = P_r dr + \frac{1}{2} P_{rr}(dr)^2 + P_t$$

$$= P_r[\alpha(\mu - r)dt + \sigma dZ] + \frac{1}{2} P_{rr}\sigma^2 + P_t$$

Using exactly the same no-arbitrage argument that we used above (p. 126), we can eliminate the dZ term by choosing the hedge ratio necessary to eliminate interest rate risk (which is what dZ represents). The partial differential equation consistent with a no-arbitrage bond market in the Vasicek model is

$$P_r[\alpha(\mu - r) + \lambda\sigma] + \frac{1}{2} P_{rr}\sigma^2 + P_t - rP = 0$$

and, as above, it must be solved subject to the boundary condition that a zero coupon bond's price at maturity equals its principal amount, 1:

$$P(r,T,T) = 1$$

The market price of risk λ is assumed to be constant. As a working assumption, we guess that the zero coupon bond price has the solution

$$P(r,t,T) = P(r,\tau) = e^{-rF(\tau) - G(\tau)}$$

where F and G are unknown functions of $\tau = T - t$. If our working assumption is correct, we will be able to obtain solutions for F and G. We know that

$$P_r = -FP$$

$$P_{rr} = F^2 P$$

$$P_t = (-rF_t - G_t)P$$

By replacing the derivatives of the zero coupon bond price P in the partial differential equation above and rearranging, we know that the following relationship must hold:

$$r[\alpha F - F_t - 1] + \left[\frac{1}{2}F^2\sigma^2 - F(\alpha\mu + \lambda\sigma) - G_t\right] = 0$$

This relationship must hold for all values of r, so the coefficient of r must be zero:

$$\alpha F - F_t - 1 = 0$$

We can solve this partial differential equation by rearranging it until we have

$$\frac{\alpha F_t}{1 - \alpha F} = -\alpha$$

We then take the integral of both sides such that

$$\int_t^T \frac{\alpha F_t(s,T)}{1 - \alpha F(s,T)}\,ds = -\int_t^T \alpha ds$$

Evaluating the integrals on both sides of the equation leaves the relationship

$$\ln[1 - \alpha F(t,T)] = -\alpha(T - t)$$

Calculating the exponential of both sides defines F:

$$F(t,T) = F(\tau) = \frac{1}{\alpha}\left(1 - e^{-\alpha\tau}\right)$$

To determine the value of the function G, we must solve the partial differential equation

$$\frac{1}{2}F^2\sigma^2 - F(\alpha\mu + \lambda\sigma) - G_t = 0$$

or

$$G_t = \frac{1}{2}F^2\sigma^2 - F(\alpha\mu + \lambda\sigma)$$

We can calculate that

$$\int_t^T F(s,T)ds = \frac{1}{\alpha}[\tau - F(\tau)]$$

and that

$$\int_t^T F^2(s,T)ds = \frac{1}{\alpha^2}[\tau - F(\tau)] - \frac{F^2(\tau)}{2\alpha}$$

We can take the integral of both sides of the equation above to solve for G:

$$\int_t^T G_s(s,T)ds = \int_t^T \left[\frac{1}{2}F(s,T)^2\sigma^2 - F(s,T)(\alpha\mu + \lambda\sigma)\right]ds$$

$$= \frac{1}{2}\sigma^2\left[\frac{1}{\alpha^2}(\tau - F(\tau)) - \frac{F^2(\tau)}{2\alpha}\right] - \frac{\alpha\mu + \lambda\sigma}{\alpha}[\tau - F(\tau)]$$

$$= \left[\frac{\sigma^2}{2\alpha^2} - \mu - \frac{\lambda\sigma}{\alpha}\right][\tau - F(\tau)] - \frac{\sigma^2}{4\alpha}F^2(\tau)$$

Since

$$\int_t^T G_s(s,T)ds = G(T,T) - G(t,T)$$

and since $G(T,T)$ must be 0 for the boundary condition that $P(T,T) = 1$, then

$$G(t,T) = G(\tau) = \left[\mu + \frac{\lambda\sigma}{\alpha} - \frac{\sigma^2}{2\alpha^2}\right][\tau - F(\tau)] + \frac{\sigma^2}{4\alpha}F^2(\tau)$$

This means that the value of a zero coupon bond in the Vasicek model is

$$P(r,t,T) = e^{-F(t,T)r - G(t,T)}$$

$$\exp\left[-rF(\tau) - \left(\mu + \frac{\lambda\sigma}{\alpha} - \frac{\sigma^2}{2\alpha^2}\right)[\tau - F(\tau)] - \frac{\sigma^2 F^2(\tau)}{4\alpha}\right]$$

The yield to maturity of zero coupon bonds in the Vasicek model is easy to derive from the expression given in Chapter 1:

$$y(\tau) = -\frac{1}{\tau}\ln[P(\tau)] = -\frac{1}{\tau}[-rF(\tau) - G(\tau)]$$

$$= \frac{F(\tau)}{\tau}r + \frac{G(\tau)}{\tau}$$

As time to maturity gets infinitely long, one can calculate the infinitely long maturity as

$$y(\infty) = \mu + \frac{\lambda\sigma}{\alpha} - \frac{\sigma^2}{2\alpha^2}$$

This yield to maturity is positive for almost all realistic sets of parameter values, correcting one of the major objections to the Merton model without the necessity to "extend" the yield curve with a time-dependent value for μ.

What does duration mean in the context of the Vasicek model? Macaulay defined duration, as we saw in Chapters 3 and 4, as the percentage change in bond prices with respect to the parallel shift in yield to maturity in a continuous time context. The parallel shift in the Macaulay model was the single stochastic factor driving the yield curve. In the Vasicek model, the short rate r is the stochastic factor. We define r-*duration* as above; it is the percentage change in the price of a bond with respect to changes in the short rate r:

$$r\text{-duration} = \frac{-P_r}{P} = \frac{F(\tau)P}{P} = F(\tau) = \frac{1}{\alpha}\left[1 - e^{-\alpha\tau}\right]$$

The hedge ratio necessary to hedge one unit of a zero coupon bond with a remaining maturity of τ_1 using a bond with remaining maturity of τ_2 is

$$w = -\frac{P_{1_r}}{P_{2_r}} = -\frac{F(\tau_1)P[\tau_1]}{F(\tau_2)P[\tau_2]}$$

a hedge ratio substantially different from that using the Merton or Ho and Lee models:

$$w = -\frac{\tau_1 P[\tau_1]}{\tau_2 P[\tau_2]}$$

In practical use, it is this difference in hedge ratios that allows us to distinguish between different models. The ability to extend a model, as in Section 5.2, renders all extendable models equally good in the sense of fitting observable data. In reality, however, the explanatory power of various term structure models can be substantially different. Ultimately, the relative performance of each model's hedge ratios and its ability to explain price movements of traded securities with the fewest parameters are what differentiate the best models from the others.

The stochastic process proposed by Vasicek allows us to calculate the expected value and variance of the short rate at any time in the future s from the perspective of current time t. Denoting the short rate at time t by $r(t)$, the expected value of the short rate at future time s is

$$E_t[r(s)] = \mu + [r(t) - \mu]e^{-\alpha(s-t)}$$

The standard deviation of the potential values of r around this mean value is

$$\text{Standard deviation}_t[r(s)] = \sqrt{\frac{\sigma^2}{2\alpha}\left[1 - e^{-2\alpha(s-t)}\right]}$$

Because $r(s)$ is normally distributed, there is a positive probability that $r(s)$ can be negative. As pointed out by Black (1995), this is inconsistent with a no-arbitrage economy in the special sense that consumers hold an option to hold cash instead of investing at negative interest rates. The magnitude of this theoretical problem with the Vasicek model depends on the level of interest rates and the parameters chosen.[5] In general, it should be a minor consideration for most applications. Very low interest rates in Japan in early 1996, with short rates well under 0.5 percent, did lead to high probabilities of negative rates using both the Vasicek and extended Vasicek models when σ was set to match observable prices of caps and floors. Although the price of a floor with a strike price of zero was positive during this period,[6] indicating that the market

5. The same objection applies to the Merton and Ho and Lee models and a wide range of other models that assume a constant volatility of interest rates, regardless of the level of short-term interest rates.
6. Lehman Brothers was quoting a floor on six-month yen Libor with a three-year maturity and a strike price of 0 at 1 basis point bid, 3 basis points offered during the fall of 1995.

perceived a real probability of negative rates, the best-fitting values of σ for all caps and floors prices indicated a probability of negative rates that was unrealistically large. For most economies, the Vasicek and extended Vasicek models are very robust, with wide-ranging benefits from practical use.

5.4 THE EXTENDED VASICEK/HULL AND WHITE MODEL

Hull and White (1990) bridged the gap between the observable yield curve and the theoretical yield curve implied by the Vasicek model by "extending" or stretching the theoretical yield curve to fit the actual market data. Having a theoretical yield curve identical to observable market data is absolutely essential in practical application, since a model that does not fit actual data will propagate errors resulting from this lack of fit into hedge ratio calculations and valuation estimates for more complex securities. No sophisticated user would be willing to place large bets on the valuation of a bond option by a model that cannot fit observable bond prices.

Hull and White apply the same logic as in Section 5.3, but they allow the market price of risk term λ to drift over time, instead of assuming it is constant, as in the Vasicek model. If we assume this term drifts over time, what are the implications for the pricing formula for zero coupon bonds? The partial differential equation changes only very slightly from Section 5.3:

$$P_r[\alpha(\mu - r) + \lambda(t)\sigma] + \frac{1}{2}P_{rr}\sigma^2 + P_t - rP = 0$$

subject to the usual requirement that the bond's price equals 1 at maturity:

$$P(r,T,T) = 1$$

We can rewrite the partial differential equation as

$$P_r[(\alpha\mu + \lambda(t)\sigma) - \alpha r] + \frac{1}{2}P_{rr}\sigma^2 + P_t - rP = 0$$

Using the definition

$$\theta(t) = \alpha\mu + \lambda(t)\sigma$$

we can simplify the partial differential equation to the point that it looks almost identical to that of the Ho and Lee model in Section 5.2:

$$P_r[\theta(t) - \alpha r] + \frac{1}{2} P_{rr}\sigma^2 + P_t - rP = 0$$

As in Section 5.3, we assume that the solution to the pricing of zero coupon bonds takes the form

$$P(r,t,T) = P(r,\tau) = e^{-rF(\tau) - G(\tau)}$$

where F and G are unknown functions of $\tau = T - t$. Using the partial derivatives of P under the assumption that we have guessed the functional form correctly, we know that the following relationship must hold:

$$r[\alpha F - F_t - 1] + \left[\frac{1}{2}F^2\sigma^2 - F\theta(t) - G_t\right] = 0$$

From Section 5.3, we can prove

$$F(t,T) = F(\tau) = \frac{1}{\alpha}\left(1 - e^{-\alpha\tau}\right)$$

We now must solve for G given the following equation:

$$G_t = \frac{1}{2}F^2\sigma^2 - F\theta(t)$$

We do this by taking the integral of both sides and making use of the integral of F^2, which was given in Section 5.3 to arrive at the solution for G:

$$G(t,T) = G(\tau) = \int_t^T F(s,T)\theta(s)ds - \frac{\sigma^2}{2\alpha^2}[\tau - F(\tau)] + \frac{\sigma^2}{4\alpha}F^2(\tau)$$

Therefore, under the extended Vasicek model, the value of a zero coupon bond is given by the formula

$$P(r,t,T) = e^{-F(t,T)r - G(t,T)}$$

$$\exp\left[-rF(\tau) - \int_t^T F(s,T)\theta(s)ds + \left(\frac{\sigma^2}{2\alpha^2}\right)[\tau - F(\tau)] - \frac{\sigma^2 F^2(\tau)}{4\alpha}\right]$$

As in the Vasicek model, the price sensitivity of a zero coupon bond is given by the formula

$$r\text{-duration} = \frac{-P_r}{P} = \frac{F(\tau)P}{P} = F(\tau) = \frac{1}{\alpha}\left[1 - e^{-\alpha\tau}\right]$$

5.5 AN EXAMPLE OF THE HEDGING IMPLICATIONS OF TERM STRUCTURE MODELS COMPARED TO THE DURATION APPROACH

So far, our discussion in this chapter has been purely theoretical, but the practical implications for hedging a position in the bond or swap market are very powerful. In order to compare the traditional duration approach with the term structure model approach, let's use a practical example. We assume that the current yield curve prevails in the money and bond markets.

Observable Market Yield Curve

Years to Maturity	Par Yield	Yield Basis	Zero Coupon Bond Price
0.5	6.000%	Actual/360	0.970481197
1.0	6.500%	Actual/360	0.938171868
1.5	6.750%	30/360	0.905037929
2.0	7.000%	30/360	0.871034604
2.5	7.500%	30/360	0.830672569
3.0	8.000%	30/360	0.787869301

As in typical U.S. or Eurocurrency money markets, we assume that the interest rates for six-month and one-year maturities are stated on an actual/360-day basis. In order to keep the example simple, we assume that there are exactly 182.5 days to maturity on the six-month instrument. Accordingly, the interest that would be paid on a money market instrument with a six-month maturity and the stated 6 percent coupon would be

$$\text{Interest} = \frac{\$100 * .06 * 182.5}{360}$$

Therefore, the zero coupon bond price with a six-month maturity can be calculated using the formula

$$\text{Zero coupon bond price} = \frac{1}{1 + \dfrac{\text{Actual days} \times \text{Coupon}}{360}}$$

The one-year instrument is also assumed to have interest paid only at maturity, like the London interbank offered rate (Libor) market, and to have interest quoted on the same actual/360-day basis. The zero coupon bond price is calculated in the same way. All of the other instruments are assumed to be standard semiannual payment bonds quoted on the normal U.S. 30/360-day basis.[7] The zero coupon bond prices associated with each maturity can be calculated recursively using the known zero coupon bond prices for shorter maturities and the following formula for the price $P[t_n]$ of a zero coupon bond with maturity t_n:

$$P[t_n] = \frac{1 - \dfrac{C}{2}\left[\sum_{i=1}^{n-1} P[t_i]\right]}{\dfrac{C}{2} + 1}$$

This formula assumes that a 6 percent coupon, for example, is stated as .06 and that it is paid semiannually on a principal amount of $1. By using this formula, we arrive at the zero coupon bond prices given above. If the data is not complete enough to use this recursive formula, we can use one of the yield curve smoothing techniques discussed in Chapter 2.

We now want to answer a very practical question: *How much of the one-year instrument should we sell short (or issue as a liability) in order to hedge the interest rate risk on a $100 position in the three-year bond?*

---

7. Note that this does *not* mean that interest is calculated on the basis of a 360-day year. A 10 percent bond would pay two equal coupons of $5 each if the principal were $100, unlike an actual/360-day instrument. The "30/360" is really shorthand that signifies that accrued interest (which is irrelevant to this example) is divided among 12 months of equal length.

Our table on p. 142 assumes that all of the instruments currently trade at present values equal to their $100 par values. We will compare three duration formulas:

- Traditional modified duration.
- The Ho and Lee model r-duration.
- The extended Vasicek r-duration.

From Chapter 1, we recall that the modified duration formula for a semiannual payment bond with an even payment period to the first coupon payment and n payments remaining is as follows:

$$\text{Modified duration} = \frac{-\dfrac{\partial NPV}{\partial y}}{NPV}$$

$$= \frac{\text{Coupon}}{2} \sum_{i=1}^{n} \frac{\dfrac{i}{2}}{\left(1+\dfrac{y}{2}\right)^{i+1}} + \frac{n}{2} \frac{\text{Principal}}{\left(1+\dfrac{y}{2}\right)^{n+1}}$$

$$= \left[\frac{1}{1+\dfrac{y}{2}}\right] \text{Duration}$$

For both the Ho and Lee and extended Vasicek models, interest rate risk is measured by r-duration, the change in value with respect to changes in the short rate of interest r. For a semiannual bond with n payments to maturity:

$$\text{Ho}-\text{Lee } r\text{-duration} = \frac{-\dfrac{\partial NPV}{\partial r}}{NPV}$$

$$= \frac{\dfrac{C}{2}\sum_{i=1}^{n} t_i P[t_i] + t_n P[t_n]}{NPV}$$

The r-duration for the extended Vasicek model is as follows:

$$\text{Extended Vasicek } r\text{-duration} = \frac{-\dfrac{\partial NPV}{\partial r}}{NPV}$$

$$= \frac{\dfrac{C}{2}\displaystyle\sum_{i=1}^{n} F[t_i]P[t_i] + F[t_n]P[t_n]}{NPV}$$

$$F[t_i] = \frac{1}{\alpha}\left[1 - e^{-\alpha t_i}\right]$$

The hedge ratio for each duration measure is consistent with the hedge ratios, labeled w above, that we have calculated throughout this chapter. For all three duration measures, the hedge ratio would be calculated as follows:

$$\text{Hedge ratio} = \frac{-D_1 V_1}{D_2 V_2}$$

where D_i is the duration for instrument i and V_i is the net present value[8] of one unit of security i. In the current example, V_i is the par value of 100 for each instrument.

The following table compares the various duration measures for the modified duration, Ho and Lee, and extended Vasicek approaches. The extended Vasicek approach can be calibrated at various speeds of mean reversion (α). Using a very low level (0.0001) and a fairly representative level for α (0.10), we can calculate the following duration measures for each instrument:

Years to Maturity	Modified Duration	Ho–Lee r-duration	Extended Vasicek r-duration for Various Alpha Values	
			0.0001	0.10
0.5	0.4852	0.4998	0.4998	0.4875
1.0	0.9382	0.9844	0.9844	0.9372
1.5	1.4042	1.4514	1.4513	1.3493
2.0	1.8365	1.9004	1.9002	1.7261
2.5	2.2416	2.3242	2.3239	2.0641
3.0	2.6211	2.7221	2.7217	2.3654

8. Recall that here we mean true present value (Price + Accrued interest), not simple price.

The Ho and Lee duration measures can be calculated as the limit of the extended Vasicek model's duration measure as α approaches 0. One might also ask what α values in the extended Vasicek model are required to match the duration as measured by the modified duration approach. A little iteration produces the matching αs:

Alpha (α) Needed to
Match Modified
Duration

Maturity	Alpha (α)
0.5	0.1188
1.0	0.0977
1.5	0.0440
2.0	0.0340
2.5	0.0291
3.0	0.0256

The modified duration approach implies a degree of "mean reversion," as measured by α, that is not consistent across maturities. How different are the hedging implications of these three models?

Using the duration measures given above, adding the extended Vasicek measures for α of 0.2 and 0.3 as well, gives the following hedge ratios:

Summary of Hedge Ratios
Hedging Three-Year Bond with
One-Year Bond

Duration Measure	Amount of One-Year Bond to Hedge $100 Three-Year Bond
Modified duration	$279.38
Ho and Lee	276.52
Extended Vasicek	
$\alpha = 0.0001$	276.49
$\alpha = 0.1000$	252.40
$\alpha = 0.2000$	231.89
$\alpha = 0.3000$	214.42

The modified duration approach results in a hedging amount of the one-year bond that is higher than any other model: $279.38. One would sell short or issue $279.38 of the one-year bond to hedge a three-year bond position of 100 under the modified duration measure. The Ho and Lee model indicates a hedge of $276.52, and the extended Vasicek model indicates hedging amounts ranging from the Ho and Lee value (as α approaches 0) and $214.42 when α is 0.3. All three models "fit" the observable yield curve perfectly. Only the extended Vasicek model, however, can be parameterized to fit actual market conditions by adjusting α. Neither the modified duration approach nor the Ho and Lee approach contains an extra degree of freedom to allow this kind of adjustment. This is one of the primary reasons why the extended Vasicek approach is increasingly popular among practitioners.

Note also that the level of interest rate volatility σ does not impact hedge ratios as long as both the instrument being hedged and the hedging tool come from the same market and are subject to interest rate shocks with the same σ. We will come back to this point in later chapters.

5.6 CONCLUSION

In this chapter, we have reviewed four popular term structure models, their derivation, and their use in the hedging of coupon-bearing bonds. A practical example shows that only the extended Vasicek model is adjustable to reflect the actual sensitivity of the long end of the yield curve to movements in shorter-term interest rates. This allows a precise adjustment of hedges to fit market conditions unique to the submarket or the country being considered. It also requires care in the choice of this parameter, α, for an erroneous choice has significant implications. We return to the parameter estimation problem in Chapter 19. Suffice it to say that in a carefully implemented hedging problem, in almost every market, using the extended Vasicek model or richer term structure models like the Heath, Jarrow, and Morton model will produce better hedges than using models that don't offer the same ability to adjust to local market conditions.

EXERCISES

For purposes of the exercises, we assume that zero coupon bond prices have the same values as in Chapter 1. We assume that today is January 15, 2000, and that the prevailing market prices in the government bond market for the following zero coupon bonds are as follows:

April 15, 2000	.974
October 15, 2000	.949
April 15, 2001	.921
October 15, 2001	.892
April 15, 2002	.862
October 15, 2002	.831
April 15, 2003	.798
October 14, 2003	.763
April 15, 2004	.725

5.1 Assume we know that α is 0.05 and σ is 0.01 for the extended Vasicek model, which best fits observable derivatives securities prices. What is the r-duration for each of the zero coupon bonds above?

5.2 What is the volatility of the price of each of the zero coupon bonds above?

5.3 Using the definition of convexity in Chapter 4, what is the "r-convexity" of each of the zero coupon bonds above?

5.4 Given the r-durations of the bonds in Exercise 5.1, how much of the April 15, 2004, zero coupon bond should be shorted to hedge a position of $3,000 principal amount of the April 15, 2003, zero coupon bonds?

5.5 What is the r-duration of a semiannual payment bond with a coupon of 6 percent and a maturity of April 25, 2003?

5.6 How much of the April 15, 2004, zero coupon bond should be shorted to hedge a position of $100,000 principal amount of the bond in Exercise 5.5?

5.7 The ABC Bond Index is the key index by which fixed-income investment managers' performance is measured, in terms of both risk and return. The index consists of two bonds, an 8 percent coupon bond due April 15, 2003, with principal outstanding of $1,000, and a 5 percent coupon bond due April 15, 2004, with principal outstanding of $2,000. Both bonds pay semiannually. What is the r-duration of the ABC Bond Index?

5.8 Amalgamated Insurance Company (AIC) invests the proceeds from life insurance premium payments to match the ABC Bond Index. AIC can borrow or lend an infinite amount of money at the overnight rate of interest. It is currently holding assets in cash of $1 billion. The investment committee of AIC has authorized the chief investment officer to buy the 7 percent semiannual bonds maturing April 15, 2002, in whatever amount necessary, in combination with overnight lending or borrowing, so the interest rate risk (defined as r-duration) of AIC's portfolio matches the ABC Bond Index. What should the chief investment officer do?

5.9 What values of r, α, σ, μ, and the market price of risk λ produce Vasicek model bond prices that best match the zero coupon bond prices in the market? (Hint: Use common spreadsheet software to minimize the sum of squared errors of estimated versus actual zero coupon bond prices.)

5.10 Convert the zero prices given above and the zero prices from the best-fitting Vasicek model zero prices at the same maturities to continuously compounded yields. How much "extension" (difference in yields) is necessary on this particular day?

REFERENCES

Black, Fischer. "Interest Rates as Options." *Journal of Finance,* December 1995, pp. 1371–1376.

Chen, Ren-raw. "Exact Solutions for Futures and European Futures on Pure Discount Bonds." *Journal of Financial and Quantitative Analysis,* March 1992, pp. 97–107.

Cox, John C.; Jonathan E. Ingersoll, Jr.; and Stephen A. Ross. "A Theory of the Term Structure of Interest Rates." *Econometrica* 53, 1985, pp. 385–407.

Dothan, L. Uri. "On the Term Structure of Interest Rates." *Journal of Financial Economics* 6, 1978, pp. 59–69.

Duffie, Darrell. *Dynamic Asset Pricing Theory*. Princeton, NJ: Princeton University Press, 1996.

Heath, D.; R. Jarrow; and A. Morton. "Bond Pricing and the Term Structure of Interest Rates: A New Methodology for Contingent Claims Valuation." *Econometrica* 60, January 1992, pp. 77–105.

Ho, Thomas S. Y., and Sang-Bin Lee. "Term Structure Movements and Pricing Interest Rate Contingent Claims." *Journal of Finance* 41, December 1986, pp. 1011–29.

Hull, John, and Alan White. "One-Factor Interest-Rate Models and the Valuation of Interest-Rate Derivative Securities." *Journal of Financial and Quantitative Analysis* 28, June 1993, pp. 235–54.

Hull, John and Alan White. "Pricing Interest Rate Derivative Securities." *Review of Financial Studies* 3, Winter 1990, pp. 573–592.

Ingersoll, Jonathan E., Jr. *Theory of Financial Decision Making*. Savage, MD: Rowman & Littlefield, 1987.

Jarrow, Robert A. *Modelling Fixed Income Securities and Interest Rate Options*. New York: McGraw-Hill, 1996.

Merton, Robert C. "A Dynamic General Equilibrium Model of the Asset Market and Its Application to the Pricing of the Capital Structure of the Firm." Working Paper No. 497-70. Cambridge, MA: A. P. Sloan School of Management, Massachusetts Institute of Technology, 1970. Reproduced as Chapter 11 in Robert C. Merton, *Continuous Time Finance* (Cambridge, MA: Blackwell, 1993).

Vasicek, Oldrich A. "An Equilibrium Characterization of the Term Structure." *Journal of Financial Economics* 5, November 1977, pp. 177–88.

CHAPTER 6

Risk-Neutral Interest Rates and European Options on Bonds

In this chapter, we introduce a general approach for the valuation of fixed-income derivatives. In this chapter and the rest of this book, we focus on the Vasicek model rather than the extended Vasicek model. The Vasicek model allows for easier exposition and provides a solid foundation for the financial market participant or serious student of finance who wants to "extend" the results of derivatives securities valuation in the Vasicek model to find the extended Vasicek result. For most derivative securities, this extension is a modest one. We emphasize the Vasicek model and its rich array of closed-form solutions because our financial market experience has convinced us that closed-form solutions should be used whenever possible. Closed-form solutions offer faster calculation time, more accurate first and second derivatives, and therefore more accurate hedge ratio calculation and risk analysis. Most large financial institutions in the insurance and banking industries have literally millions of transactions with embedded derivatives, with the number of transactions outstanding typically ranging between 20 million and 50 million in a large bank. A calculation method that minimizes the need to summarize these transactions will ultimately produce much more accurate results.

In this chapter, we introduce the concept of risk-neutral interest rates and the relationship between this powerful concept and the term structure models we discussed in Chapter 5. We then use the insights of the risk-neutral approach to value European options on bonds.

6.1 AN INTRODUCTION TO RISK-NEUTRAL INTEREST RATES AND THE NO-ARBITRAGE ASSUMPTION

Over the last 50 years, monetary economists have devoted a considerable amount of time to the discussion of "liquidity premiums" embedded in the term structure of interest rates. Ingersoll (1987) gives a very lucid summary of the theories that seek to explain the liquidity premium. Usually, the discussions of the liquidity premium focus on the long-standing debate about whether forward rates represent only the market's expectations of future interest rates or whether forward rates also include a premium for risk. One of the most popular theories of the term structure is the "local expectations hypothesis," which holds that bond market participants are indifferent to risk and that the expected return on bonds of all maturities must therefore equal the short-term risk-free rate of interest. The linkage between this theory of the term structure of interest rates and the Vasicek model helps illustrate the risk-neutral approach.[1]

In Chapter 5, we introduced the Vasicek model, in which short-term interest rates move randomly according to the stochastic process

$$dr = \alpha(\mu - r)dt + \sigma dz$$

Using the hedging argument from Chapter 5, riskless arbitrage requires that zero coupon bonds for all maturities are related to the market price of risk λ by the following equation:

$$\frac{P_r \alpha(\mu - r) + \frac{1}{2}\sigma^2 P_{rr} + P_t - rP}{\sigma P_r} = -\lambda$$

This bond market version of the Sharpe ratio says that the ratio of expected return on the bond less the risk-free return on the bond rP divided by its standard deviation must be the same for bonds

---

1. See Ingersoll (1987) for an in-depth discussion of the links between the local expectations hypothesis and term structure models.

of all maturities. If λ is positive,[2] investors receive an extra return, or liquidity premium, for holding bonds with higher price volatility. If λ is 0, investors are risk neutral and the expected return on all bonds is the risk-free rate. When λ is 0, we can rearrange the equation above such that

$$\frac{P_r\alpha(\mu - r) + \frac{1}{2}\sigma^2 P_{rr} + P_t}{P} = r$$

The numerator of this expression is the expected change in the bond's price that we get by calculating dP using Ito's lemma, as in Chapters 4 and 5, and then taking its expected value.[3] The expression says

$$\frac{dP}{P} = r$$

The percentage return on bonds of all maturities equals the risk-free rate. If investors are risk neutral, then the Vasicek model with lambda $(\lambda) = 0$ applies.

What if investors are *not* risk neutral? Is the concept of risk neutrality useful in valuing fixed-income and foreign exchange derivatives? The answer is definitely yes. For any degree of risk aversion, as measured by the market price of risk λ, we can derive a related stochastic process for interest rates that is consistent with a pseudo economy where investors are risk neutral and the same bond prices would prevail.[4] We assume that observable interest rates move according to the Vasicek model stochastic process above. For what stochastic process would (*a*) the same bond prices prevail and (*b*) investors be risk neutral? We guess that the stochastic process has the form

$$d\tilde{r} = a(\tilde{r},t)dt + \sigma dz$$

---

2. Note that P_r is negative and that the minus sign in front of λ corrects for the fact that the denominator on the left-hand side of the equation, the volatility of the bond's price, is negative.

3. The expected value of any function h times the stochastic term $dz\ E(h\ dz)$ is 0, so the random term in the Ito's lemma expansion disappears on taking the expectation. See Shimko (1992) for an artistic exposition of this point.

4. See Jarrow (1996) for an extensive discussion of the construction of the pseudo probabilities behind the risk-neutral stochastic process for interest rates.

where the tilde denotes the risk-neutral process. If the process is truly risk neutral, the expected return on all bonds will equal the short rate r, which by standard assumption is equal to the current risk-neutral interest rate:

$$\frac{P_{\tilde{r}}a(\tilde{r},t) + \frac{1}{2}\sigma^2 P_{\tilde{r}\tilde{r}} + P_t}{P} = r = \tilde{r}$$

We rearrange this equation and divide by σ times the first derivative of the bond's price P_r to get

$$\frac{P_{\tilde{r}}a(\tilde{r},t) + \frac{1}{2}\sigma^2 P_{\tilde{r}\tilde{r}} + P_t - \tilde{r}P}{\sigma P_{\tilde{r}}} = 0$$

This is the equilibrium bond pricing equation under the risk-neutral interest rate process. For what value of the function a is this valuation equation identical to the valuation equation using the observable stochastic process given above? It is identical if

$$a(\tilde{r},t) = \alpha(\mu - r) + \lambda\sigma$$

so the equivalent risk-neutral stochastic process for interest rates is simply a shift in the drift term of the short-term interest rate:

$$d\tilde{r} = [\alpha(\mu - \tilde{r}) + \lambda\sigma]dt + \sigma dz$$

The risk-neutral process is always assumed to be such that the risk-neutral short rate at the current time t and the observable short rate at that time are equal. There is a close link between the existence of this risk-neutral-equivalent stochastic process and the assumption of a no-arbitrage economy.

Jamshidian (1990) summarizes these links by noting that for any one-factor model of interest rates, there are eight equivalent conditions that assure a no-arbitrage economy:

1. The market price of risk is the same for bonds of all maturities.
2. The expected drift in the observable short rate r can be expressed as the product of the difference between the volatility of a bond with maturity T and the market

price of risk times the volatility of the observable short rate.

3. The short rate r at an arbitrary point t in the future can be expressed as a particular stochastic integral of the volatilities of bond prices plus the forward rate for time t prevailing at time 0.

4. The forward rate at time T, as of an arbitrary point t in the future, can be expressed as a particular stochastic integral of the volatilities of bond prices plus the forward rate for time T prevailing at time 0.

5. Bond prices prevailing at any point in time equal the risk-neutral discounted expected value of future risk-neutral short-term interest rates.

6. The relative prices of a zero coupon bond with maturity T and a money market fund consisting of the compounded reinvestment of $1 at time 0 at the short-term risk-neutral rate of interest are martingales[5] with respect to the risk-neutral process for interest rates.

7. The forward rates as of time T from the perspective of time t are martingales with respect to a "T-maturity forward-risk-adjusted expectation."

8. Forward bond prices are martingales with respect to the forward-risk-adjusted expectation.

See Heath, Jarrow, and Morton (1992) and Jamshidian (1990) for a precise mathematical specification of these points.

6.2 RELATIONSHIP BETWEEN THE EXPECTED SHORT RATE, EXPECTED RISK-NEUTRAL SHORT RATE, AND FORWARD RATES

The local expectations hypothesis holds that the expected return on bonds of all maturities is the short rate of interest. In addition, most debates on the nature of the liquidity premium in the term structure of interest rates revolve around the relationship between

---

5. Informally, a variable is a martingale if its expected value for a given stochastic process (in this case, the risk-neutral process) at some point in the future equals its current value. See Arnold (1974) or Karatzas and Shreve (1991) for a formal mathematical definition. See Jarrow (1996) for more on the money market fund analogy.

forward rates and expected future short rates. In the Vasicek model, it is important to make it very clear that neither the expected observable short rate of interest nor the expected risk-neutral short rate at some arbitrary future date will in general equal the forward rate prevailing for that maturity.

Vasicek (1977)[6] showed that the observable short rate r expected to prevail at time s in the future from the perspective of time t is

$$E_t[r(s)] = \mu + [r(t) - \mu]e^{-\alpha(s-t)}$$

Jamshidian[7] shows that the expected value of the risk-neutral short rate expected to prevail at time s in the future from the perspective of current time t[8] is

$$E_t[\tilde{r}(s)] = \mu + \frac{\lambda\sigma}{\alpha} + \left[r(t) - \left(\mu + \frac{\lambda\sigma}{\alpha}\right)\right]e^{-\alpha(s-t)}$$

$$= E_t[r(s)] + F(s-t)\lambda\sigma$$

where

$$F(s-t) = \frac{1}{\alpha}\left[1 - e^{-\alpha(s-t)}\right]$$

The forward rate f prevailing at time t for maturity at time s is

$$f_t(s) = \mu + \frac{\lambda\sigma}{\alpha} + \left[r(t) - \left(\mu + \frac{\lambda\sigma}{\alpha}\right)\right]e^{-\alpha(s-t)} - \frac{\sigma^2}{2}F(s-t)^2$$

$$= E_t[\tilde{r}(s)] - \frac{\sigma^2}{2}F(s-t)^2$$

$$= E_t[r(s)] + F(s-t)\lambda\sigma - \frac{\sigma^2}{2}F(s-t)^2$$

These formulas clearly show that forward rates will not equal either the expected value of the observable short rate or

---

6. See Equation 25 in Vasicek.
7. See page 208 of Jamshidian (1989).
8. Remember that the current short rate r and the current risk-neutral short rate are equal by assumption, so no notational distinction is necessary.

the expected value of the risk-neutral short rate unless interest rate volatility σ is 0. This is true even under the local expectations hypothesis ($\lambda = 0$). This distinction between forward rates and the two variations on expected future short rates will be important to keep in mind in Section 6.3.

6.3 A GENERAL VALUATION FORMULA FOR VALUATION OF INTEREST RATE–RELATED SECURITIES IN THE VASICEK MODEL

In this section, we present the general Jamshidian solution for the valuation of interest rate–related securities under the Vasicek model. It is simplest to do this in terms of the risk-neutral interest rate process. Using the results from Section 6.1, we define the "risk-neutral drift" in the risk-neutral short-term interest rate to be consistent with Jamshidian as

$$\tilde{\mu} = \mu + \frac{\sigma\lambda}{\alpha}$$

so we can write the risk-neutral stochastic process for the short rate as

$$d\tilde{r} = [\alpha(\mu - \tilde{r}) + \lambda\sigma]dt + \sigma dz$$

$$= \alpha(\tilde{\mu} - \tilde{r})dt + \sigma dz$$

Following Jarrow (1996) and Jamshidian (1989), we can also define the value of a money market fund with an original principal amount at beginning time t of \$1 and which is continually reinvested at the risk-neutral interest rate until time s as

$$B(t,s) = e^{Y(t,s)}$$

where

$$Y(t,s) = \int_t^s \tilde{r}(u)\,du$$

What is the value of a security that pays a continuous cash flow at a function $h[r(t),t]$, which depends on time t and the level of the observable (not risk-neutral[9]) short rate r and a terminal cash flow $g[r(T),T]$ when it matures at time T?

We know from Chapter 5 that a zero coupon bond must satisfy a partial differential equation that restricts its excess expected return over the observable short-term interest rate r, all divided by the price volatility of the security, to equal the market price of risk λ. In the Vasicek model, the market price of risk λ is assumed to be a constant.[10] Shimko (1992) shows that the same concept applies for a security that has cash flow prior to maturity according to some function $h[r(t),t]$. The value of a security paying continuous cash flow h and cash flow g at maturity must satisfy the partial differential equation[11] for its value V such that

$$\alpha(\tilde{\mu} - r)V_r + \frac{1}{2}\sigma^2 V_{rr} + V_t - rV + h(r,t) = 0$$

subject to the boundary condition that at maturity T

$$V(r,T) = g(r)$$

There are two different expressions for the general solution to this valuation problem. The first solution is useful for numerical solution techniques like binomial and trinomial lattice techniques:

$$V(r,t) = E_{r,t}\left[\frac{g[\tilde{r}(T)]}{B(t,T)} + \int_t^T \frac{h[\tilde{r}(s),s]}{B(t,s)}ds\right] \tag{6.1}$$

Jamshidian, citing Friedman (1975), shows that the value V of any security can be written simply as the (risk-neutral) expected value of the terminal cash flow g at time T divided by the value of the money fund $B(t,T)$, plus the continuous sum of the continuous cash flow h at time s divided by the value of the money fund $B(t,s)$,

---

9. Derivative contracts, for instance, pay based only on observable interest rates, not risk-neutral rates.

10. This assumption is relaxed in the extended Vasicek (Hull and White) version of the model. The derivation that follows is almost identical for the extended version of the Vasicek model.

11. Note again that the observable short rate r and the risk-neutral rate are the same at current time t.

but cash flows g *and* h *are determined as functions of the risk-neutral interest rate instead of the observable interest rate* r. This is the heart of the lattice calculation techniques, which are constructed based on the risk-neutral interest rate process, use cash flows determined by risk-neutral interest rates, and discount by the value of the money fund *B*. We discuss how to construct such lattices in Chapter 12.

The most convenient form of the solution formula for *V* to use in obtaining closed-form solutions for security values is given as Jamshidian's Equation 5:

$$V(r,t) = P(r,t,T)E[g(R_{r,t,T})] + \int_t^T P(r,t,s)E[h(R_{r,t,s},s)]ds \quad (6.2)$$

The value *V* is the simple present value of the "expected" cash flows from functions *g* and *h* except that expected cash flows are *not* evaluated based on the probability distribution for either the observable short rate *r* or the risk-neutral short rate. Instead, cash flows are evaluated as if the short rate *R* has

$$\text{Mean}_R(r,t,s) = f(r,t,s) = re^{-\alpha(s-t)} + \alpha F(s-t)\tilde{\mu} - \frac{\sigma^2}{2}F(s-t)^2$$

$$\text{Variance}_R = var_{r,t}[r(s)] = v^2(t,s) = \frac{\sigma^2}{2\alpha}\left[1 - e^{-2\alpha(s-t)}\right]$$

$$F(s-t) = \frac{1}{\alpha}\left[1 - e^{-\alpha(s-t)}\right]$$

In other words, we evaluate the expected values of the cash flows *g* and *h* as if the short rate had a mean equal to the forward rate with maturity equal to the timing of the cash flow and the same variance as the observable short rate will have at that time (say time *s*) from the perspective of current time *t*. How can this be? We know from Section 6.2 that the forward rate equals neither the expected observable short rate nor the expected risk-neutral short rate. The reason for this surprising conclusion is given in Section 6.4. We illustrate the use of Equation 6.2 to evaluate European bond options in Section 6.5.

6.4 DERIVATION OF THE CLOSED-FORM VALUATION FORMULA

Equation 6.1, in which cash flows are determined by risk-neutral interest rates and discounted by the value of the money market fund B, comes directly from stochastic process mathematics. It is important to understand how Equation 6.2 is related to Equation 6.1, which has become popular for numerical valuation of fixed-income securities and interest rate derivatives. The closed-form valuation formula in Equation 6.2 is just as powerful, as we shall see in Section 6.5, so we devote considerable effort here to rationalizing these two solutions, which appear at first glance to be at odds with each other, by elaborating on the derivation shown in the appendix to Jamshidian (1989).

Jamshidian shows that the expected value in Equation 6.1 can be rewritten in terms of the multivariate normal probability density function p, which depends on the initial short rate r, current time t, future time s, the risk-neutral interest rate at time s r', and the yield on the money market fund $Y(t,s)$ since r' and Y are both random and jointly normally distributed:

$$V(r,t) = \int_{-\infty}^{\infty} \int_{-\infty}^{\infty} \frac{g(r')}{B(t,T)} p[r,t,T,r',Y(t,T)]dYdr'$$

$$+ \int_{t}^{T} \int_{-\infty}^{\infty} \int_{-\infty}^{\infty} \frac{h(r',s)}{B(t,s)} p[r,t,s,r',Y(t,s)]dYdr'ds$$

To link the numerical solution, Equation 6.1, and the closed-form solution, Equation 6.2, we need to evaluate further the integral

$$G(r,r',t,s) = \int_{-\infty}^{\infty} \frac{1}{B(t,s)} p(r,t,s,r',Y)dY = \int_{-\infty}^{\infty} e^{-Y(t,s)} p(r,t,s,r',Y)dY \tag{6.3}$$

To do this, we make use of the following facts concerning the mean, variance, and covariance of risk-neutral rates and the money market yield Y:

$$E_{r,t}[\tilde{r}(s)] = m_r = e^{-\alpha\tau}r + \alpha F(\tau)\tilde{\mu}$$

$$var_{r,t}[\tilde{r}(s)] = v_r^2 = \frac{\sigma^2}{2\alpha}\left[1 - e^{-2\alpha\tau}\right]$$

$$E_{r,t}[Y(t,s)] = m_y = \tau\tilde{\mu} + (r - \tilde{\mu})F(\tau)$$

$$var_{r,t}[Y(t,s)] = v_y^2 = \frac{\sigma^2}{2\alpha^3}\left[4e^{-\alpha\tau} - e^{-2\alpha\tau} + 2\alpha\tau - 3\right]$$

$$cov_{r,t}[\tilde{r}(s),Y(t,s)] = \rho v_r v_y = \frac{\sigma^2}{2}F(\tau)^2$$

$$\tau = s - t$$

Now the probability density function for any two variables x_1 and x_2 with a joint multivariate normal distribution, means m_1 and m_2, standard deviations s_1 and s_2, and correlation ρ can be written

$$f(x_1,x_2) = \frac{1}{2\pi\sigma_1\sigma_2\sqrt{(1-\rho^2)}}$$

$$\exp\left[\frac{-1}{2(1-\rho^2)}\left[\left(\frac{x_1-m_1}{\sigma_1}\right)^2 - 2\rho\left(\frac{x_1-m_1}{\sigma_1}\right)\left(\frac{x_2-m_2}{\sigma_2}\right) + \left(\frac{x_2-m_2}{\sigma_2}\right)^2\right]\right]$$

After a tedious calculation, it is possible to show that

$$f(x_1,x_2) = n(x_1,m_1,\sigma_1)\, n\left(x_2, m_2 + \sigma_2\rho\left[\frac{x_1-m_1}{\sigma_1}\right], \sigma_2\sqrt{1-\rho^2}\right)$$

where n is the single variate normal density function for variable x with mean m and standard deviation σ such that

$$n(x,m,\sigma) = \frac{1}{\sigma\sqrt{2\pi}}e^{\frac{-1}{2}\left(\frac{x-m}{\sigma}\right)^2}$$

It can also be shown that

$$\int_{-\infty}^{a} e^{bs}n(s,m,\sigma)ds = e^{b\left(m+\frac{b\sigma^2}{2}\right)}N(a,m+b\sigma^2,\sigma) \qquad (6.4)$$

where $N(a,m,\sigma)$ is the cumulative normal distribution function for a variable a with mean m and standard deviation σ. Accordingly, we can rewrite Equation 6.3 as follows:

$$G(r,r',t,s) = \int_{-\infty}^{\infty} e^{-Y} f(r',Y) dY$$

$$= \int_{-\infty}^{\infty} e^{-Y} n(r',m_r,v_r)\, n\!\left(Y, m_y + v_y \rho\left[\frac{r'-m_r}{v_r}\right], v_y\sqrt{1-\rho^2}\right) dY$$

$$= n(r',m_r,v_r) \int_{-\infty}^{\infty} e^{-Y} n\!\left(Y, m_y + v_y \rho\left[\frac{r'-m_r}{v_r}\right], v_y\sqrt{1-\rho^2}\right) dY$$

$$= P(r,t,s) n[r', f(s-t), v_r]$$

which is Jamshidian's Equation 13. The $f(s - t)$ is the forward rate for maturity at time s from the perspective of time t. This bridges the gap between Equations 6.1 and 6.2 and shows why the forward rate becomes the mean of the distribution used to evaluate closed-form solutions even though neither the mean of the observable short rate nor the mean of the risk-neutral short rate equals the forward rate.

6.5 THE VALUE OF EUROPEAN OPTIONS ON A ZERO COUPON BOND

We can use Equation 6.2 to value a European call option on a zero coupon bond. Assume that the call option is to be valued at current time t. It is an option to purchase a zero coupon bond with maturity at time T_2 that is exercisable at a purchase price K at time T_1. Because it is a European option exercisable only at time T_1, there is no intermediate cash flow (function $h = 0$ in Equations 6.1 and 6.2) and cash flow g at maturity is

$$g(R,T_1) = P(R,T_2 - T_1) - K \ \text{ if } R < s^*$$
$$= 0 \ \text{ if } R \geq s^*$$

The call option has a payoff only if the price of a zero coupon bond with maturity at T_2 is greater than K as of time T_1. This comes about only if the short rate R as of time T_1 is less than a critical level s^* defined by solving this equation for s^*:

$$K = P(s^*, \tau) = e^{-F(\tau)s^* - G(\tau)}$$

where, using the notation of Chen (1992),

$$\tau = T_2 - T_1$$

$$F(\tau) = \frac{1}{\alpha}\left(1 - e^{-\alpha\tau}\right)$$

$$D = \tilde{\mu} - \frac{\sigma^2}{2\alpha^2} = \mu + \frac{\sigma\lambda}{\alpha} - \frac{\sigma^2}{2\alpha^2}$$

$$G(\tau) = D[\tau - F(\tau)] + \frac{\sigma^2}{4\alpha}F(\tau)^2$$

so that

$$s^* = -\frac{\ln(K) + G(\tau)}{F(\tau)}$$

The value of the call option as of time t given the observable short rate r is

$$V(r,t,T_1,T_2,K) = P(r,t,T_1) \int_{-\infty}^{s^*} \left(e^{-sF(\tau) - G(\tau)} - K\right)n[s,f,v]ds \qquad (6.5)$$

where n is the normal density function, f is the forward rate as of time t prevailing for maturity at time T_1, and v is the standard deviation of the short rate (both observable and risk neutral) that will prevail as of T_1 from the perspective of time t:

$$f(r,t,T_1) = re^{-\alpha(T_1-t)} + \alpha F_1\tilde{\mu} - \frac{\sigma^2}{2}F_1^2$$

$$v(r,t,T_1) = \sqrt{\frac{\sigma^2}{2\alpha}\left(1 - e^{-2\alpha(T_1-t)}\right)}$$

We use the abbreviations

$$F(T_i - t) = F_i$$

$$G(T_i - t) = G_i$$

$$F(T_2 - T_1) = F_\tau$$

$$G(T_2 - T_1) = G_\tau$$

$$f(T_1 - t) = f_1$$

We can quickly simplify Equation 6.5 using the formula in Equation 6.4 so that

$$V(r,t,T_1,T_2,K) =$$

$$P(r,t,T_1)\left[e^{-G(\tau)} \int_{-\infty}^{s^*} e^{-sF(\tau)} n[s,f_1,v]\,ds - K \int_{-\infty}^{s^*} n(s,f_1,v)\,ds \right]$$

$$V(r,t,T_1,T_2,K) =$$

$$P(r,t,T_1)\left[e^{-F_\tau f_1 - G_\tau + \frac{F_\tau^2 v^2}{2}} N\!\left(F_\tau v + \frac{s^* - f_1}{v} \right) - KN\!\left(\frac{s^* - f_1}{v} \right) \right]$$

This expression can be simplified considerably using the fact that

$$-G_\tau - f_1 F_\tau + \frac{F_\tau^2 v^2}{2} = -\ln[P(r,t,T_1)] + \ln[P(r,t,T_2)]$$

and that

$$\frac{s^* - f_1}{v} = \frac{\ln\!\left(\dfrac{P(r,t,T_2)}{KP(r,t,T_1)} \right)}{vF_\tau} - \frac{1}{2}vF_\tau$$

to arrive at Jamshidian's formulation for the value of a European option on a zero coupon bond:

$$V(r,t,T_1,T_2,K) = P(r,t,T_2)N(h) - P(r,t,T_1)KN(h - \sigma_P)$$

where N is the standard cumulative normal distribution and we use the following definitions:

$$h = \frac{1}{\sigma_P}\ln\left[\frac{P(r,t,T_2)}{KP(r,t,T_1)}\right] + \frac{\sigma_P}{2}$$

$$\sigma_P = vF_\tau$$

The latter expression is the standard deviation of the price of the T_2 maturity zero coupon bond's price.

Readers familiar with the Black-Scholes options model will notice a very strong similarity to the pricing formula in that model. The similarities occur because the zero coupon bond's price is lognormally distributed, since its yield is linear in the short rate of interest and the yield is therefore normally distributed. There are, however, very important differences in this formulation compared to the Black-Scholes model that are worth noting:

- The volatility of the bond's price declines over time and reaches 0 at maturity, which is fully captured by the Jamshidian formulation. It is not captured by the Black-Scholes model if applied to bond options, since the bond price volatility is assumed to be constant in the Black-Scholes model.

- The Jamshidian formulation looks through bond price fluctuations to the economic source of the fluctuations, random interest rates, and provides an internally consistent methodology for bond option valuation. The Black-Scholes model for bond options pricing relies on the dangerous inconsistency that bond options are being valued using a model that assumes interest rates are constant.

- The Jamshidian formula, in combination with the Vasicek or extended Vasicek term structure model, provides a consistent approach that allows cross-hedging of a one-year option on a three-year zero coupon bond with the appropriate hedging amount of two-year bonds. The Black-Scholes model does not provide an explanation of the relationship between price changes on bonds with different maturities.

- The Jamshidian formulation provides all of the same richness of hedging tools, including the term structure model equivalent of the "Greeks":

$$r\text{Delta} = \frac{\partial V}{\partial r}$$

$$r\text{Gamma} = \frac{\partial^2 V}{\partial r^2}$$

$$r\text{Vega} = \frac{\partial V}{\partial \sigma}$$

$$r\text{Theta} = \frac{\partial V}{\partial t}$$

The Jamshidian formulation is far more powerful in explaining observable caps and floors prices, as we will see in Chapter 9.

6.6 EUROPEAN PUTS ON ZERO COUPON BOND PRICES

The Jamshidian technique applies to European put options as well. In the case of a European put, the general valuation formula becomes

$$V(r,t,T_1,T_2,K) = P(r,t,T_1)\left[K \int_{s^*}^{\infty} n(s,m,v)\,ds - \int_{s^*}^{\infty} e^{-sF\tau - G\tau} n(s,m,v)\,ds \right]$$

$$= P(r,t,T_1)KN(-h + \sigma_P) - P(r,t,T_2)N(-h)$$

using exactly the same approach as in Section 6.5. Put–call parity requires that the sum of a long position in a European call and a short position in a European put is the equivalent of a long position in a forward contract on the zero coupon bond with maturity T_2 at an exercise price of K at time T_1. The present value of the forward bond contract, which we know from Chapter 1 and review again in Chapter 7, can be shown to be

$$\text{Call}(r,t,T_1,T_2,K) - \text{Put}(r,t,T_1,T_2,K) = P(r,t,T_2) - P(r,t,T_1)K$$

as it should be. This results simply from the fact that

$$N(-h) = 1 - N(h)$$

because of the symmetry of the normal cumulative distribution function.

6.7 OPTIONS ON COUPON-BEARING BONDS

Jamshidian notes that the price of any security with a positive amount of contractual cash flows a_i at n points of time in the future is a monotonically decreasing function of the short rate of interest r. Therefore, the zero coupon bond formulas for European options can be applied directly to the problem of European options on coupon-bearing bonds. For each cash flow date, the strike price K_i is set to equal the zero coupon bond price as of the exercise date T such that the present value of the remaining payments on the security as of time T exactly equals the true strike price on the entire security K. The interest rate r^* is the short-term interest rate at which this is true:

$$\sum_{i=j}^{n} a_i P(r^*,T,T_i) = K$$

and

$$K_i = P(r^*,T,T_i)$$

Jamshidian shows that the value of a European option on the entire security is the weighted sum of options on each cash flow:

$$\text{Option}(r,t,T,K) = \sum_{i=j}^{n} a_i \text{Option}(r,t,T,T_i,K_i)$$

An example of the use of this formula is given in the next section.

6.8 AN EXAMPLE

Throughout the first half of the 1990s, step-up coupon bonds were popular among issuers and investors alike. In this section, we analyze a step-up coupon bond with a six-year maturity and semiannual coupons at 6 percent for the first three years and 8 percent for the last three years. We assume that the bonds are callable at par on the interest payment date three years from now (after interest has been paid on that date). The rising coupon structure on this type of bond was rarely relevant to issuers, who typically combined the bonds with an interest rate swap to convert the proceeds to a floating-rate instrument tied to the London interbank offered rate (Libor) at a spread well below the normal financing costs available to the issuer. The issuers were beneficiaries of a large arbitrage due to the fact that many investors, enamored by the higher coupon in the latter half of the life of the bond, placed a lower value on the issuer's ability to "call" the bonds than did most market participants. In this section, we use the Jamshidian bond pricing formula to price this hypothetical step-up coupon bond issue.

The bond is composed of two securities. The first part is the bond itself, which we analyze as if it were noncallable by taking the simple present value of cash flows.

Step-up Coupon Bond
Scheduled Cash Flow

Maturity	Interest	Principal	Total
0.5	30		30
1.0	30		30
1.5	30		30
2.0	30		30
2.5	30		30
3.0	30		30
3.5	40		40
4.0	40		40
4.5	40		40
5.0	40		40
5.5	40		40
6.0	40	1,000	1,040

We do this present value calculation using the parameters for the Vasicek term structure model given below:

Step-up Coupon Bond
Present Value of Scheduled Payments

Term Structure Model Parameters

α	0.05000
μ	0.08000
σ	0.01500
λ	0.01000
r	6.7500%

Maturity	$F(T-t)$	D	$G(T-t)$	Zero Price	Cash Flow	Present Value
0.5	0.49380	0.03800	0.00051	0.96672	30	29.00
1.0	0.97541	0.03800	0.00200	0.93441	30	28.03
1.5	1.44513	0.03800	0.00443	0.90305	30	27.09
2.0	1.90325	0.03800	0.00775	0.87265	30	26.18
2.5	2.35006	0.03800	0.01191	0.84321	30	25.30
3.0	2.78584	0.03800	0.01687	0.81472	30	24.44
3.5	3.21086	0.03800	0.02259	0.78716	40	31.49
4.0	3.62538	0.03800	0.02902	0.76053	40	30.42
4.5	4.02968	0.03800	0.03614	0.73481	40	29.39
5.0	4.42398	0.03800	0.04391	0.70997	40	28.40
5.5	4.80856	0.03800	0.05229	0.68601	40	27.44
6.0	5.18364	0.03800	0.06125	0.66289	1,040	689.41

Total present value of cash flows	996.59

The bonds, if we ignore the value of the call option, have a present value of $996.59. This is the value many investors believed they were receiving when they were offered the bonds at a price plus accrued interest of, say, 98 percent of par, or $980. Unfortunately, we now have to calculate the value of the call option and subtract this value from the simple present value of the bonds to get the true value of this "packaged" security.

Step 1 is to determine what value of the short rate r, assuming it is now three years hence, will cause the bonds to have a present value of exactly $1,000 (par value) on that date. Using the "solver" function in a common spreadsheet software package, we see that the break-even level of r is 7.8412 percent.

Calculation of Break-even r at Three-Year Point

Break-even r in 3 years: 7.8412%

Maturity	$F(T-t)$	D	$G(T-t)$	Zero Price	Cash Flow	Present Value
0.5	0.49380	0.03800	0.00051	0.96153	40	38.46
1.0	0.97541	0.03800	0.00200	0.92451	40	36.98
1.5	1.44513	0.03800	0.00443	0.88892	40	35.56
2.0	1.90325	0.03800	0.00775	0.85471	40	34.19
2.5	2.35006	0.03800	0.01191	0.82186	40	32.87
3.0	2.78584	0.03800	0.01687	0.79032	1,040	821.94

Total present value of cash flows　　　　　　　　　　　　　　　　　1,000.00

As shown in Section 6.7, we can now calculate a call option on this step-up coupon bond even though it has more than one cash flow by combining the values of call options on each cash flow using the zero prices in the chart immediately above as the adjusted strike prices. This calculation shows that the total value of the call option is $32.96.

Calculation of European Call Option Value

Break-even r in 3 years: 7.8412%

T1 Maturity	T2 Maturity	$P(T1)$	$P(T2)$	Strike Price K	$F(T2-T1)$	$v(T1)$	σ_P	h	Value of Call on $1	Cash Flow	Total Call Value
3.0	3.5	0.81472	0.78716	0.96153	0.49380	0.02415	0.01192	0.41052	0.00593	40	0.24
3.0	4.0	0.81472	0.76053	0.92451	0.97541	0.02415	0.02355	0.42215	0.01136	40	0.45
3.0	4.5	0.81472	0.73481	0.88892	1.44513	0.02415	0.03490	0.43350	0.01632	40	0.65
3.0	5.0	0.81472	0.70997	0.85471	1.90325	0.02415	0.04596	0.44456	0.02083	40	0.83
3.0	5.5	0.81472	0.68601	0.82186	2.35006	0.02415	0.05675	0.45535	0.02493	40	1.00
3.0	6.0	0.81472	0.66289	0.79032	2.78584	0.02415	0.06727	0.46587	0.02864	1,040	29.79

Total value of European option to call the bond　　　　　　　　　　32.96

The total value of the package offered to investors is $996.59 − $32.96, or $963.63. Investors who thought they were getting a bargain at $980 actually paid more than $16 too much.

Differences of opinion about the right price of securities are what makes a market. As we have seen in this chapter, bond option pricing is more of a science and somewhat less of an art than it has been in the past thanks to the pioneering work of Black, Scholes, Vasicek, and Jamshidian, who combined both approaches to reach the conclusions of this chapter. With these tools, both issuers and investors will have a more accurate view of fair value.

EXERCISES

6.1 Using the Vasicek parameter assumptions of Section 6.8 (p. 168), what is the value at the beginning of the six-year period of a three-year call option to buy a six-year zero coupon bond at a price of $88?

6.2 What is the price of a three-year put option at the same strike price of $88?

6.3 What is the present value of a three-year forward contract to buy a zero coupon bond with current maturity of six years at a price of $98?

6.4 What combination of European calls and European puts on this six-year zero coupon bond replicates the value of a three-year forward contract at a price of $88?

6.5 What is the value of this combination?

6.6 How does that value compare to the answer you gave to Exercise 6.3?

6.7 What is the value of a three-year put at par value on the step-up coupon bond described in Section 6.8? Do this calculation without using Jamshidian's put option formula.

6.8 Calculate the "Greeks" for the term structure model European call option formula: rDelta, rGamma, rTheta, and rVega. Should there be another Greek for the speed of mean reversion factor, Alpha? Even if you think the answer is no, calculate "rAlpha" anyway.

6.9 Recalculate the value of the call option in Section 6.8 for maturities of 0.5, 1, 1.5, 2, 2.5, 3.5, 4, 4.5, 5, and 5.5 years.

6.10 What relationship should an American call option on this bond have to the European call options in Section 6.8 and Exercise 6.9?

6.11 Calculate the value of the step-up coupon bonds in Section 6.8 for r of 2, 4, 6, 8, and 10 percent on two bases: assuming the bonds are noncallable and assuming they are callable after three years as described. Describe the differences in interest rate sensitivity that you observe.

6.12 Assume you are the new chief investment officer at a life insurance company that owns more step-up coupon bonds than it should. Your predecessor has gone on to manage money for a well-known southern California municipality under considerable duress. You own $1,000 principal amount of the callable step-up bond in Section 6.8, and you want to hedge the risk that the bonds will be called with a four-year zero coupon bond (the only maturity at which you have any liquidity). How much of that four-year zero should you buy or sell? Remember, hedge the call option only.

REFERENCES

Arnold, Ludwig. *Stochastic Differential Equations: Theory and Applications*. New York: John Wiley & Sons, 1974.

Chen, Ren-raw. "Exact Solutions for Futures and European Futures Options on Pure Discount Bonds." *Journal of Financial and Quantitative Analysis*, March 1992, pp. 97–107.

Friedman, A. *Stochastic Differential Equations and Applications*, vol. 1. New York: Academic Press, 1975.

Geske, Robert. "The Valuation of Compound Options." *Journal of Financial Economics*, March 1979, pp. 63–81.

Heath, D.; R. Jarrow; and A. Morton. "Bond Pricing and the Term Structure of Interest Rates: A New Methodology for Contingent Claims Valuation." *Econometrica* 60, January 1992, pp. 77–105.

Ingersoll, Jonathan E. *Theory of Financial Decision Making*. Savage, MD: Rowman & Littlefield, 1987.

Jamshidian, Farshid. "An Exact Bond Option Formula." *Journal of Finance*, March 1989, pp. 205–9.

———. *Bond and Option Evaluation in the Gaussian Interest Rate Model.* Financial Strategies Group, Merrill Lynch, New York 1990.

Jarrow, Robert A. *Modelling Fixed-Income Securities and Interest Rate Options.* New York: McGraw-Hill, 1996.

Karatzas, Ioannis, and Steven E. Shreve. *Browian Motion and Stochastic Calculus.* New York: Springer-Verlag, 1991.

Shimko, David C. *Finance in Continuous Time: A Primer.* Miami: Kolb, 1992.

Vasicek, Oldrich. "An Equilibrium Characterization of the Term Structure." *Journal of Financial Economics*, November 1977, pp. 177–88.

CHAPTER 7

Forward and
Futures Contracts

Financial forward and futures contracts are critical everyday tools of risk management and investment management. Their popularity is probably best summarized by the three-month Eurodollar contract traded on the Chicago Mercantile Exchange. Open interest on March 25, 1996, represented underlying principal of $2.3 trillion, and contracts were outstanding at maturities ranging from April 1996 to December 2005. Even the December 2005 contract had open interest representing underlying principal of $948 million.[1] This chapter illustrates the important distinctions between forward and futures contracts of different types using the tools of Chapter 6. We start first with various forward contracts and then cover futures contracts.

7.1 FORWARD CONTRACTS ON ZERO COUPON BONDS

The most basic forward contract is a forward contract on the price of a zero coupon bond. In this section and the rest of this chapter, we need to make an important distinction between the *value* of an existing contract on the books of an investment manager, insurance firm, or bank and the *price* of the forward contract quoted in

---

1. Source: *The Wall Street Journal*, March 26, 1996.

the market. Before making this distinction clear, a real-world example of a forward contract on zero coupon bonds is useful. In this case, the best example is provided by the 90-day bank bill futures contract traded on the Sydney Futures Exchange. For purposes of this section, we will ignore daily mark-to-market requirements and analyze this contract as a forward, not a futures, contract. We will do the true futures analysis in Section 7.4.

Contract: 90-day bank bills, Sydney Futures Exchange
Quotation basis: 100-yield in percent, quoted to two decimal places
Assumed maturity of underlying bill: 90 days
Valuation formula:

$$\text{Bank bill contract price} = \frac{365(1,000,000)}{365 + \frac{90 * \text{yield}}{100}}$$

The bank bill contract assumes the underlying instrument pays simple interest on an actual/365-day basis and has a maturity of 90 days. Essentially, the price of the contract is the price of a 90-day zero coupon bond with principal amount of A\$ 1 million at maturity. The calculation is the same as those we used in Chapter 1. One of the key features of the Sydney bank bill contract, as opposed to the Libor contracts we discuss below, is that the value of a 0.01 percent change in yield depends on the level of interest rates rather than being a constant dollar amount like the Eurodollar contract:

Yield	A\$ Value of 0.01% Yield Increase
9.00%	A\$ 23.60
10.00%	A\$ 23.49
11.00%	A\$ 23.37
12.00%	A\$ 23.26

Note that the quotation method (100-yield) is irrelevant to valuation: only the underlying cash flow described by the valuation formula matters for valuation purposes.

For notational convenience, we do the valuation analysis assuming that the principal amount on the underlying instrument is A\$ 1 instead of A\$ 1 million. We know from Chapter 1 that the forward price of this bond should be the ratio of zero coupon bond prices

$$\text{Forward bond price}(r,t,T_1,T_2) = \frac{P(r,t,T_2)}{P(r,t,T_1)}$$

where T_2 is the maturity date of the underlying instrument (in years), T_1 is the maturity date of the forward contract, and t is the current time. This result doesn't depend on any particular term structure model since it can be derived using arbitrage arguments alone. How is this result relevant to the valuation of a forward zero coupon bond forward using the Vasicek model and the results of Chapter 6? Noting that

$$T_2 = T_1 + \frac{90}{365}$$

in the case of the Sydney contract, we analyze the value of a Sydney bank bill *forward*. Like all of the valuation formulas in Chapters 4, 5, and 6, the value V of this existing contract must satisfy the general Vasicek model partial differential equation

$$V_r \alpha(\tilde{\mu} - r) + \frac{1}{2}\sigma^2 V_{rr} + V_t - rV = 0$$

We assume that the existing forward contract has a zero coupon bond exercise price K, which equates to a quoted exercise yield Y^* by inverting the valuation formula like this:

$$Y* = \frac{36{,}500}{90}\left[\frac{1{,}000{,}000}{K} - 1\right]$$

Using the notation of Section 6.5, the exercise price is equivalent to an instantaneous short rate in the Vasicek model of s^* such that

$$K = P(s^*,T_1,T_2) = e^{-F\tau s^* - G\tau}$$

where F and G are as defined in Section 6.5 and the subscript refers to the maturity $T_2 - T_1$:

$$\tau = T_2 - T_1$$

We know from Jamshidian's general valuation formula that the value of the forward contract is equal to the present value of the expected value of the cash flow on the contract's maturity date, evaluated as if the mean of the short rate is equal to the instantaneous forward rate for T_1:

$$V(r,t,T_1,T_2,K) = P(r,t,T_1) \int_{-\infty}^{\infty} \left(e^{-sF\tau - G\tau} - K \right) n[s,f_1,v] ds$$

with f_1 denoting the instantaneous forward rate prevailing at time t with maturity time T_1 and with v representing the same standard deviation of the short rate as of time T_1 from the perspective of time t. Using Equation 6.4 and simplifying shows that

$$V(r,t,T_1,T_2,K) = P(r,t,T_1) \left[\frac{P(r,t,T_2)}{P(r,t,T_1)} - K \right]$$

$$= P(r,t,T_2) - P(r,t,T_1)K$$

The price of an existing zero coupon bond forward contract equals the current value of the underlying instrument (the price of a zero coupon bond maturing at T_2) less the present value of the strike price, valued with maturity equal to the exercise date.

What about the observable market price of a forward contract on a zero coupon bond? We call this observable market price Q. We know that no cash is required to purchase such a contract; therefore, its value must be zero or arbitrage would be possible. We also know that at the instant a contract is purchased, the strike price K will equal the quoted market price Q. Therefore, we can solve for Q to get the same result we found in Chapter 1:

$$V(r,t,T_1,T_2,K) = 0 = P(r,t,T_1) \left[\frac{P(r,t,T_2)}{P(r,t,T_1)} - Q \right]$$

So

$$Q(r,t,T_1,T_2) = \frac{P(r,t,T_2)}{P(r,t,T_1)} = \text{Forward zero coupon bond price}$$

The observable market price (in zero coupon bond terms) equals the forward bond price. In yield terms as quoted on the Sydney Exchange, the quoted yield will be

$$Y* = \frac{36{,}500}{90}\left[\frac{1{,}000{,}000}{\text{Forward zero coupon bond price}} - 1\right]$$

As in Chapter 6, all of the term structure model equivalents of the "Greeks" apply to both V and Q, with the key statistics being the first derivatives with respect to the random short rate r in the Vasicek model:

$$r\text{Delta}(V) = \frac{\partial V}{\partial r}$$

$$r\text{Delta}(Q) = \frac{\partial Q}{\partial r}$$

7.2 FORWARD RATE AGREEMENTS

The design of the Sydney Futures Exchange bank bill contract is one of a relatively small number of contracts where the underlying instrument is a zero coupon bond. It is most common for the underlying instrument to be expressed in terms of an interest rate. Perhaps the most common forward contract with this structure is the forward rate agreement (FRA), where the counterparties agree on a strike rate K at maturity T_1 based on an underlying rate for an instrument maturing at T_2. The cash flow at time T_2 from the FRA is proportional to the FRA rate at maturity and the strike rate K:

$$\text{Cash flow} = B\left(\text{FRA rate}[T_1] - K\right)$$

where the coefficient B reflects the notional principal amount, the maturity of the underlying instrument, and the interest quotation method used for the FRA contract (i.e., actual/360 days, actual/

365 days, etc.). In this section, we analyze the case where this interest differential is paid at the maturity of the underlying instrument, T_2. Conventional FRAs normally pay in an economically equivalent way, paying the present value of this interest rate differential at the maturity of the FRA contract, T_1.

We value the contract as if cash flowed at time T_1 by taking the simple present value of T_2 cash flow from the perspective of time T_1 (the standard FRA convention):

$$\text{Present value}[T_1] = P(\tau)B[(FRA\ rate) - K]$$

$$= P(\tau)B\left[\frac{1}{P(\tau)} - 1 - K\right]$$

$$= B[1 - P(\tau)(1 + K)]$$

Using Jamshidian's formula and the approach in Section 6.5, we know the value of an existing FRA contract that pays at time T_2 is the present value of expected T_1 cash flow (present value), evaluated on the assumption that the short rate r has a mean equal to the instantaneous forward rate at time T_1:

$$V(r,t,T_1,T_2,K) = P(r,t,T_1) \int_{-\infty}^{\infty} B\left[1 - e^{-sF_\tau - G_\tau}(1 + K)\right]n(s,f_1,v)ds$$

$$= B\left[P(r,t,T_1) - (1 + K)P(r,t,T_2)\right]$$

$$= BP(r,t,T_2)\left[\text{Forward rate} - K\right]$$

The value of an existing FRA contract that pays at the T_2 maturity of the underlying instrument is the present value (based on a T_2 maturity) of the difference between the forward rate and the strike price.

What will be the observable FRA quotation Q for a contract which pays at the maturity of the underlying instrument? As in Section 7.1, for a newly quoted instrument the value must be 0 and the strike price K will be equal to Q. Solving for Q gives

$$Q(r,t,T_1,T_2) = \frac{P(r,t,T_1)}{P(r,t,T_2)} - 1 = \text{Forward rate}$$

What if the rate differential between the FRA rate and K is paid on an undiscounted basis at time T_1? We answer that question in Section 7.3.

7.3 EURODOLLAR FUTURES-TYPE FORWARD CONTRACTS

What if the market convention regarding FRA payment were that the forward rate agreement pays its cash flow

$$\text{Cash flow} = B\big(\text{FRA rate}[T_1] - K\big)$$

at the T_1 maturity of the FRA contract instead of its present value at time T_1 or payment in cash at the T_2 maturity of the underlying instrument? An FRA that pays in this manner is essentially equivalent to a Eurodollar futures contract with no mark-to-market margin (i.e., a Eurodollar futures-type forward). Such a Eurodollar futures-type forward, if modeled after the Chicago Mercantile Exchange Eurodollar futures contract, would pay \$25 for every one-basis-point differential between the settlement yield on the futures-type forward and the strike price. Unlike the bank bill future in Section 7.1, the dollar value of a basis point change in quoted yield is the same for all levels of interest rates under this type of contract. The cash flow at time T_1 under this kind of contract is figured as follows:

$$\text{Cash flow} = B\left(\frac{1}{P(\tau)} - 1 - K\right)$$

so we can use Jamshidian's formula to calculate the value of a Eurodollar futures-type forward contract with strike K:

$$V(r,t,T_1,T_2,K) = P(r,t,T_1) \int_{-\infty}^{\infty} B\left(\frac{1}{P(\tau)} - [1+K]\right) n(s,f_1,v_1)ds$$

Again using Equation 6.4 and simplifying gives

$$V(r,t,T_1,T_2,K) = BP(r,t,T_1)\left[\left(\frac{P(r,t,T_1)}{P(r,t,T_2)}\right)e^{F_{\tau}^2 v_1^2} - (1+K)\right]$$

$$= BP(r,t,T_1)\left[(\text{Forward rate} + 1)e^{F_{\tau}^2 v_1^2} - (1+K)\right]$$

The value of a true forward rate agreement in place at a strike price of K is the present value of the difference between an adjustment factor times 1 plus the forward rate less the sum of 1 plus the strike rate. This adjustment factor reflects the volatility of the short rate at time T_1 from the perspective of time t:

$$v_1^2 = \frac{\sigma^2}{2\alpha}\left[1 - e^{-2\alpha(T_1-\tau)}\right]$$

If the volatility of interest rates σ is 0, then v_1 becomes 0 and the Eurodollar futures-type forward becomes a simple present value times the difference between the forward rate and the strike price. We will see later also that a zero value for σ causes futures prices to equal forward prices. As long as interest rate volatility σ is not 0, however, a volatility adjustment is necessary for correct valuation of outstanding Eurodollar futures-type forwards.

What will be the market price of a Eurodollar futures-type forward that pays at its maturity T_1? As in Sections 7.1 and 7.2, the value of a new contract must be zero and its market price Q will equal the strike price of that contract. The quoted price of such a contract will be

$$Q(r,t,T_1,T_2) = \left(\frac{P(r,t,T_1)}{P(r,t,T_2)}\right)e^{F_\tau^2 v_1^2} - 1$$

$$= [\text{Forward rate} + 1]e^{F_\tau^2 v_1^2} - 1$$

The forward rate observable in the market equals 1 plus the forward rate, times a volatility adjustment factor, less 1. When interest rate volatility is 0, the Eurodollar futures-type forward contract rate will equal the simple forward rate.

7.4 FUTURES ON ZERO COUPON BONDS: THE SYDNEY FUTURES EXCHANGE BANK BILL CONTRACT

From this point on in the chapter, we will deal with true futures contracts. A "true" futures contract has daily mark-to-market requirements, with cash flow on an existing contract occurring continuously through its life. Ending cash flow is essentially 0, since the full amount of the change in observable futures prices over the life of the contract will have already been paid in cash through the continuous mark-to-market requirements. We will ignore initial margin payments and the return of these initial payments since they represent a simple zero coupon bond-type adjustment to the formulas that follow.

As in the previous three sections, there is an important distinction between the market value of an existing futures position V and the observable market price of a futures contract Q. Sections 7.1–7.3 showed the distinct differences between V and Q for three different types of forward contracts. In this section and in the remainder of this chapter, we note the following:

> The market value V of an existing futures position will always be 0 since (a) the market price of a new futures contract must be 0 to avoid arbitrage and (b) a previously taken futures position is continuously made equivalent to a new position by continuous margin payments. The observable market price Q of the futures contract and the initial strike rate K on the futures transaction, put in place at time t_0, are related by the fact that cash payments of at least $M = K - Q$, the cumulative net loss (gain) on the futures contract, must have been made to (withdrawn from) the margin account since initiation of the transaction at time t_0. The balance of the margin account is unknown since parties with a positive margin balance may use the cash proceeds for any purpose.

These theoretical truisms require a careful vocabulary to bridge the gap between the slang of market participants and financial reality. To a market participant, the "value of a futures contract" is $Q - K$, even though the margin account balance would be $\text{Max}(0, K - Q)$ rather than always being $Q - K$. These same market participants are rarely aware of the margin account balance, which is normally managed by an operational group. To a financial economist, the value is 0. Fortunately, the interest rate risk of a futures position to both groups is the change in Q that results from a change in interest rates, as captured by movements in the single stochastic factor r. Taking care to remember this distinction between viewpoints, we ignore the market value of an existing futures position V and concentrate on determining the observable market price Q.

For the rest of this chapter, we deviate temporarily from the solution technique we used in Chapter 6 and the first half of this chapter and return to the trial-and-error solution techniques used in Chapters 4 and 5. The reason, as noted by Chen (1992), is that "trading in futures markets requires no initial investment"[2] and, moreover, that value V is always 0 due to margin requirements. Therefore, when we derive the partial differential equation for the observable market price of a futures contract Q, the usual term rQ that results from the no-arbitrage condition is missing:

$$Q_r \alpha(\tilde{\mu} - r) + \frac{1}{2}\sigma^2 Q_{rr} + Q_t = 0$$

This equation represents the fundamental partial differential equation for the determination of the observable futures price. For every futures contract, the boundary condition at maturity requires that the futures price at expiration equals the market price of the underlying instrument.

Returning to the Sydney Futures Exchange bank bill futures contract, the boundary condition requires that the observable market price of a futures contract at expiration T_1 equals the market price of a zero coupon bond (a bank bill) with the maturity of the instrument underlying the futures contract:

$$Q(r,T_1,T_1,T_2) = P(r,T_1,T_2) = P(\tau)$$

We guess that the solution to the price of a Sydney Futures Exchange bank bill futures contract (zero coupon bond futures contract) takes the form

$$Q(r,t,T_1,T_2) = \left[\frac{P(r,t,T_2)}{P(r,t,T_1)}\right] e^{-Z} = e^{-r(F_2 - F_1) - (G_2 - G_1) - Z}$$

on the assumption that the forward bond price must be important to the solution. Solving for Z gives us the formula for a futures contract on a zero coupon bond:

$$Q(r,t,T_1,T_2) = \left[\frac{P(r,t,T_2)}{P(r,t,T_1)}\right] e^{-\frac{\sigma^2}{2}F\tau F_1^2}$$

$$= (\text{Forward zero coupon bond price}) e^{-\frac{\sigma^2}{2}F\tau F_1^2}$$

---

2. See page 99 of Chen (1992).

The zero coupon bond futures contract will have an observable market price equal to the forward zero coupon bond price times an adjustment factor that depends on the volatility of interest rates σ and the interest rate sensitivity F_1 of a zero coupon bond with maturity of T_1. If interest rate volatility σ is 0, the futures price will equal the forward price of a zero coupon bond. Note also that the exponent of the adjustment factor contains the term σF_1, which is the instantaneous price variance of a zero coupon bond with maturity T_1. As the contract nears maturity, this variance reduces to 0.

The interest rate risk of a position in the Sydney bank bill futures contract, or any other zero coupon bond futures contract, can be calculated using the usual term structure model "Greeks" for sensitivity analysis.

$$r\text{Delta} = \frac{\partial Q}{\partial r}$$

$$r\text{Gamma} = \frac{\partial^2 Q}{\partial r^2}$$

$$r\text{Theta} = \frac{\partial Q}{\partial t}$$

$$r\text{Vega} = \frac{\partial Q}{\partial \sigma}$$

$$r\text{Alpha} = \frac{\partial Q}{\partial \alpha}$$

7.5 FUTURES ON COUPON-BEARING BONDS: EXAMPLE USING THE SIMEX JAPANESE GOVERNMENT BOND FUTURE

Futures contracts on coupon-bearing bonds are a modest extension of the zero coupon bond price futures formula. Consider the contract specifications of the Singapore International Monetary Exchange's (SIMEX's) Japanese government bond (JGB) contract:

Notional principal: ¥50 million
Maturity: 10 years
Coupon rate: 6 percent

In actual operation, there will be a number of actual JGB issues "deliverable" under the SIMEX contract. The seller of the futures contract has a "delivery option" that allows the seller of the futures contract to deliver the "cheapest-to-deliver" bond if the seller of the futures contract chooses to hold the contract to maturity. If there are N deliverable bonds, the exchange will calculate a delivery factor F_i, which specifies the ratio of the principal amount on the ith deliverable bond to the notional principal of ¥50 million that is necessary to satisfy delivery requirements.

One of the bonds at any given time is the cheapest to deliver. After multiplying the yen coupon amounts and yen principal amount on this bond by the delivery factor, one will have the j maturities and cash flow amounts underlying the bond future. The market price of the bond future (as long as only one bond is deliverable) is the sum of zero coupon bond futures prices (assuming ¥1 of principal on each zero coupon bond future) times these cash flow amounts C_i:

$$Q_{\text{Bond}}(t,T_0) = \sum_{i=1}^{j} Q(r,t,T_i)C_i$$

T_0 is the maturity date of the bond futures contract. The sensitivity analysis of bond futures, assuming only one bond is deliverable, is the sum of the sensitivities for the zero coupon bond futures portfolio that replicates the cash flows on the bond.

What about the value of the delivery option? Assume there are two deliverable bonds. Using the insights of Jamshidian's (1989) approach, we know that there will be a level of the short rate r, which we label s^*, such that the two bonds are equally attractive to deliver as of time T_0. Above s^*, bond 1 is cheaper to deliver. Below s^*, bond 2 is cheaper to deliver. We can solve the partial differential equation for futures valuation subject to the boundary conditions that the futures price converges to bond 1's deliverable value above s^* and to bond 2's deliverable value below s^*. We also impose the condition that the first and second derivatives of the futures price are smooth at a short-rate level of s^*. The result is a special weighted average of the futures prices that would have prevailed if each bond were the only deliverable bond under the futures contract. There are other options embedded in common U.S. and Japanese bond tracks that can be analyzed in a related way.

7.6 EURODOLLAR, EUROYEN, AND EUROMARK FUTURES CONTRACTS

Money market futures have evolved to a fairly standard structure around the world. The SIMEX futures contracts in U.S. dollars, yen, and deutsche marks are all on three-month instruments with a constant currency amount paid at maturity per basis point change in the price of the contract. The per-basis-point value of rate changes under each contract is as follows:

U.S. dollars	25.00
Yen	2,500
Deutsche marks	25

In each case, the futures price must converge to the underlying three-month interest rates, multiplied by the notional principal amount and the appropriate day count factor to convert the rate to an annual basis. At maturity, the futures price (actually, the futures "rate" times the notional principal) Q must meet this boundary condition:

$$Q(r,T_1,T_1,T_2) = B\left[\frac{1}{P(r,T_1,T_2)} - 1\right]$$

B represents the notional principal and annualization factor; T_1 is the maturity of the futures contract in years; and T_2 is the maturity of the underlying three-month instrument — so T_2 is roughly 0.25 greater than T_1.

The futures contract must satisfy the same partial differential equation as in Section 7.4:

$$Q_r \alpha(\tilde{\mu} - r) + \frac{1}{2}\sigma^2 Q_{rr} + Q_t = 0$$

The solution to this equation, subject to the boundary condition on the futures price at its maturity date, is

$$Q(r,t,T_1,T_2) = B\left[\left(\frac{P(r,t,T_1)}{P(r,t,T_2)}\right)e^{-\frac{\sigma^2}{2\alpha^2}\left[(F_2 - F_1)(1 + \alpha F_2) - (F_\tau + \alpha F_\tau^2)\right]} - 1\right]$$

The market price of the futures contract (ignoring the annualization factor and notional principal embedded in B) is 1 over the forward bond price, multiplied by an adjustment factor, minus 1.

This formula reduces to the forward rate if interest rate volatility σ is 0. It shows that there are significant differences in the interest sensitivity of money market futures contracts that pay a constant currency amount per basis point and futures contracts on zero coupon bonds. Interest rate sensitivity parameters are calculated in the same way as in the prior sections.

E X E R C I S E S

For the exercises that follow, assume that the parameters of the Vasicek term structure model are as follows:

alpha (α), speed of mean reversion	.05
sigma (σ), interest rate volatility	.015
lambda (λ), market price of risk	.01
mu (μ), long-run expected value of r	.09
r, current short rate of interest	.06

7.1 What would be the observable market price for a forward contract on a zero coupon bond whose maturity today is three years if the maturity of the forward contract is one year?

7.2 What would be the value of an existing forward contract on the bond in Exercise 7.1 if the exercise price on the forward contract is 0.83?

7.3 What would be the quoted yield on the 90-day bank bill forward contract with one year to expiration if the terms of the contract were identical to the Sydney Futures Exchange's 90-day bank bill future, except for the fact that the contract is a forward rather than a future?

7.4 What would be the quoted yield on the 90-day bank bill contract in Exercise 7.3 if the contract were a futures contract, not a forward contract?

7.5 What would be the observable market price on a forward contract with one year to maturity on a six-month instrument where the cash payment in one year would be $25 per basis point of rate differential between the forward rate at expiration and the forward rate at initiation of the contract?

7.6 What would be the observable market price of the contract in Exercise 7.5 if it were a futures contract instead of a forward contract?

7.7 What would be the observable market price on a forward rate agreement with the terms in Exercise 7.6?

7.8 What would be the observable market price for a bond futures contract with one year to maturity on an underlying instrument that has five years to maturity, a principal amount of $100,000, and an annual coupon of 8 percent?

7.9 (Advanced.) Calculate analytical expressions for the rDeltas for

   a. A forward contract on a zero coupon bond.

   b. A forward rate agreement.

   c. A forward contract like a forward rate agreement except that the cash amount paid at the expiration of the contract is $25 per basis point of rate differential, not the present value of the rate differential at the expiration of the underlying instrument.

   d. A futures contract on a zero coupon bond.

   e. A futures contract that pays like the forward contract in Exercise 7.9c.

   f. A bond futures contract with N semiannual coupons of C and principal B.

7.10 (Advanced.) Use your answers to Exercise 7.9 to solve the following hedging problem: An insurance company has a two-year security with quarterly interest payments in its portfolio. The principal amount is $10 million, and the coupon level is 6 percent. The company will hedge the first year of interest rate risk by issuing a one-year security with quarterly interest payments. The second year of interest rate risk exposure can be hedged using the following instruments, all of which have maturity dates identical to the payment dates on the two-year loan:

   a. Forward contracts on a three-month zero coupon bond.

b. Forward rate agreements on a three-month instrument paying on an actual/365-day basis.

c. A forward contract that pays $25 per basis point at the maturity of the forward contract according to the rate differential between the original forward rate and the rate on the underlying three-month instrument.

d. Futures contracts on three-month zero coupon bonds.

e. A futures contract that pays like the forward contract in Exercise 7.10c.

Assume that there is no credit risk on either the two-year security or the futures contracts. Assume also that forward and futures contracts come in any denomination. How much of the one-year security should be issued, in combination with the futures contracts, for zero interest rate risk? (The answer is *not* the obvious answer.) How many of each of the futures contracts (using solely one type of contract at a time) would be employed to complete the hedge?

REFERENCES

Chen, Ren-raw. "Exact Solutions for Futures and European Futures Options on Pure Discount Bonds." *Journal of Financial and Quantitative Analysis*, March 1992, pp. 97–107.

Cox, J. C.; J. E. Ingersoll; and S. A. Ross. "The Relationship between Forward Prices and Futures Prices." *Journal of Financial Economics*, December 1981, pp. 321–46.

Jamshidian, Farshid. "An Exact Bond Option Formula." *Journal of Finance*, March 1989, pp. 205–9.

_____. *Bond and Option Evaluation in the Gaussian Interest Rate Model.* Financial Strategies Group, Merrill Lynch, New York 1990.

Jarrow, Robert A. *Modelling Fixed Income Securities and Interest Rate Options.* New York: McGraw-Hill, 1996.

Shimko, David C. *Finance in Continuous Time: A Primer.* Miami: Kolb, 1992.

Vasicek, Oldrich. "An Equilibrium Characterization of the Term Structure." *Journal of Financial Economics*, 1977, pp. 177–88.

CHAPTER 8

European Options on Forward and Futures Contracts

8.1 VALUING OPTIONS ON FORWARDS AND FUTURES

Valuing options on forward and futures contracts can be done in three ways. First, as in the original Black-Scholes article on stock options, one can specify a partial differential equation and appropriate boundary conditions and solve for the correct option pricing formula. Second, we can take advantage of the first Jamshidian general solution for security pricing under the Vasicek model, which we then use to find numerical solutions. We explain how to do this in Chapter 12. Third, we can use the second Jamshidian valuation formula from Chapter 6 to obtain analytical solutions. Market participants generally prefer analytical solutions over numerical solutions because both the speed and the accuracy of the analytical solution are superior, assuming the underlying term structure model would be used in both the analytical and the numerical approaches.

In this chapter, we take frequent advantage of the following notation, adapted from Chen (1992):

$$F_i = F(t,T_i) = \frac{1}{\alpha}\left[1 - e^{-\alpha(T_i-t)}\right]$$

$$F_{ij} = F(T_i, T_j) = \frac{1}{\alpha}\left[1 - e^{-\alpha(T_j - T_i)}\right]$$

$$F_{ij} = \frac{F_i - F_j}{\alpha F_i - 1}$$

$$D = \mu + \frac{\sigma\lambda}{\alpha} - \frac{\sigma^2}{2\alpha^2} = \tilde{\mu} - \frac{\sigma^2}{2\alpha^2}$$

$$G_i = G(t, T_i) = D[T_i - t - F_i] + \frac{\sigma^2 F_i^2}{4\alpha}$$

$$G_{ij} = D[T_j - T_i - F_{ij}] + \frac{\sigma^2 F_{ij}^2}{4\alpha}$$

$$v_i = v(t, T_i) = \sqrt{\frac{\sigma^2}{2\alpha}\left(1 - e^{-2\alpha(T_i - t)}\right)}$$

$$v_{ij} = v(T_i, T_j) = \sqrt{\frac{\sigma^2}{2\alpha}\left(1 - e^{-2\alpha(T_j - T_i)}\right)}$$

$$P_i = P(r, t, T_i) = e^{-rF_i - G_i}$$

$$P_{ij} = P(r, T_i, T_j) = e^{-rF_{ij} - G_{ij}}$$

Otherwise, using the same notation as in Chapters 6 and 7, we denote the forward rate from the perspective of current time t and maturity T_i as f_i. We know from Chapter 6 that

$$-G_{ij} - f_i F_{ij} + \frac{F_{ij}^2 v_i^2}{2} = \ln\left[\frac{P(r, t, T_j)}{P(r, t, T_i)}\right]$$

Using this expression and Equation 6.4 provides a useful formula we use in Section 8.3 in valuing options on forward rate agreements (FRAs):

$$\int_{-\infty}^{\infty} P_{0i}\, n(s, f_0, v_0)\, ds = \frac{P_i}{P_0}$$

We can also use Equation 6.4 to derive a useful expression for the expected value of the ratio of two coupon bonds with maturities T_i and T_j, evaluated as of time T_0 on the assumption that the short rate r has a normal density function n with mean f_0 and standard deviation v_0:

$$\int_{-\infty}^{\infty} \frac{P(s,T_0,T_j)}{P(s,T_0,T_i)} n(s,f_0,v_0)ds = \frac{P(r,t,T_j)}{P(r,t,T_i)} e^{v_0^2\left(F_{0i}^2 - F_{0i}F_{0j}\right)}$$

These powerful formulas are central to the results of this chapter.

8.2 EUROPEAN OPTIONS ON FORWARD CONTRACTS ON ZERO COUPON BONDS

Consider a European call option on a forward contract with maturity T_1 on a zero coupon bond with maturity T_2. We also assume that the maturity of the option is T_0. What is the value of the option if the exercise price is K and the current time is time t? We know from the Jamshidian formula in Chapter 6 that the value of the option is

$$V(r,t,T_0,T_1,T_2,K) = P_0 \int_{-\infty}^{s*} \left[\frac{P_{02}}{P_{01}} - K\right] n(s,f_0,v_0)ds$$

The constant $s*$ is the value of the short rate r at time T_0 at which the forward bond price exactly equals the strike price K:

$$s* = -\left[\frac{\ln(K) + G_{02} - G_{01}}{F_{02} - F_{01}}\right]$$

The forward bond price will only be greater than K when r at time T_0 is less than $s*$. Using the equations in Section 8.1 and Equation 6.4 gives the solution to the value of a European call option on a forward zero coupon bond contract:

$$V(r,t,T_0,T_1,T_2,K) = P_0\left(\frac{P_2}{P_1}\right)e^{v_0^2\left(F_{01}^2 - F_{01}F_{02}\right)}$$

$$N\left(\frac{s*-f_0}{v_0} + v_0[F_{02} - F_{01}]\right) - P_0 K N\left(\frac{s*-f_0}{v_0}\right)$$

As mentioned in Chapter 6, this term structure model–based option on forward bonds provides two critical improvements over the Black constant–interest rate extension of the Black-Scholes model to futures contracts: It recognizes that the volatility of the forward bond's price is declining over time, and it provides a full explanation of term structure movements, which allows for "delta hedging," via the rDelta calculation, of the option position with bonds of any maturity.

8.3 EUROPEAN OPTIONS ON FORWARD RATE AGREEMENTS

In this section, we analyze the European option to "buy" a forward rate agreement at the FRA strike rate of K. We assume that the option expires at time T_0, the FRA matures at time T_1, and the underlying zero coupon bond matures at time T_2. The cash flow on the option at time T_0 is the time T_0 value of the FRA, less K:

$$\text{Cash flow} = BP_{02}\left[\left(\frac{P_{01}}{P_{02}} - 1\right) - K\right]$$

where B is a factor that represents both the underlying notional principal and the annualization factor (i.e., actual days/360, actual days/365), which goes into the FRA cash flow calculation. Simplifying the cash flow expression and applying the Jamshidian valuation formula from Chapter 6, we get the value of the option on the FRA:

$$V(r,t,T_0,T_1,T_2,K) = P_0\int_{s^*}^{\infty}\left[BP_{01} - (1+K)BP_{02}\right]n(s,f_0,v_0)ds$$

Using the equations in Section 8.1, noting that cash flows only when r at time T_0 is *above* $s*$, gives the option value:

$$V(r,t,T_0,T_1,T_2,K) =$$

$$B\left[P_1N\left(\frac{f_0 - s*}{v_0} - v_0F_{01}\right) - (1+K)P_2N\left(\frac{f_0 - s*}{v_0} - v_0F_{02}\right)\right]$$

Like all of the other term structure model–based formulas in this book, the complete array of sensitivity parameters, including rDelta and rGamma, is available to market participants.

8.4 EUROPEAN OPTIONS ON A EURODOLLAR FUTURES-TYPE FORWARD CONTRACT

In this section, we analyze an option based on the observable market price of a Eurodollar futures-type option that pays a constant currency amount per basis point at the maturity of the forward contract. The underlying forward contract is the forward contract counterpart to the terms for standard three-month U.S. dollar, yen, and deutsche mark futures contracts. We let the factor B represent both the notional principal and an annualization factor. The time T_0 cash flow will be nonzero only if the short rate r at time T_0 is above a critical level $s*$.

Consider an option whose cash flow is proportional to the difference between the forward contract rate and the strike price K on the exercise date K. The cash flow at time T_0, using the formula for Eurodollar futures-type forwards from Chapter 7, is

$$\text{Cash flow} = B\left[\left(\frac{P_{01}}{P_{02}}e^{F_{12}^2 v_{01}^2} - 1\right) - K\right]$$

if the short rate at time T_0 is greater than a critical level $s*$. This critical level is the short-rate level at which the Eurodollar futures-type forward rate just equals the strike rate K. The rate $s*$ is implied by the equality of the forward rate and K:

$$\frac{P_{01}}{P_{02}}e^{F_{12}^2 v_{01}^2} - 1 = K$$

The level of $s*$ for which this is true is

$$s* = -\left[\frac{\ln(1+K) + G_{01} - G_{02} - F_{12}^2 v_{01}^2}{F_{01} - F_{02}}\right]$$

Using the Jamshidian formula and the relationships in Section 8.1 leads to the solution

$$V(r,t,T_0,T_1,T_2,K) = P_0 \int_{s*}^{\infty}\left(\frac{P_{01}}{P_{02}}e^{F_{12}^2 v_{01}^2} - 1 - K\right)n(s,f_0,v_0)ds$$

This expression, like the other formulas in this chapter, can be rearranged to closely resemble the Black-Scholes options formula:

$$V(r,t,T_0,T_1,T_2,K) = P_0 \frac{P_1}{P_2} e^{F_{12}^2 v_{01}^2 + v_0^2(F_{02}^2 - F_{01}F_{02})}$$

$$N\left(\frac{f_0 - s*}{v_0} - v_0(F_{01} - F_{02})\right) - P_0(1 + K)N\left(\frac{f_0 - s*}{v_0}\right)$$

8.5 EUROPEAN OPTIONS ON FUTURES ON ZERO COUPON BONDS

Chen (1992) provides the solution for the valuation of options on zero coupon bond futures like the Sydney Futures Exchange bank bill futures contract. The cash flow on such an option is as follows:

$$\text{Cash flow} = \frac{P_{02}}{P_{01}} e^{-\frac{\sigma^2}{2} F_{12}F_{01}^2} - K$$

where the left-hand side of this expression is the value of the underlying futures contract as of time T_0. This cash flow occurs as long as the short rate r at time T_0 is less than a critical level $s*$, at which the value of the futures contract at time T_0 exactly equals K. This occurs where

$$-s*(F_{02} - F_{01}) - (G_{02} - G_{01}) - \frac{\sigma^2}{2} F_{12}F_{01}^2 = \ln(K)$$

or

$$s* = -\left[\frac{\ln(K) + G_{02} - G_{01} + \frac{\sigma^2}{2} F_{12}F_{01}^2}{F_{02} - F_{01}}\right]$$

The value of the option fits the Jamshidian formulation

$$V(r,t,T_0,T_1,T_2,K) = P_0 \int_{-\infty}^{s*} \left(\frac{P_{02}}{P_{01}} e^{-\frac{\sigma^2}{2} F_{12}F_{01}^2} - K\right) n(s,f_0,v_0)ds$$

Evaluating this integral using the same approach as in previous sections leads to the option value

$$V(r,t,T_0,T_1,T_2,K) = P_0 \frac{P_2}{P_1} e^{v_0^2 \left(F_{01}^2 - F_{01}F_{02} \right) - \frac{\sigma^2}{2} F_{12}F_{01}^2}$$

$$N\left(\frac{s* - f_0}{v_0} + v_0(F_{02} - F_{01}) \right) - P_0 K N\left(\frac{s* - f_0}{v_0} \right)$$

This expression can be rearranged to show the relationship between the option and the futures price, as in Chen:

$$V(r,t,T_0,T_1,T_2,K) = P_0 \frac{P_2}{P_1} e^{\frac{\sigma^2}{2} F_0^2 (F_{02} - F_{01}) - \frac{\sigma^2}{2} F_{12}F_1^2}$$

$$N\left(\frac{s* - f_0}{v_0} + v_0(F_{02} - F_{01}) \right) - P_0 K N\left(\frac{s* - f_0}{v_0} \right)$$

$$= P_0 [\text{Futures price}] e^{\frac{\sigma^2}{2} F_0^2 (F_{02} - F_{01})}$$

$$N\left(\frac{s* - f_0}{v_0} + v_0(F_{02} - F_{01}) \right) - P_0 K N\left(\frac{s* - f_0}{v_0} \right)$$

All the usual term structure model sensitivity calculations, including rDelta and rGamma, can be done on these expressions, although one should take care to note that the forward rate prevailing at time t for maturity at time T_0, which we write as f_0, is a function of the short rate r.

8.6 EUROPEAN OPTIONS ON FUTURES ON COUPON-BEARING BONDS

As noted in Chapter 7, a future on a coupon-bearing bond can be analyzed as a collection of futures contracts on zero coupon bonds. Similarly, a European option on a coupon-bearing bond futures contract can be analyzed using the Jamshidian approach to options on coupon-bearing bond options, discussed in Chapter 6. Actual bond futures contracts have embedded in them other options, such as the delivery option, discussed in Chapter 7. Even with these complications, the approach of this chapter can provide a surprisingly tractable analytical answer for European option values without the need to resort unnecessarily to numerical solutions that introduce approximation error due to computer science, not to financial theory. For more information on this approach, please contact the authors. American options require numerical techniques, which we discuss in Chapter 12.

8.7 OPTIONS ON EURODOLLAR, EUROYEN, AND EUROMARK FUTURES CONTRACTS

From Chapter 7, we know that the observable market price at time T_0 of a money market futures contract maturing at time T_1 on an underlying instrument maturing at time T_2 and paying a constant currency amount per basis point of rate change will be

$$Q(r,T_0,T_1,T_2) = B\left[\frac{P_{01}}{P_{02}}e^{-\frac{\sigma^2}{2\alpha^2}[(F_{02} - F_{01})(1 + \alpha F_{02}) - (F_{12} + \alpha F_{12}^2)]} - 1\right]$$

if the notional principal is \$1. We analyze the case of a "call option" on a futures contract like the U.S.-dollar Libor futures contract traded in Chicago. Although almost all market participants concentrate on the futures rate, say 12 percent, the contract is actually quoted on the basis of an index, defined as

Index = 100 − Futures rate

A call option to buy the index at 90 will pay the buyer of the call the index value at maturity (say 92, corresponding to a rate of 8 percent) less the strike price (90) times the notional principal amount consistent with the futures contract. Under this call option, the buyer receives payment when the futures rate drops (i.e., the index rises) below (above) his exercise rate (exercise index level). Therefore, the cash payoff on this call option is

Cash flow = $K - Q(r,T_0,T_1,T_2)$

for r below a critical level $s*$, defined as the level of r at T_0 where the futures rate just equals the strike rate K. The critical level $s*$ is

$$s* = -\left[\frac{\ln(1 + K) + (G_{01} - G_{02}) + \frac{\sigma^2}{2\alpha^2}\left[\begin{matrix}(F_{02} - F_{01})(1 + \alpha F_{02})\\ + (F_{12} + \alpha F_{12}^2)\end{matrix}\right]}{F_{01} - F_{02}}\right]$$

The value of this European call option is

$$V(r,t,T_0,T_1,T_2,K) =$$

$$-BP_0\frac{P_1}{P_2}e^{-\frac{\sigma^2}{2\alpha^2}\left[(F_{02} - F_{01})(1 + \alpha F_{02}) - (F_{12} + \alpha F_{12}^2)\right] + v_0^2(F_{02}^2 - F_{01}F_{02})}$$

$$N\left(\frac{s* - f_0}{v_0} - v_0(F_{01} - F_{02})\right) + P_0B(1 + K)N\left(\frac{s* - f_0}{v_0}\right)$$

EXERCISES

For purposes of the exercises that follow, assume that the parameters of the Vasicek term structure model are as follows:

alpha (α), speed of mean reversion	.05
sigma (σ), interest rate volatility	.015
lambda (λ), market price of risk	.01
mu (μ), long-run expected value of r	.09
r, current short rate of interest	.06

8.1 What is the value of a one-year European option to buy a forward contract with two years remaining on a three-year zero coupon bond, if the exercise price on the option is $0.90?

8.2 What is the value of a European put option on the same forward contract at the same exercise price and same maturity for the option as in Exercise 8.1?

8.3 What is the value of a one-year option to exercise a forward rate agreement with a two-year maturity on an underlying instrument that will have a three-month maturity at the maturity of the FRA, if the "strike FRA rate" on the option is 6 percent?

8.4 What is the value of the same option as in Exercise 8.3 if the underlying two-year contract pays $25 per basis point for every basis point that the forward contract closes above the 6 percent strike rate at the maturity of the forward contract?

8.5 What is the value of a one-year option to buy a two-year futures contract on a zero coupon bond that currently has three years to maturity at a strike price of $0.95?

8.6 What is the value of a one-year call option to buy the U.S.-dollar three-month Libor Eurodollar futures contract with a two-year maturity at an index rate of 91 (futures interest rate of 9 percent)?

REFERENCES

Black, Fischer and Myron Scholes. "The Pricing of Options and Corporate Liabilities." *Journal of Political Economy* 81, May–June 1973, pp. 637–654.

Chen, Ren-raw. "Exact Solutions for Futures and European Futures Options on Pure Discount Bonds." *Journal of Financial and Quantitative Analysis*, March 1992, pp. 97–107.

Cox, J. C.; J. E. Ingersoll; and S. A. Ross. "The Relationship between Forward Prices and Futures Prices." *Journal of Financial Economics*, December 1981, pp. 321–46.

Jamshidian, Farshid. "An Exact Bond Option Formula." *Journal of Finance*, March 1989, pp. 205–9.

Vasicek, Oldrich. "An Equilibrium Characterization of the Term Structure." *Journal of Financial Economics*, November 1977, pp. 177–88.

CHAPTER 9

Caps and Floors

9.1 INTRODUCTION TO CAPS AND FLOORS

Interest rate caps and floors have become perhaps the most popular interest rate option–based instrument. They provide an invaluable tool for financial managers interested in controlling their exposure to extremely high or extremely low interest rates. Common uses of caps and floors include the following:

- Limiting the maximum rate paid on a floating-rate loan by purchasing a cap.
- Limiting the exposure to a floor on nonmaturity consumer deposit rates paid by the bank by purchasing a floor in the open market.
- Hedging the prepayment risk on a mortgage portfolio.
- Hedging the cancellation risk on a portfolio of life insurance policies.
- Insuring that the performance of a fixed-income portfolio can only improve as rates rise.

The purchaser of a cap purchases an insurance policy against interest rate increases. Consider a hedger who has a floating-rate loan tied to the three-month U.S.-dollar Libor. By purchasing a 10 percent cap, the hedger insures that he will never pay more than 10 percent on the loan after subtracting payments from the seller of the cap. If rates rise to 12 percent, he pays 12 percent on the loan but receives 2 percent from the person who sold the cap, for a net expense of 10 percent.

Caps and floors are both traded outright and embedded in common banking and insurance industry assets and liabilities. A number of market conventions deserve mention here. First, payment for the cap or floor typically takes place at time 0 when the contract is traded outright. Embedded in a loan or deposit, the cap or floor price would be disguised as an interest rate differential relative to the identical loan or deposit with no cap or floor. Second, the cap or floor strike rate is stated on the same basis as the underlying interest rate. For example, the buyer of the Libor cap above is quoted a strike rate of 10 percent versus Libor. Both Libor and the cap strike rate interest amounts are calculated on an actual/360-day basis. In other markets, actual/365-day calculations are common. Both the Libor rate and the cap or floor rate will normally be set from the same reference point (the same "screen" provided by a vendor of real-time information, such as Reuters, Telerate, or Bloomberg) and use the same method for counting business days and the same holiday convention.

In this chapter, we abstract from these market conventions to ease exposition. For purposes of this chapter, a strike rate quoted as 10 percent for a Libor cap on a 91-day period would be converted to a decimal strike rate K using the following formula:

$$ K = .10\left[\frac{91}{360}\right] $$

In applying the formulas below, the strike rate should be converted to this "K format" to allow us to abstract from day count and accrual methods in what follows.

Another important market convention is the use of Black's (1976) futures model for the quotation of cap and floor prices. The Black-Scholes (1973) option model was perhaps the biggest innovation in financial theory in the 20th century, but its well-justified popularity should not obscure the reasons cited in Chapter 6 for instead using a term structure model approach to model interest rate derivatives. Hull (1993) presents a lucid explanation of the use of the Black (1976) approximation to cap and floor valuation, and the reasons why a term structure model approach works better.

A commonly asked question is this: If most of the traders in the market are using the Black model, won't I be making a mistake by using something else? The short answer is an emphatic no. We show in Chapter 19 that the term structure model approach fits actual quoted prices better than the Black model, which has to be "bent" considerably to fit observable prices. We also show in Chapter 17 that the term structure model approach fits observable foreign exchange options data better than the conventional modification of the Black-Scholes model for the foreign exchange market. Finally, the true test of a model is whether it provides the best hedge. As we noted in Chapter 6, the Black-Scholes model assumes constant interest rates and, to find a hedge, one has to do a two-stage analysis that incorporates term structure model analytics after the fact. We think it's better to do this from the outset, and that's confirmed by the data in Chapter 19. The market convention of quoting cap and floor prices in terms of Black-Scholes volatilities means market participants have to convert the quotation into an up-front dollar price for analysis, valuation, and hedging, which is true even for traders who still rely solely on the Black model for their analytics.

At this point, we take advantage of our work in previous chapters to illustrate cap and floor pricing under a term structure model approach.

9.2 CAPS AS EUROPEAN OPTIONS ON FORWARD RATE AGREEMENTS

In Chapter 8, we analyzed the European option to "buy" a forward rate agreement at the FRA strike rate of K. We assumed in Chapter 8 that the option expires at time T_0, the FRA matures at time T_1, and the underlying zero coupon bond matures at time T_2. The cash flow on the option at time T_0 is the time T_0 value of the FRA, less K:

$$\text{Cash flow} = BP_{02}\left[\left(\frac{P_{01}}{P_{02}} - 1\right) - K\right]$$

where B is a factor that represents both the underlying notional principal and the annualization factor (i.e., actual days/360, actual days/365), which goes into the FRA cash flow calculation. Cash flow will be positive if r at time T_0 exceeds the critical level $s*$

$$s* = -\left[\frac{\ln(1 + K) + G_{01} - G_{02}}{F_{01} - F_{02}}\right]$$

The value of an option on an FRA was given in Chapter 8 as

$$V(r,t,T_0,T_1,T_2,K) =$$

$$B\left[P_1 N\left(\frac{f_0 - s*}{v_0} - v_0 F_{01}\right) - (1 + K)P_2 N\left(\frac{f_0 - s*}{v_0} - v_0 F_{02}\right)\right]$$

Looking at the cash flows for an option on an FRA shows that a cap is really just a special case of an option on an FRA, where the exercise date of the option on the FRA (T_0 in Chapter 8) is the same as the expiration date of the FRA, T_1. We make this change to the valuation formula for an option on an FRA. All subscripts of 0 become 1, and we note that F_{11} and G_{11} are both 0. The value of a "caplet" that matures at time T_1 and with a cap at the rate K (subject to the qualifications mentioned in Section 9.1) on an interest rate derived from an underlying instrument maturing at time T_2 is

$$V(r,T_1,T_2,K) = B\left[P_1 N\left(\frac{f_1 - s*}{v_1}\right) - (1 + K)P_2 N\left(\frac{f_1 - s*}{v_1} - v_1 F_{12}\right)\right]$$

where

$$s* = \frac{\ln(1 + K) - G_{12}}{F_{12}}$$

B is the notional principal, and

$$P_i = P(r,t,T_i)$$

This formula is also identical to the put option formula for zero coupon bonds in Chapter 6. It represents a put on $1 + K$ units of a zero coupon bond with maturity T_2 and a strike price of 1 at time T_1 on the sum of those $1 + K$ units.

9.3 FORMING OTHER CAP-RELATED SECURITIES

A wide variety of cap and floor derivatives can be constructed with this basic building block as a tool:

- Floor prices are calculated in an equivalent way using the formula for a call option on a zero coupon bond in Chapter 6.
- Longer-term caps are constructed as the sum of a number of caplets.
- Longer-term floors are constructed as the sum of a number of floorlets.
- Collars represent a combination of caps and floors (typically purchasing a cap and selling a floor).
- Costless collars are created by finding the floor rate K_f such that the value of the floor exactly equals the value of the cap with cap rate K_c (or vice versa).

EXERCISES

For the exercises that follow, assume that the parameters of the Vasicek term structure model are as follows:

alpha (α), speed of mean reversion	.05
sigma (σ), interest rate volatility	.015
lambda (λ), market price of risk	.01
mu (μ), long-run expected value of r	.09
r, current short rate of interest	.06

Assume that three-month periods are exactly 0.25 years long and that Libor is quoted on an actual/365-day basis (instead of market practice of actual/360).

9.1   What are the values of each of the eight caplets that make up the value of a two-year cap on three-month Libor at 10 percent? (Note: K = .025.)

9.2   What is the value of the two-year cap?

9.3   What are the values of each of the eight floorlets that make up the value of a floor on three-month Libor at 6 percent? (Note: K = .015.)

9.4   What is the value of the two-year floor?

9.5   What is the value of a two-year collar on three-
month Libor with a cap at 10 percent and a floor at
6 percent?

9.6   What is the rDelta of each caplet?

9.7   What is the rDelta of the two-year cap?

9.8   What is the rDelta of each floorlet?

9.9   What is the rDelta of the two-year floor?

9.10   What is the rDelta of the two-year collar?

9.11   You are the derivative trader for caps and floors at
Golden, Spats & Co., a major Newark dealer. You
have been ordered to hedge your position in the
two-year collar with zero coupon bonds. (You sold
the collar to an industrial company, Placem &
Gamble.) All quarterly maturities are available out to
two years with good liquidity. What should be your
position in each zero coupon bond? Assume you
believe that one-factor term structure models are a
good approximation to reality but that it's safer to
"match maturities" whenever possible to get the
best fit, even if the term structure model turns out
to be less than perfect.

REFERENCES

Black, F. "The Pricing of Commodity Contracts." *Journal of Financial Economics*,
March 1976, pp. 167–79.

Black, F., and M. Scholes. "The Pricing of Options and Corporate Liabilities."
Journal of Political Economy, May–June 1973, pp. 637–54.

Hull, John. *Options, Futures, and Other Derivative Securities.* 2nd ed. Englewood
Cliffs, NJ: Prentice Hall, 1993.

Jamshidian, Farshid. "An Exact Bond Option Formula." *Journal of Finance*,
March 1989, pp. 205–9.

Vasicek, Oldrich. "An Equilibrium Characterization of the Term Structure." *Journal of Financial Economics*, November 1977, pp. 177–88.

CHAPTER 10

Interest Rate Swaps and Swaptions

10.1 INTRODUCTION TO INTEREST RATE SWAPS

Interest rate swaps have become the most successful over-the-counter derivative security in the world. The most common "plain vanilla" swap between two counterparties calls for counterparty A to make "fixed-rate" payments at even intervals (normally semiannual) to counterparty B, and for counterparty B to make "floating-rate" payments, typically at three-month or six-month intervals, to counterparty A. Seen from the perspective of counterparty A, the swap has the same net cash flow as if counterparty A issued a fixed-rate bond and purchased a floating-rate bond. From the perspective of counterparty B, the swap cash flows are identical to the case where counterparty B purchases a fixed-rate bond with the proceeds of a floating-rate bond issue.

Why are interest rate swaps so popular? The primary reasons include the vast liquidity of the swap markets in the major currencies, the low "issuance" costs compared to traditional bonds even under a medium-term note program or shelf registration, the ease of reversing a position with an offsetting transaction, and the lack of daily mark-to-market margin requirements for swap market participants of good quality.

Most market participants value swaps as if both the fixed and the floating side involved principal payments at maturity. Since the amounts net to zero, this is a good approximation when both parties have zero credit risk. As the credit risk of each party diverges from zero, this becomes a more dangerous assumption, so we won't use it in this chapter. We explore the issue of credit risk in more detail in Chapter 16.

10.2 VALUING THE FLOATING-RATE PAYMENTS ON A SWAP

In Chapter 1, we valued various floating-rate securities on the assumption that principal came due at maturity. In this section, we value only the floating-rate payments and ignore the ending principal payments. Consider the value at an interest rate reset date T_0 of interest paid at then-current market levels on an underlying bond with maturity at T_1. The present value of this interest payment as of time T_0 is

$$\text{Present value} = P_{01}\left(\frac{1}{P_{01}} - 1\right) = 1 - P_{01}$$

Using the Jamshidian valuation formula in Chapter 6 and Equation 6.4 gives us the value of the interest rate payment as of the current time t:

$$V(r,t,T_0,T_1) = P_0 \int_{-\infty}^{\infty} (1 - P_{01})n(s,f_0,v_0)ds = P_0 - P_1$$

If in the future we will receive N floating-rate payments at dates $T_1, \ldots, T_N$ priced on reset dates $T_0, T_1, \ldots, T_{N-1}$, the stream of floating-rate payments will be worth

$$V(r,t,T_0,T_N) = \sum_{i=1}^{N} V(r,t,T_{i-1},T_i) = \sum_{i=1}^{N}(P_{i-1} - P_i) = P_0 - P_N$$

The values of floating-rate payments at market levels equal the difference between values of a zero coupon bond maturing at the first reset date and one maturing on the last payment date. If the current time t is the first reset date,

$$V(r,t,t,T_1) = 1 - P_N$$

If we had analyzed the problem as a floating-rate bond with principal paid at time T_N, the present value of principal would be P_N and the sum of the principal and interest portions would be par value, or 1. If the first coupon has already been set (on a previous reset date) to a currency amount C_0 and there is a spread over the pricing index with a constant currency amount s, the value of the floating-rate payments consistent with Chapter 1 is

$$V(r,t,T_0,T_N,s,C_0) = P_0C_0 + P_0 - P_N + s\sum_{i=1}^{N}P_i$$

10.3 THE OBSERVABLE FIXED RATE IN THE SWAP MARKET

A fixed-rate swap normally pays a fixed currency amount C at each payment date. The present value of this payment on M payment dates is straight from Chapter 1:

$$\text{Value}(r,t,T_1,T_M) = C\sum_{i=1}^{M}P_i$$

How could we calculate the market value on a swap if for some reason we could not observe it on dealing screens? Aside from the bid-offered spread, the market value of a new swap should be 0. Therefore, the market level of the fixed-rate payment C will be the level C such that the present value of the fixed-rate payments exactly equals the present value of the floating-rate payments:

$$C\sum_{i=1}^{M}P_i = 1 - P_N$$

If T_N and T_M are the same dates, the preceding equation effectively requires that C be set at the level such that the present value of a bond with coupon C equals par value:

$$C\sum_{i=1}^{N}P_i + P_N = 1$$

10.4 AN INTRODUCTION TO SWAPTIONS

A swaption is an agreement between two counterparties that allows counterparty A to enter into an interest rate swap with a preagreed fixed-rate payment C at the option of counterparty A. Swaptions come in two forms. The "constant maturity" form of swaption prescribes that the interest rate swap have a set maturity, say five years, regardless of when the swaption was exercised. For example, if the exercise period on the swaption is two years, the underlying swap would end up being a five-year swap regardless of whether the swaption was entered into after 3 months, 12 months, or two years. The "fixed maturity date" swaption prescribes a maturity date for the swap at the signing date of the contract, and therefore the effective maturity of the swap will shorten if exercise is delayed. Consider a 3-year swaption of the fixed maturity type on a swap with an original maturity of 10 years. If the swaption is exercised after two years, the swap will have an eight-year life.

Both forms are common. If the swaption is a European swaption, the two methods are equivalent.

10.5 VALUATION OF EUROPEAN SWAPTIONS

The valuation of European swaptions is a direct application of Jamshidian's formula for options on coupon-bearing bonds. As shown in Section 10.3, the market value of a new swap must be such that the fixed rate on the swap would cause a coupon-bearing bond with the same payment frequency and maturity date[1] to trade at par. This means we can ignore the floating-rate side of the swap for purposes of valuation.[2] Therefore, a swaption that allows the holder to receive the fixed-rate side of the swap is a call option to buy the equivalent underlying *bond*. A swaption that allows the holder to pay the fixed-rate side of the swap is a put option on the equivalent underlying *bond*. Having made this translation, the formula is identical to that of Section 6.7.

---

1. And for purposes of this chapter, credit risk.
2. We could not ignore the floating side if the floating side involved a nonzero spread from the pricing index.

10.6 VALUATION OF AMERICAN SWAPTIONS

Because of the intervening cash flows on swaps, there is the possibility of early exercise on an American swaption; therefore, the European swaption valuation approach is only a rough approximation to the value of an American swaption. Correct valuation requires the numerical methods we analyze in Chapter 12.

E X E R C I S E S

For the exercises that follow, assume that the parameters of the Vasicek term structure model are as follows:

alpha (α), speed of mean reversion	.05
sigma (σ), interest rate volatility	.015
lambda (λ), market price of risk	.01
mu (μ), long-run expected value of r	.09
r, current short rate of interest	.06

10.1 What is the present value of an existing $100 million swap with three years and three months to maturity, semiannual Libor payments, a spread to Libor of 0, a fixed rate of 8 percent, and a current floating-rate coupon of 6.5 percent? (Use actual/365-day interest for simplicity.) Assume you pay fixed rate and receive floating.

10.2 What is the rDelta of this swap position?

10.3 If you were going to hedge the interest rate risk of this swap with a position in two-year zero coupon bonds, what should be the size and direction (long or short) of the two-year zero coupon bond position?

10.4 How much would you pay for the right, two years from today, to enter into a five-year swap with semiannual payments, a fixed rate of 7 percent, and a notional principal of $50 million? Assume the floating-rate side is "Libor flat."

10.5 What would be the value of the same swaption as in Exercise 10.4 if the exercise period were one year? Three years? Four years? Five years? Which European swaption price would best approximate the value of an American swaption that allowed you to enter into the five-year 7 percent swap at any time in the next five years?

10.6 What is the *r*Delta of the swap in Exercise 10.4?

10.7 Assume that 10 seconds ago you bought the swaption giving you the right to pay fixed on the 7 percent five-year swap two years from now. Five seconds ago, your boss, anticipating adverse market movements, ordered all open-trading positions hedged immediately. Your only outlet is a bond broker offering a two-way price in a four-year zero coupon bond. What should you do? Assume immediate resignation is not an option, since bonuses are paid next month.

REFERENCES

Jamshidian, Farshid. "An Exact Bond Option Formula." *Journal of Finance*, March 1989, pp. 205–9.

Vasicek, Oldrich. "An Equilibrium Characterization of the Term Structure." *Journal of Financial Economics*, November 1977, pp. 177–88.

CHAPTER 11

Exotic Swap and Option Structures

11.1 INTRODUCTION TO EXOTIC SWAPS AND OPTIONS

A difference of opinion makes a market, and that is the major rationale for the development of the market in exotic swaps and exotic options. A second and less happy rationale is the willingness of some market participants to buy and sell securities without much knowledge of their true value. The purpose of this chapter is to show how the techniques of Chapters 6–10 can be used to value securities that, at least at one point in their life, were considered exotic. *Exotic* means both "strange" and "difficult to value," and it is the latter that often motivates the originators of exotic structures. The following examples are taken from the swap portfolio of some major U.S.-government-guaranteed agencies.

11.2 ARREARS SWAPS

In most interest rate swaps, the floating-rate payment is based on Libor in the relevant currency. If the swap calls for six-month Libor, the Libor rate is set on a reference date approximately six months before the cash interest payment will normally be made. In an arrears swap, the Libor rate and payment amount will be made "in arrears," that is, shortly before the cash payment must be made. How do we value this kind of swap?

We start by analyzing the value of one arrears payment. We want the value at current time t of an arrears swap where the payment is determined and made at time T_0 based on a reference rate derived from a zero coupon bond with a maturity at time T_1. The cash flow at time T_0 is

$$\text{Cash flow} = \frac{1}{P_{01}} - 1$$

if we assume a notional principal of \$1.

The value at current time t of a security that pays this amount at time T_0 comes from the general Jamshidian valuation formula

$$V(r,t,T_0,T_1) = P_0 \int_{-\infty}^{\infty} \left(\frac{1}{P_{01}} - 1 \right) n(s,f_0,v_0)ds$$

which we can simplify using Equation 6.4 to derive the value at time t as

$$V(r,t,T_0,T_1) = \frac{P_0^2}{P_1} e^{F_{01}^2 v_0^2} - P_0$$

The value of N arrears payments made at $T_1, \ldots, T_N$ is

$$V(r,t,T_1,T_N) = \sum_{i=1}^{N} V(r,t,T_i,T_{i+1}) = \sum_{i=1}^{N} \left[\frac{P_i^2}{P_{i+1}} e^{F_{i,i+1}^2 v_i^2} - P_i \right]$$

Equilibrium pricing calls for the net value of an arrears swap versus a traditional floating-rate swap plus a spread s (which may be positive or negative) to have a net value of 0.[1] Since the market value of the floating side of a traditional swap with dollar spread s to Libor is

$$V(r,t,T_1,T_N) = 1 - P_N + s \sum_{i=1}^{N} P_i$$

---

1. Again, we ignore the bid-offered spread.

The equilibrium spread s for which an arrears swap has an [efficient] market value of 0 is

$$s = \frac{P_N - 1 + \sum_{i=1}^{N}\left[\dfrac{P_i^2}{P_{i+1}} e^{F_{i,i+1}^2 v_i^2} - P_i\right]}{\sum_{i=1}^{N} P_i}$$

In an efficient market, new swaps will be priced at this spread over Libor. Existing swaps would be priced based on the existing terms using the formulas above.

11.3 DIGITAL OPTIONS

Another category is the "digital" category of derivatives that pays either 1 or 0 depending on the level of a random variable. Given our focus on fixed-income derivatives, consider the value of a derivative security that pays \$1 at time T_0 if a short-term interest rate (such as Libor) is less than or equal to a critical level K. We assume that the underlying instrument has a maturity of time T_1. Cash flow is nonzero at time T_0 only if the short-term interest rate is below a critical level $s*$ such that

$$s* = \frac{\ln(1 + K) - G_{01}}{F_{01}}$$

According to Chapter 6, and Equation 6.4 in particular, the value of such a security is

$$V(r,t,T_0,T_1,K) = P_0 \int_{-\infty}^{s*} 1\, n(s,f_0,v_0)ds$$

$$= P_0 N\left(\frac{s* - f_0}{v_0}\right)$$

11.4 DIGITAL RANGE NOTES

What if the security described in Section 11.3 pays \$1 only if the short-term rate is between critical levels K_1 and K_2? These critical levels translate into short rates s_1 and s_2 such that

$$s_i = \frac{\ln(1 + K_i) - G_{01}}{F_{01}}$$

The value of one payment of these "digital range notes," viewed from the perspective of time t, is

$$V(r,t,T_0,T_1,s_1,s_2) = P_0 \int_{s_2}^{s_1} 1 \, n(s,f_0,v_0) ds$$

$$= P_0 \left[N\left(\frac{s_1 - f_0}{v_0} \right) - N\left(\frac{s_2 - f_0}{v_0} \right) \right]$$

11.5 RANGE FLOATERS

Another popular derivative is the so-called range floater. Consider a security that pays Libor when Libor is less than a critical level K, and 0 otherwise. Cash flow is determined at time T_0 based on the level of an underlying zero coupon bond with maturity T_1. The security pays Libor only if the short rate is below a critical level s_i, defined as follows:

$$s_i = \frac{\ln(1 + K_i) - G_{01}}{F_{01}}$$

The value of this single payment of a range floater as of current time t is

$$V(r,t,T_0,T_1,s_i) = P_0 \int_{-\infty}^{s_i} P_{01} \left(\frac{1}{P_{01}} - 1 \right) n(s,f_0,v_0) ds$$

$$= P_0 N\left(\frac{s_i - f_0}{v_0} \right) - P_1 N\left(\frac{s_i - f_0}{v_0} + v_0 F_{01} \right)$$

What about the case where the range floater pays only between critical Libor levels K_1 and K_2, which translate into critical levels of the short rate at time T_0 of s_1 and s_2 (defined as s_i above)? One payment of this range floater can be shown to be

$$V(r,t,T_0,T_1,s_1,s_2) = P_0 \int_{s_2}^{s_1} P_{01}\left(\frac{1}{P_{01}} - 1\right)n(s,f_0,v_0)ds$$

$$= P_0\left[N\left(\frac{s_1 - f_0}{v_0}\right) - N\left(\frac{s_2 - f_0}{v_0}\right)\right]$$

$$- P_1\left[N\left(\frac{s_1 - f_0}{v_0} + v_0 F_{01}\right) - N\left(\frac{s_2 - f_0}{v_0} + v_0 F_{01}\right)\right]$$

11.6 MIN-MAX FLOATERS

Another security that was extremely popular for a time was the "min-max floater." The security paid Libor as long as Libor was below a critical level X, which translated into a critical short rate level s^* at time T_0 of

$$s^* = \frac{\ln(1 + X) - G_{01}}{F_{01}}$$

Above X, the security pays K – Libor. The general Jamshidian solution to this valuation problem is given by

$$V(r,t,T_0,T_1,X,K) = P_0 \int_{-\infty}^{s^*} P_{01}\left(\frac{1}{P_{01}} - 1\right)n(s,f_0,v_0)ds$$

$$+ P_0 \int_{s^*}^{\infty} P_{01}\left[K - \left(\frac{1}{P_{01}} - 1\right)\right]n(s,f_0,v_0)ds$$

The solution again relies on Equation 6.4 and gives the value for one min-max floater payment as

$$V(r,t,T_0,T_1,X,K) = \left(P_0 - P_1\right)N\left(\frac{s^* - f_0}{v_0}\right)$$

$$- \left[P_0 - (1 + K)P_1\right]\left[1 - N\left(\frac{s^* - f_0}{v_0}\right)\right]$$

11.7 OTHER DERIVATIVE SECURITIES

Literally almost any fixed-income derivative structure can be analyzed in this framework due to the generality of the solutions in Chapter 6 and the richness of the Vasicek term structure model. All of these analytical solutions have related sensitivity statistics, of which rDelta is the most important. As a result, explicit hedge ratios can be calculated directly. The largest area of derivatives that cannot be valued in this type of analytical, closed-form solution is that of derivatives that include an American option. We turn to that problem in Chapter 12.

E X E R C I S E S

For the exercises that follow, assume that the parameters of the Vasicek term structure model are as follows:

alpha (α), speed of mean reversion	.05
sigma (σ), interest rate volatility	.015
lambda (λ), market price of risk	.01
mu (μ), long-run expected value of r	.09
r, current short rate of interest	.06

11.1 What is the value of a security that pays the three-month Libor rate one year from now on a notional principal of $100 million if the three-month Libor rate is determined (*a*) on the payment date (an arrears swap payment) and (*b*) three months before the payment date (the normal method)?

11.2 What is the rDelta of each of the securities in Exercise 11.1?

11.3 What is the value of a security that pays $1 at the beginning of every quarter for four quarters beginning one year from now if three-month Libor is
a. 8 percent or below?
b. between 10 percent and 8 percent?
Assume Libor is measured on the first day of the quarter and payment is made that day.

11.4 What is the value of a security that pays Libor quarterly for the next four quarters only if Libor is between 6 percent and 7 percent?

11.5 What is the value of a security that pays
  a. Libor quarterly if Libor is less than 8 percent?
  b. 17 percent – Libor if Libor is greater than 8 percent?
  Assume the security has a one-year maturity and the first coupon has already been set at 8 percent.

11.6 What is the *r*Delta of the security in Exercise 11.5?

11.7 What amount of one-year zero coupon bonds is necessary to hedge a position in the security in Exercise 11.5?

11.8 Is the security in Exercise 11.5 suitable for investment by a government entity? Why or why not?

REFERENCES

Jamshidian, Farshid. "An Exact Bond Option Formula." *Journal of Finance*, March 1989, pp. 205–9.

Vasicek, Oldrich. "An Equilibrium Characterization of the Term Structure." *Journal of Financial Economics*, November 1977, pp. 177–88.

CHAPTER 12

American Fixed-Income Options

12.1 INTRODUCTION TO AMERICAN OPTIONS

In Chapters 6–11, we emphasized the valuation of securities where the option embedded in the security was exercisable at only one date. These European options, as we have shown, generally have explicit analytical solutions in the Vasicek family of models, so numerical techniques are neither necessary nor desirable. As we will see below, numerical techniques have disadvantages that are usually due to computer science considerations: they are normally more calculation intensive, which reduces speed, and almost all steps taken to improve speed by reducing the complexity of the numerical calculation introduce errors that often can be significant.

American options, in order to avoid arbitrage, must satisfy the same partial differential equation that we used in the Vasicek model in Chapter 5. In addition, there is a boundary condition similar to the boundary condition imposed in Chapters 5 and 6 that requires the value of the security at maturity to equal its cash flow at maturity. In the case of American options, however, there is an additional boundary condition that requires the holder of the option to act rationally throughout the period during which the option can be exercised.[1] Consider the typical

---

1. We relax this assumption in Chapter 13.

Japanese or American fixed-rate mortgage. We cover this topic in detail in Chapter 14, but here we can briefly summarize the nature of these securities by saying that the holder receives a constant cash flow C. If the option to prepay is exercised, the holder of the cash flow receives a principal amount B, which depends on the time to maturity τ. Rational behavior requires the holder of this prepayment option to act to minimize the value of the security, so at any time to maturity τ the value of the security is

$$\text{Value}[\tau] = \text{Minimum}\begin{bmatrix} B(\tau), \text{Value if prepayment} \\ \text{option unexercised} \end{bmatrix}$$

If ever the value of the security if not prepaid were greater than the value of prepaying, the holder prepays according to this boundary condition. We will see that the imposition of this seemingly simple constraint creates a problem so complex that, generally speaking, no analytical solutions for value are known. We devote the remainder of this chapter to discussing the alternative valuation techniques and their strengths and weaknesses. Most of the weaknesses revolve around the ability of the various techniques to mimic the boundary condition above. We concentrate through most of the chapter on Hull and White's (1990, 1993, 1994) popular trinomial lattice to illustrate the principles of the valuation of American options.

The reason for devoting much of this and the two following chapters to American fixed-income options is that almost all financial institutions have the bulk of their balance sheets devoted to American fixed-income options, explicitly or implicitly. A brief list of examples shows how critical this topic is. Typical American options on financial institution balance sheets include the following:

- The right to terminate a life insurance policy in return for receipt of its surrender value.
- The right to resign as the customer of an investment management firm.
- The right to prepay a mortgage loan.
- The right to withdraw as a bank from the consumer-deposit-gathering business.

- The right to withdraw almost any consumer bank deposit either at par or upon the payment of an early withdrawal penalty.
- The right of a corporate borrower to declare bankruptcy.
- The right of a financial institution to pay dividends.
- The right to exercise a foreign exchange option.
- The right to exercise a standard swaption contract.

The list of examples is almost endless. Needless to say, the topic at hand is a critical one.

12.2 AN OVERVIEW OF NUMERICAL TECHNIQUES FOR FIXED-INCOME OPTION VALUATION

Financial market participants generally use one of six approaches to the valuation of fixed-income options:

- Analytical solutions.
- Monte Carlo simulation.
- Finite difference methods.
- Binomial lattices.
- Bushy trees.
- Trinomial lattices.

We all turn first to analytical solutions, like the present value formula and the Black-Scholes model, when we are aware that such analytical solutions exist. That is why the first 11 chapters of this book were devoted to analytical solutions. In the case of American fixed-income options, we generally have no alternative but to turn to a numerical technique. In Sections 12.3–12.7, we discuss the five alternatives in turn.

12.3 MONTE CARLO SIMULATION

Monte Carlo simulation is justifiably popular in financial markets, but it must be used with great care. Adams and van Deventer (1993) have discussed in detail the reasons for such caution. In

general, Monte Carlo simulation is slow and is a rough approximation best restricted to problems that cannot be solved by any
other method (i.e., by analytical methods, lattice approaches, or
finite difference methods).

It is most appropriately used for problems that involve path
dependence[2] or three or more random variables.[3] Monte Carlo
simulation has a number of liabilities, however. In Chapter 14, on
mortgage-backed securities, we discuss a number of specific problems with Monte Carlo simulation. In general, however, Monte
Carlo simulation's limitations can be summarized as follows:

• As Hull notes, "one limitation of the Monte Carlo simulation
approach is that it can be used only for European-style derivative
securities."[4] The boundary condition, which we specified above,
cannot be correctly analyzed in Monte Carlo simulation since it is a
forward-looking technique that projects from today into the future.
To correctly value an American option, one measures value (as we
see below) by working backward from maturity to calculate value,
assuming at each decision point that the option holder does the
rational thing. Monte Carlo works by projecting one interest rate
"path" at a time, so there is not enough information at any point on
that path to correctly analyze whether or not an American option
holder should prepay. For this reason, Monte Carlo simulation almost always requires the user to specify a decision rule regarding
what the holder of the option should do in any given interest rate
scenario, often in the form of a prepayment table or prepayment
function in the case of a prepayment option. This is putting the
cart before the horse, since the user has to guess how the option
will be exercised before the user knows what the option is worth.
Rather than going through this error-filled exercise, we think most
users would get better results by just guessing the value of the
option directly!

• The calculation speed of Monte Carlo techniques is slow
for problems where there is a small number of random variables.
It does have a speed advantage for problems with a large number
of random variables.

---

2. Even in the case of path dependence, however, the use of Monte Carlo simulation is
   technically incorrect, as noted by Hull (1993).
3. See Hull (1993), pp. 329–34, for more on this point.
4. See Hull (1993), p. 334.

• Monte Carlo simulation by definition does not use all possible scenarios for valuation. There are an infinite number of interest rate scenarios, and Monte Carlo simulation, due to its speed problems, inevitably requires the user to use too few "scenarios" in the interests of time.

• As a result, Monte Carlo simulations have sampling error, which results from "throwing the dice" too few times. Many users of Monte Carlo simulation are under the mistaken impression that the beautiful probability distribution that is displayed on their computer screen reflects the true uncertainty about the value of a security as measured by Monte Carlo. Nothing could be further from the truth. If you call a major securities firm to get a bid on a mortgage security, you get a bid in the form of one number, not a probability distribution. The beautiful probability distribution reflects the inaccuracy or sampling error of the technique itself, and this kind of graph reflects a weakness of Monte Carlo, not a strength. This kind of sampling error can lead to very serious problems when calculating hedge amounts.

• To reduce sampling error to a meaningful level, a very large number of simulations are normally required to get a stable answer and a sampling error small enough to allow decisions to be based on the Monte Carlo results.[5]

• Sampling error becomes even more important when basing hedges on the results of Monte Carlo simulation. The authors feel that the primary purpose of the calculations in this book are to define action rather than simply to describe the amount of risk an institution currently has. With Monte Carlo simulation, safe action is harder to find than high-class companionship in a Manhattan bar on a Friday night. Consider a hedger who values his portfolio using 200 simulations via Monte Carlo. The result shows a value of 100 and a sampling error standard deviation of, say, 2. This means that there is roughly a 65 percent probability that the true value lies between 98 and 102. In order to determine the

---

5. In discussions with sophisticated institutions that have many years' experience with Monte Carlo simulation, Bank of America executives stated that 2,000 to 10,000 iterations were necessary for a stable answer, while Tokyo Mitsubishi Bank argued that 5,000 to 10,000 runs were essential. A risk management expert at a very large New York bank expressed extreme concern that some line units in his bank were basing management actions on as few as 100 iterations per Monte Carlo calculation.

proper amount of the hedge, the analyst shifts rates up by 10 basis points and repeats the analysis, getting a value of 99 and a sampling error standard deviation of 2 again. The analyst concludes that the "delta" of his portfolio is $100 - 99 = 1$ and wants to base his hedge on this result. This is fine, as far as it goes, but the delta has sampling error also. The sampling error on the delta is a function of the sampling error on the two simulation runs, and it is calculated as follows:

$$\sigma_{\text{hedge }\Delta} = \sqrt{\sigma^2_{\text{run }1} + \sigma^2_{\text{run }2}}$$

In the example given, the sampling error of the hedge delta of 1.00 works out to 2.828. What does it mean for the precision of the hedge? It means that there is a 36.2 percent chance that the hedge amount is not only the wrong magnitude but the *wrong sign!* This is a career-ending type of error that has happened often enough on Wall Street that it's become a familiar story.[6]

• The "delta" from a Monte Carlo simulation can only be derived from doing the calculation twice (or preferably three times for securities with high convexity), further aggravating its speed disadvantages.

• Monte Carlo simulations must be done on the basis of the risk-neutral distributions of all random variables, an adjustment that many users fail to make.

On the plus side, Monte Carlo simulation has a number of advantages that should not be overlooked:

• It is sometimes the only alternative where the cash flow is path-dependent, as imprecise as it might be in that case.

• It has speed advantages for problems with a large number of variables. Generally, this means three or more variables.

• It is relatively simple to implement.

---

6. A major New York bank reported a loss of more than $100 million after discovering the Monte Carlo simulation routine it was using to value its portfolio was producing a "gamma" (or second derivative) with the wrong sign; the loss was the magnitude of the mark-to-market error discovered after using a more sophisticated technique to value the same portfolio.

What are our conclusions about Monte Carlo simulation? First, it is a tool that all users should have access to. Monte Carlo simulation is widely available for less than $400 as an add-in to common spreadsheet software and, at this price, everyone should buy it. (More sophisticated software packages that don't clearly display the sampling error of both value and hedges derived from Monte Carlo simulation calculations should be used with extreme caution.) Finally, however, any of the other techniques in this chapter is a superior approach and we feel that Monte Carlo simulation should only be used as a calculation of last resort. In almost no case should it be necessary to use Monte Carlo simulation to value a European option.

12.4 FINITE DIFFERENCE METHODS

Compared to Monte Carlo simulation, finite difference methods are more complex but more general solution methods commonly used in engineering applications. Finite difference methods provide a direct general solution of the partial differential equation (which defines the price of a callable security), unlike lattice methods, which model the evolution of the random variables. These methods fall into two main groups: *explicit* and *implicit* finite difference methods. The explicit finite difference methods are equivalent to the trinomial lattice methods. Implicit methods are more robust in the types of problems that they can handle, but implicit methods are computationally more difficult. Both methods usually use a grid-based calculation method, rather than the lattice approach, to arrive at numerical solutions.

Finite difference methods can be used to solve a wide range of derivative product valuation problems, and they are not restricted to a small number of stochastic processes (i.e., normal or lognormal) that describe how the random variable moves. These methods can be used to value both American- and European-style options. Like lattice methods, the valuation by finite difference methods is performed by stepping backward through time. This is a one-stage process under the finite difference method; there is no need to model the evolution of the random variable before the valuation can be performed.

The authors believe that the finite difference method, in its grid rather than lattice implementation, is an essential tool for most institutions.

12.5 BINOMIAL LATTICES

A binomial lattice (sometimes called a binomial tree) is a discrete time model for describing the movement of a random variable whose movements at each node on the tree can be reduced to an up or down movement with a known probability. The model is usually specified so that an upward movement followed by a downward movement gives the same value as a downward movement followed by an upward movement; this means there will be three possible values of the random variable at the end of the second time interval and $k + 1$ possible values at the end of time interval k.

Starting at a known value, x_0, of the variable at time 0, the two possible values of the variable at the end of the first time interval can be predicted by multiplying by two carefully calculated values u and d:

$$\text{Higher value} = u * x_0$$

$$\text{Lower value} = d * x_0$$

Since each node has two branches, the process can be repeated to predict the values at all the nodes in the tree. The values of u and d depend on the stochastic process for x; usually, the binomial tree approach is used for valuing "securities" that have movements that can be described by a lognormal distribution without mean reversion. This is a good assumption for stock prices, but not for interest rates. If the coefficients of the equation describing how the stock price moves are constant, then there are simple formulas for the values of u and d that best approximate the true movement in the stock price.

Valuation with the binomial tree requires two passes through the lattice; on the first pass, which is forward from time 0, the values of the stock price or interest rate at each node are calculated and on the second pass, which is backward, the values of the derivative security at each node are calculated. The proper fitting of the lattice is much like the process described below for the trinomial lattice. The evolution of the random variable in the first pass through the lattice is determined by the parameters of the stochastic process and the size of the discrete time step. Unlike the Monte Carlo method, subsequent forward passes will always produce the same values.

The binomial lattice can be used to value American-style options as well as European-style options. However, interest rate derivative securities often assume a more complicated stochastic process for interest rates, for which the trinomial tree method presents some advantages.

12.6 BUSHY TREES

Lattice techniques are computationally efficient in that the lattices "recombine": an interest rate increase followed by a decrease leads to the same interest rate as a decrease followed by an increase. For some stochastic processes, this recombination does not occur, particularly in the context of attractive assumptions about forward rate movements under the Heath, Jarrow, and Morton (1992) model. In this case, that lattice takes on the structure of a "bushy tree" whose branches split over and over but never recombine with other branches. The result is a very efficient process for approximating the assumed stochastic process for interest rates and the ability to value complex securities that are path-dependent or that involve American options. The technique offers many of the advantages but few of the disadvantages of Monte Carlo simulation. See Jarrow (1996) for a clear, thorough illustration of how the bushy tree technique should be employed.

12.7 TRINOMIAL LATTICES

In a number of papers with important theoretical and practical implications, Hull and White (1990, 1993, 1994) developed the trinomial lattice valuation technique, which has quickly established itself as the standard valuation technique, not only for the Vasicek model and its extended version (the Hull and White model) but also for a number of other single-factor term structure models that are Markov in nature. This section borrows heavily from Hull and White (1994) in describing the workings of the trinomial lattice. A trinomial lattice (sometimes called a trinomial tree) is a discrete time model for describing the movement of a random variable whose movements at each node on the tree can be reduced to one of three possibilities: an upward movement, a downward movement, or no change. The model is specified so that an upward movement followed by a downward movement and a downward movement followed by an upward movement give the same value as two movements where no change occurs; this means there will be three possible values of the random variable at the end of the first time interval and $k + 2$ possible values at the end of time interval k. This recombining feature maximizes the efficiency of the calculation.

The additional outcome at each node provides an additional degree of freedom, which enhances the power of the model; trinomial lattices can be used to model almost any Markov stochastic process, including ones in which the parameters are functions of time and the random variable itself. In modeling interest rate–related derivatives, it allows rates to be modeled so that the current term structure of interest rates and term structure of rate volatility are matched exactly by the modeling process. This offsets the more complicated calculations of the values at the ends of each branch. The trinomial lattice can be used to value American- as well as European-style options.

Four basic constraints are imposed on the three branches at each node of the tree.

1. The sum of the probabilities of each branch must be 1. We call these probabilities p_u, p_m, and p_d (for the *up*, *middle*, and *down* probabilities).

$$p_u + p_m + p_d = 1$$

2. The mean change in the short-term interest rate from the given node to the attached three nodes must be consistent with the theoretical expected change for the term structure model used.

3. The variance of change in the short rate from the current node to the next three nodes must be consistent with the theoretical value for the variance.

4. The probabilities must all be positive.

A fifth constraint may appear necessary to experienced users of lattice techniques or market participants who experienced yen Libor rates near 3/8 percent in 1995–96. The Vasicek model and its extended version allow a theoretical possibility of negative interest rates, even with a no-arbitrage derivation. Jamshidian (1989) calls this *local no-arbitrage,* since, as pointed out by Black (1995), interest rates should be considered as options. If rates are negative and market participants have the alternative of holding cash with zero interest, they will. If market participants have the option of holding cash, nominal interest rates can never turn negative, or "global arbitrage" would be possible. Black (1995) proposes a method of avoiding these problems, but space does not allow us to devote the attention to this refinement that it deserves. We assume that the possibility of negative rates does not pose practical problems for the rest of the chapter. The four constraints above have a number of implications for the lattice. We follow the implementation procedure prescribed by Hull and White (1994). In the prior 11 chapters of this book, we focused on the Vasicek model, in which the observable short-term rate of interest follows the stochastic process

$$dr = \alpha[\mu - r]dt + \sigma dz$$

In Chapters 7–11, we used Jamshidian's valuation equation, Equation 6.2, where securities were valued as if the short rate of interest had a normal distribution with mean equal to the forward rate at a given maturity and the same variance as the Vasicek model's short rate. In implementing the trinomial lattice, we turn now to Jamshidian's Equation 6.1, where securities are valued in a different way; cash flow dependent on the short-term rate of interest r is calculated as if r has the distribution of the risk-neutral short-term interest rate. The discount factor is the accumulated value of the "money market account" (see Jarrow, 1996, for more on this approach), which is defined as the accumulated value of an account with an initial balance of $1, which is continually reinvested in the money market account.

The stochastic process for the risk-neutral short rate (which we call r in this section) in the Hull and White (extended Vasicek) model is

$$dr = [\theta(t) - \alpha r]dt + \sigma dz$$

where θ has the definition

$$\theta(t) = \frac{\tilde{\mu}(t)}{\alpha}$$

using the notation of Chapters 5 and 6.

Hull and White construct a trinomial lattice for the risk-neutral short rate where the time steps have length Δt. If r_0 is the initial value of r at time 0 on the lattice, the value of r at any subsequent node takes the form

$$r = r_0 + k\Delta r$$

where k is an integer and can be either positive or negative. Step 1 in the Hull and White process for construction of the lattice is to build an interim tree for r under the simplified assumptions that

$$\theta(t) = 0$$

$$r_0 = 0$$

This effectively means that risk-neutral r has the stochastic process

$$dr = -\alpha r dt + \sigma dz$$

This is a special case of the Vasicek model where

$$\mu = 0$$

We know in the Vasicek model that the expected value of r at any time in the future is, when μ is 0,

$$E_t[r(s)] = r(t)e^{-\alpha(s-t)}$$

Over the time interval Δt, we know by subtracting the initial r from both sides that

$$E[r(t + \Delta t) - r(t)] = r(t)[e^{-\alpha \Delta t} - 1] = r(t)M$$

where

$$M = e^{-\alpha \Delta t} - 1$$

The variance of the change in the short rate over this interval Δt is the same as in the Vasicek model:

$$V = \frac{\sigma^2}{2\alpha}\left[1 - e^{-2\alpha\Delta t}\right]$$

We then determine the size of the time step Δt and set

$$\Delta r = \sqrt{3V}$$

in order to minimize the errors of the numerical solution. Hull and White define node (i,j) on the tree as the node where $t = i\Delta t$ and $r = j\Delta r$. At most tree branches, there is an upshift in r of Δr, a middle branch with no change, and a downshift of Δr. In this case, the probabilities that meet the first three constraints are

$$p_u = \frac{1}{6} + \frac{j^2 M^2 + jM}{2}$$

$$p_m = \frac{2}{3} - j^2 M^2$$

$$p_d = \frac{1}{6} + \frac{j^2 M^2 - jM}{2}$$

This will not always be the case, given constraint number 4, which requires all of the probabilities to be positive. For positive α, for large values of j, the branching style has to change from the normal pattern

Up branch $= +\Delta r$

Middle branch $= 0$

Down branch $= -\Delta r$

to the *downshift pattern:*

Up branch $= 0$

Middle branch $= -\Delta r$

Down branch $= -2\Delta r$

This change to the downshift pattern should occur at the smallest integer greater than $-0.184\,M$ (the non-integer value of j at which probabilities would otherwise become 0). Hull and White call this value j_{max}. When the downshift pattern applies, the probabilities on the tree should be

$$p_u = \frac{7}{6} + \frac{j^2M^2 + 3jM}{2}$$

$$p_m = -\frac{1}{3} - j^2M^2 - 2jM$$

$$p_d = \frac{1}{6} + \frac{j^2M^2 + jM}{2}$$

Likewise, when j is small (a large negative number) it becomes necessary to switch to the *upshift pattern:*

$$\text{Up branch} = +2\Delta r$$

$$\text{Middle branch} = +\Delta r$$

$$\text{Down branch} = 0$$

This should happen, Hull and White recommend, at a j_{min} value equal to $-j_{max}$.

We now illustrate the construction of these probabilities with a specific example. We construct a lattice with two time steps, one at two years and another at four years. We label the lattice starting point node A. The tree splits into three branches at the two-year maturity. The up node is labeled B, the middle node C, and the down node is D. At four years, the three branches from node B are E (up), F (middle), and G (down). From node C, the branches in the same order are F, G, and H. From node D, they are G, H, and I. At both two years and four years, zero coupon bond prices are observable. The values are 0.88163 and 0.77018. We seek to construct a tree that matches these prices exactly. We will then use it to price bond options. See Exhibit 12–1.

In order to later use Jamshidian's European bond option formula, these zero prices are actually 100 percent consistent with the Vasicek (not extended Vasicek) model. We used an α value of 0.08, interest volatility of 0.02, a market price of risk of 0.01, and a long-run expected value of the short rate of .10 (10 percent). We assumed a short rate of .06, and using the notation of Chapters 5–6 we calculated the zero prices cited above. We now proceed to lattice construction.

E X H I B I T   12-1

Base Case Tree:
Outline of Nodes

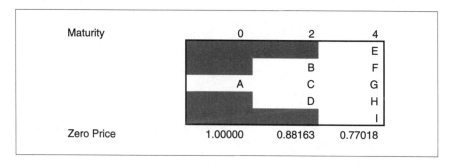

α =		0.08000
σ =		0.02000
λ =		0.01000
μ =		0.10000
ΔT =	size of time step =	2.00000
M =	expected value of [Δ r/r] =	−0.14786
V =		0.00068
Δr =		0.04532
r =		0.06000
D		0.07125

Maturity	2	4
F	1.84820	3.42314
G	0.01509	0.05575
Zero bond price	0.88163	0.77018

Delta r is 0.04532 on this lattice. Using these parameters, the up, middle, and down probabilities associated with node A are 0.16667, 0.66667, and 0.16667, respectively.

Once the probabilities have been determined, the next step is to determine the value of $1 received in the event a given node is reached. We call these values $Q(i,j)$. The values of Q for all the nodes $m + 1$ time steps from the start of the lattice are given by

$$Q_{m+1,j} = \sum_k Q_{m,k}\, prob(k,j)\, e^{-(y_m + k\Delta r)\Delta t}$$

where k denotes all of these rate paths that connect with node $Q_{m+1,j}$. All other rate paths are excluded from the calculation. The variable y_m is a parallel shift up or down in the interest rates for all nodes m time steps from the start of the lattice. We assume that we have observable zero coupon bond prices $P(0,m)$ consistent with the economy at time 0 with maturities consistent with all time steps, including time step m. The variable y_m is calculated such that

$$P(0, m+1) = \sum_{j=-n_m}^{n_m} Q_{m,j} e^{-(y_m + j\Delta r)\Delta t}$$

The coefficient of Δt in the exponent we refer to as "adjusted r." After rewriting this equation

$$P(0, m+1) = e^{-y_m \Delta t} \left[\sum_{j=-n_m}^{n_m} Q_{m,j} e^{-j\Delta r \Delta t} \right]$$

we can solve for y_m:

$$y_m = -\frac{1}{\Delta t} \ln \left[\frac{P(0, m+1)}{\sum_{j=-n_m}^{n_m} Q_{m,j} e^{-j\Delta r \Delta t}} \right]$$

With this as background, we can solve for all of the probabilities, Q values, and y values that exactly price a portfolio of zero coupon bonds with maturities equal to the maturity at each time step. We know y_0 is given by the zero coupon bond price $P(0,1)$ with maturity equal to the maturity of the first time step. We also know that the $Q(0,0)$ value is 1. We fill out the lattice as follows:

1. Fill in the Q values for time step 1.
2. Solve for y_1.
3. Using y_1, solve for the Q values for time step 2.
4. Solve for y_2.
5. Continue until the end of the lattice.

We know the short rate for the first period, which is calculated from the two-year zero coupon bond price using Chapter 1. The continuously compounded rate is 6.2989 percent. Given this rate for r, we can calculate the present value of a security that pays a

$1 if we end up at node B. The Q value for node B is 0.14694. The values for nodes C and D are 0.58776 and 0.14694.

Using the formulas above for our sample lattice, we get the following results:

Trinomial Lattice Worksheet

Node	A	B	C	D	E	F	G	H	I
j	0	1	0	−1	2	1	0	−1	−2
Initial r	0.00000	0.04532	0.00000	−0.04532	0.09064	0.04532	0.00000	−0.04532	−0.09064
Up probability	0.16667	0.10367	0.16667	0.25153	0.06253	0.10367	0.16667	0.25153	0.35825
Mid probability	0.66667	0.64481	0.66667	0.64481	0.57922	0.64481	0.66667	0.64481	0.57922
Down probability	0.16667	0.25153	0.16667	0.10367	0.35825	0.25153	0.16667	0.10367	0.06253
$P_u + P_m + P_d$	1.00000	1.00000	1.00000	1.00000	1.00000	1.00000	1.00000	1.00000	1.00000
Q		0.14694	0.58776	0.14694	0.01214	0.16095	0.40658	0.17596	0.01455
Shift		0.06826	0.06826	0.06826					
Adjusted r (y)		0.11358	0.06826	0.02294					

12.8 VALUING SECURITIES ON THE LATTICE: EUROPEAN AND AMERICAN CALLS

We now use this simple lattice to value a European call option on a zero coupon bond with four years to maturity. We assume that the exercise period on the option is two years. We know from Chapter 6 that the value of this call option is

$$V(r,2,4,K) = P(r,4)N(h) - KP(r,2)N(h - \sigma_P)$$

where

$$\sigma_P = \left(\frac{\sigma^2}{2\alpha}\left[1 - e^{-2\alpha 2}\right] \right)^{\frac{1}{2}} \frac{1}{\alpha}\left[1 - e^{-\alpha 2}\right]$$

and

$$h = \frac{\ln\left[\dfrac{P(r,4)}{P(r,2)K}\right]}{\sigma_P} + \frac{\sigma_P}{2}$$

We can calculate this option value for a wide variety of strike prices and compare to the values indicated by the lattice.

How is the lattice used to calculate this option value? In practice, we would use a lattice with many time steps to minimize errors. For illustration purposes, we will use the simple lattice we have constructed already in spite of the errors that will result. Exercise is a possibility at nodes B, C, and D. At node B, the cash flow from exercising the option will be the maximum of 0 and the difference between the value of a four-year zero coupon bond (which now has two years remaining) and the strike price K:

$$\text{Cash flow} = \text{Maximum}\left(0, e^{-\text{adjusted } r \, \Delta t} - K\right)$$

We make the same cash flow calculation at nodes C and D. The value of the option is

$$\text{Lattice option value} = Q_B \text{Cash flow}_B + Q_C \text{Cash flow}_C$$
$$+ Q_D \text{Cash flow}_D$$

In order to illustrate some basic principles of the use of lattices, we compiled a chart of theoretical (Jamshidian) call option values at various strike prices and the lattice valuations at the same strike prices (see Exhibit 12–2).

E X H I B I T   12–2

Comparison of Lattice and Jamshidian Closed-Form Solution for Call Option on Zero Coupon Bond with Maturity of Four Years and Exercise Period on Call of Two Years

Jamshidian calculations					
σ_P		0.002344			
		Jamshidian Model			
Strike Price	**Yield to Strike**	**h**	**Value**	**Lattice Value**	**Difference**
0.00	1381.55%	11732.45	0.77018	0.77018	0.00000
0.05	149.79%	1220.60	0.72609	0.72609	0.00000
0.10	115.13%	924.84	0.68201	0.68201	0.00000
0.15	94.86%	751.83	0.63793	0.63793	0.00000
0.20	80.47%	629.07	0.59385	0.59385	0.00000
0.25	69.31%	533.86	0.54977	0.54977	0.00000
0.30	60.20%	456.06	0.50568	0.50568	0.00000
0.35	52.49%	390.29	0.46160	0.46160	0.00000
0.40	45.81%	333.31	0.41752	0.41752	0.00000
0.45	39.93%	283.05	0.37344	0.37344	0.00000
0.50	34.66%	238.09	0.32936	0.32936	0.00000

E X H I B I T   12–2

(cont.)

Strike Price	Yield to Strike	Jamshidian Model		Lattice Value	Difference
		h	Value		
0.55	29.89%	197.43	0.28528	0.28528	0.00000
0.60	25.54%	160.30	0.24119	0.24119	0.00000
0.65	21.54%	126.14	0.19711	0.19711	0.00000
0.70	17.83%	94.52	0.15303	0.15303	0.00000
0.75	14.38%	65.08	0.10895	0.10895	0.00000
0.76	13.72%	59.43	0.10013	0.10013	0.00000
0.77	13.07%	53.85	0.09132	0.09132	0.00000
0.78	12.42%	48.35	0.08250	0.08250	0.00000
0.79	11.79%	42.91	0.07368	0.07368	0.00000
0.80	11.16%	37.54	0.06487	0.06534	−0.00047
0.81	10.54%	32.24	0.05605	0.05799	−0.00194
0.82	9.92%	27.01	0.04723	0.05065	−0.00341
0.83	9.32%	21.84	0.03842	0.04330	−0.00488
0.84	8.72%	16.73	0.02960	0.03595	−0.00635
0.85	8.13%	11.68	0.02079	0.02861	−0.00782
0.86	7.54%	6.68	0.01197	0.02126	−0.00929
0.87	6.96%	1.75	0.00318	0.01391	−0.01073
0.88	6.39%	−3.12	0.00000	0.01104	−0.01104
0.89	5.83%	−7.95	0.00000	0.00957	−0.00957
0.90	5.27%	−12.71	0.00000	0.00810	−0.00810
0.91	4.72%	−17.43	0.00000	0.00663	−0.00663
0.92	4.17%	−22.09	0.00000	0.00516	−0.00516
0.93	3.63%	−26.71	0.00000	0.00370	−0.00370
0.94	3.09%	−31.27	0.00000	0.00223	−0.00223
0.95	2.56%	−35.78	0.00000	0.00076	−0.00076
0.96	2.04%	−40.25	0.00000	0.00000	0.00000
0.97	1.52%	−44.67	0.00000	0.00000	0.00000
0.98	1.01%	−49.05	0.00000	0.00000	0.00000
0.99	0.50%	−53.38	0.00000	0.00000	0.00000
1.00	0.00%	−57.67	0.00000	0.00000	0.00000

For strike prices from 0 up to 0.79, the lattice values are identical to the Jamshidian theoretical values. For strike prices between 0.80 and 0.95, the lattice values begin to deviate significantly from theoretical values, as you would expect given that we are essentially

EXHIBIT   12-3

Errors in Using Simple Trinomial Lattice, as Percentage of
Lattice Value, Plotted by Zero Coupon Bond Option Strike Price

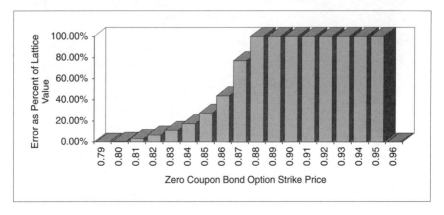

trying to replicate the theoretical value with a one-step lattice that
has only three branches. The deviations can be displayed graphi-
cally to summarize the strike regions in which error is serious. (See
Exhibit 12–3.)

Errors basically grow large because the highly simplified version of the lattice represented in Exhibit 12–3 continues to show
some value to the call option from strike prices of 0.88 or over,
even when the theory would indicate that the option should be
essentially worthless in this strike price range. (See Exhibit 12–4.)

This exercise simply illustrates that error is inevitable when
using numerical methods. In some cases, the technique will work
perfectly over a wide range of values, as this simple example
indicates. For particular strike prices, errors creep in. The user
has to take care to adjust the characteristics of the lattice (chiefly
the number of time steps), input parameters, and so on to minimize errors and not expect an overly precise answer from any
numerical technique. Benchmarking against known theoretical
answers is essential.

American Call Option

If the option were an American call option, the calculation we
have just done would be the calculation done on the expiration

EXHIBIT 12–4

Actual Values versus Lattice Estimated Values of Two-Year Option to Buy Four-Year Zero Coupon Bond, as Function of Exercise Price

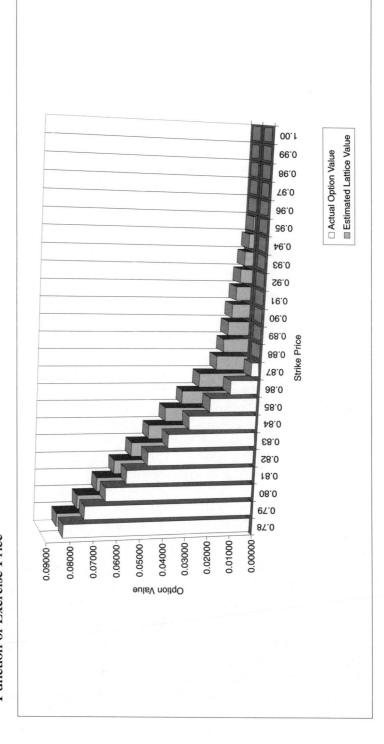

date of the American call, say at time step m. Step one time step forward, back toward the start of the lattice to time step $m - 1$. At time step $m - 1$, cash flow will be

$$\text{Cash flow} = \text{Maximum}\left(\begin{array}{c}\text{value if exercised at time} \\ \text{step } m, \ e^{-\text{adjusted } r \,\Delta t} - K\end{array}\right)$$

The value, if left unexercised, to time step m is simply the one period present value, weighted by the probabilities, of the cash flow above:

$$\begin{array}{c}\text{Value if exercised} \\ \text{at time step } m\end{array} = \sum_{j=\text{up,mid,down}} e^{-\text{adjusted } r_{m-1} \,\Delta t}$$

$$\text{probability}(m, j)$$
$$\text{Maximum}(0, e^{-\text{adjusted } r_{m,j}\Delta t} - K)$$

In this manner, almost any fixed-income security or derivative security can be valued on the lattice with a level of precision consistent with the analyst's choice of the size of the time steps.

In Chapter 13, we modify our approach to allow for the irrational exercise of options, and in Chapter 14, we apply this combined discipline to mortgage-related securities.

E X E R C I S E S

For the exercises that follow, assume that the parameters of the Vasicek term structure model are as given in the example above (p. 234).

12.1 What would be the six-year zero coupon bond price?

12.2 Using this zero coupon bond price, calculate the adjusted short rates that would prevail at nodes E, F, G, H, and I on the lattice above.

12.3 What is the theoretical price of a four-year European option on a six-year zero coupon bond with a strike price of 0.75?

12.4 What is the trinomial lattice valuation of the four-year European option?

12.5 What would the option value be if it were a four-year American option on a six-year zero coupon bond?

12.6 What is the economic intuition behind your answer to Exercise 12.5?

12.7 What is the value of a four-year American option on a six-year bond with principal of $100 that pays $20 of interest every two years? Assume there is no interest due at time 0.

REFERENCES

Adams, Kenneth J., and Donald R. van Deventer. "Monte Carlo Simulation: The Pros and the Cons." *Balance Sheet* 2, no. 3, Autumn 1993, pp. 18–24.

Black, Fischer. "Interest Rates as Options." *Journal of Finance*, December 1995, pp. 1371–76.

Boyle, P. "Options: A Monte Carlo Approach." *Journal of Financial Economics* 4, May 1977, pp. 323–28.

Brennan, M., and E. Schwartz. "A Continuous Time Approach to the Pricing of Bonds." *Journal of Banking and Finance* 3, July 1979, pp. 133–55.

Chen, R. "Exact Solutions for Futures and European Futures Options on Pure Discount Bonds." *Journal of Financial and Quantitative Analysis* 27, March 1992, pp. 97–108.

Cox, J. C.; S. A. Ross; and M. Rubinstein. "Option Pricing: A Simplified Approach." *Journal of Financial Economics*, September 1979, pp. 229–63.

Dunn, K. B., and C. Spatt. "Private Information and Incentives: Implications for Mortgage Contract Terms and Pricing." *Journal of Real Estate Finance and Economics* 1, April 1988, pp. 47–60.

Flannagan, C. T.; M. D. Herskovitz; and H. T. Loy. "Understanding and Modelling Cost of Funds ARMs Prepayments." Mortgage-Backed Securities Research, Merrill Lynch, February 1989.

Flesaker, Bjorn. "Testing the Heath-Jarrow-Morton/Ho-Lee Model of Interest Rate Contingent Claims Pricing." *Journal of Financial and Quantitative Analysis*, December 1993, pp. 483–95.

Heath, David; Robert Jarrow; and Andrew Morton. "Bond Pricing and the Term Structure of Interest Rates: A Discrete Time Approach." *Journal of Financial and Quantitative Analysis*, December 1990, pp. 419–40.

———. "Bond Pricing and the Term Structure of Interest Rates: A New Methodology for Contingent Claims Valuation." *Econometrica* 60, January 1992, pp. 77–105.

Ho, Thomas S. Y., and Sang-Bin Lee. "Term Structure Movements and Pricing Interest Rate Contingent Claims." *Journal of Finance* 41, December 1986, pp. 1011–29.

Hull, J. *Options, Futures, and Other Derivative Securities*. 2nd ed. Englewood Cliffs, NJ: Prentice Hall, 1993.

Hull, J., and A. White. "Valuing Derivative Securities Using the Explicit Finite Difference Method." *Journal of Financial and Quantitative Analysis* 25, March 1990a, pp. 87–100.

_____. "Pricing Interest-Rate Derivative Securities." *Review of Financial Studies* 3 Winter 1990b, pp. 573–92.

_____. "One Factor Interest Rate Models and the Valuation of Interest Rate Derivative Securities." *Journal of Financial and Quantitative Analysis,* June 1993, pp. 235–54.

_____. "Numerical Procedures for Implementing Term Structure Models I: Single Factor Models." *Journal of Derivatives,* Fall 1994, pp. 7–16.

Ingersoll, Jonathan. *Theory of Modern Financial Decision Making.* New York: Rowman & Littlefield, 1987.

Jamshidian, Farshid. "An Exact Bond Option Formula." *Journal of Finance,* March 1989, pp. 205–9.

Rendleman, R., and B. Bartter. "Two-State Option Pricing." *Journal of Finance,* December 1979, pp. 1093–1110.

Richard, S. F., and R. Roll. "Prepayments on Fixed-Rate Mortgage-Backed Securities." *Journal of Portfolio Management* 15, Spring 1989, pp. 73–82.

Schwartz, E., and W. Torous. "Prepayment and the Valuation of Mortgage-Backed Securities." *Journal of Finance* 44, June 1989, pp. 375–92.

Vasicek, Oldrich A. "An Equilibrium Characterization of the Term Structure." *Journal of Financial Economics* 5, November 1977, pp. 177–88.

CHAPTER 13

Irrational Exercise of Fixed-Income Options

13.1 IRRATIONALITY

One of the reasons that analysis of consumer-related financial products is so complex is the so-called irrationality of consumers. Perhaps the most prominent example from a Wall Street perspective is the mortgage market, which we address in detail in Chapter 14. Mortgages are often prepaid when current mortgage rates are higher than the borrower's mortgage rate, and many borrowers fail to prepay even when rates have fallen far below the rate on their loan. As a working assumption, the hypothesis that borrowers are not very intelligent runs contrary to the assumptions behind all developments in modern financial theory over the 20 years since the Black-Scholes options formula was first published. The perception of irrationality is simply a shorthand description for the fact that lenders and academic researchers do not have enough data to "see through" the individual loan or pool data to understand that the individual borrower's behavior may be more rational than it appears at first glance. The authors have come to feel even more strongly that the underlying assumption of rationality is the right one since one of us has failed to refinance his own mortgage loan, even though it must seem irrational from the bank's perspective. The bank clearly is unaware that writing this book is more important than earning a few yen from refinancing a mortgage. Once the book is done, the "irrational" author will suddenly become rational from the bank's perspective.

However, the need to deal with hard-to-explain consumer behavior is essential for accurate risk management in the insurance, investment management, and banking industries. Insurance companies must deal with the reality that some traditional life insurance policyholders will cancel their policies in return for the surrender value when interest rates rise, "putting" the policy back to the underwriter. Investment managers who suffer poor performance know that some customers of the firm will "put" their ownership in a mutual fund back to the investment management company. Bankers who make home equity loans know that some of these loans will be "called" by the borrower. Bankers also know that some time deposit customers will "put" the deposit back to the bank and willingly pay an early withdrawal penalty when rates rise in order to earn more on their funds. Without dealing with the degree of "irrational" consumer behavior behind these products, institutions can neither price properly nor hedge their risk properly. This chapter deals explicitly with a method for dealing with irrationality.

13.2 ANALYSIS OF IRRATIONALITY: CRITERIA FOR A POWERFUL EXPLANATION

The irrationality problem is so pervasive that we deal with the problem only in general terms in this chapter. This approach has two virtues. First, it will help us deal with the problem from a fresh perspective, unburdened by conventional wisdom. Second, armed with a general solution, we can compare the general solution to the conventional wisdom and judge the relative strengths of the two approaches without prejudice. In Chapter 14, armed with the tools of this chapter, we will plunge into all the traditional practices of mortgage-related products. In this chapter, however, we need to establish principles that will solve problems in insurance, investment management, and banking. They have to apply equally well to call options, put options, and securities that are callable but have rate caps and floors as well. A few basic principles come to mind:

1. *A general approach to irrational behavior should, to as great an extent possible, take advantage of the advances in finance*

in the last 20 years. All derivative pricing theory is based on the premises of no arbitrage and rational behavior. If all consumers were totally irrational, we would not need to price the options embedded in retail finance products because the exercise of those options would be truly random and uncorrelated with economic events. Portfolio theory would allow us to argue that we can diversify away this random behavior and ignore the option altogether. The reality, however, as we shall see in Chapter 14, is that consumer behavior is highly correlated with economic variables and is not totally irrational. It is this mixture of rational and irrational behavior that makes the problem both important and difficult. We need, then, an approach that allows us to scale the degree of irrationality to fit the particular product, company, and market at hand. We need an approach that assumes consumer action is partially rational so we can use the first 12 chapters of this book.

2. *History is not generally a good guide to the future, and we want to be able to derive the level of irrationality implied by observable market prices.* Wall Street firms have spent millions of dollars examining historical data for clues to consumer behavior as reflected in historical prepayment activity. As we shall see in Chapter 14, this work has been, at best, only partially satisfactory. For financial institutions that need to make an immediate decision about the proper hedge for a security whose market price and local rate sensitivity (i.e., the value change for small changes in interest rates) is observable, the historical approach is too slow, too inaccurate, and too expensive. The parallels in the debate about the use of historical volatility versus implied volatility in the Black-Scholes options model are very strong. We want an approach that gives us the "implied" level of irrationality. Most bankers who price retail banking products that contain embedded options come to the conclusion that most products are unprofitable if the options risk is fully hedged. Bankers implicitly recognize that consumers are partially rational and that a partial hedge is necessary. How can we use market data to calculate exactly how much rationality is embedded in a given product?

3. *Any model of irrationality must be able to explain observable phenomena in pools of consumer-related "securities": path-dependent prepayment behavior, decreased interest rate sensitivity over time ("burnout"), and a lower propensity to exercise embedded options as the financial product nears its expiration.*

4. *The model must allow for very rapid calculation time and maximum use of analytical solutions for security valuation.*

One approach that meets these criteria is the transactions cost approach, which we explain in Section 13.3.

13.3 THE TRANSACTIONS COST APPROACH

Over the last 10 years, the "rational" approach to irrational behavior has steadily gained prominence among both academics (see McConnell and Singh, 1994, and Stanton, 1995, for recent examples) and practitioners as the best method to model consumer behavior. The rational, or transactions cost, approach holds that consumers are rational but exercise their options subject to transactions costs. These transactions costs can be both explicit financial costs (the "points" from refinancing a mortgage or the penalty for early withdrawal of bank deposits) and more subtle costs that reflect the fact that consumers are maximizing a utility function with more arguments in it than the present value of rational action in one specific aspect of their lives. For example, someone with a life insurance policy that rationally should be canceled and reinstituted at current market pricing may have a serious disease that would cause the applicant to be rejected at the health check on the new policy. The disease is a transactions cost that at least partially blocks rational action. J. Thurston Howell III may fail to refinance the mortgage on his ski chalet in Aspen because his yacht has run aground on some desert island without a Bloomberg screen to keep him abreast of the benefits of refinancing. In the authors' case, the principal amount of our bank time deposits is so small that the benefits of early withdrawal of our time deposits, while positive, are smaller than the cost of the time it takes to go to the bank and negotiate the transaction. The cost of our time is a transactions cost.

The objective of the transactions cost approach is to firmly divorce rational from irrational behavior. Accordingly, the transactions cost function can be any time-dependent function that is not dependent on the level of interest rates. Determinants of the level of transactions costs could be any of the following:

• The time to maturity on the security.
• The level of the coupon on the security.

- The fixed dollar cost of exercising the option embedded in the security.
- The dollar opportunity cost of the time it takes to exercise the embedded option.
- The month of the year, recognizing that the cost of refinancing a home in Alaska in January is higher than in August.
- The date of origination of the security.
- The length of time the security has been outstanding without the embedded option being exercised.

There are an endless number of factors that can go into the transactions cost function. In short, however, as of current time t, all of these factors are nonrandom functions of time. We call this transactions cost function X and make it, without loss of generality, a function of the remaining time to maturity on the security:

$$\text{Transactions cost} = X(t,T) = X(\tau)$$

We can model any degree of irrationality using this function. If the consumer is a retired Salomon Brothers partner living in Greenwich with a Bloomberg screen in his living room and a healthy bank account, $X = 0$. The consumer is totally rational. If the consumer is working hard on a book on risk management, X is infinity, the consumer is totally irrational, and no embedded options will be exercised. Any level of irrationality in between these two extremes can be modeled in the same way. We illustrate the approach for European options in Section 13.4.

13.4 IRRATIONAL EXERCISE OF EUROPEAN OPTIONS

In Chapter 6, we analyzed the value of a European option on a zero coupon bond using Jamshidian's valuation formula. The value of an option exercisable at time T_1 on a zero coupon bond with a maturity of T_2 and strike price K was given as

$$V(r,t,T_1,T_2,K) = P(r,t,T_2)N(h) - P(r,t,T_1)KN(h - \sigma_P)$$

where

$$h = \frac{1}{\sigma_P}\ln\left[\frac{P(r,t,T_2)}{KP(r,t,T_1)}\right] + \frac{\sigma_P}{2}$$

and

$$\sigma_P = v_1 F_1$$

where v and F have the same definitions as in Chapters 6–11. What if the holder of this option exercises it irrationally, subject to transactions cost X?

Since it is a European option, the time-dependent nature of X is irrelevant with regard to a single European option. Only the level of X that will prevail at time T_1 matters, so we drop the time-dependent notation. We know from Jamshidian's valuation formula that the solution to the valuation of an irrationally exercised option is

$$V(r,t,T_1,T_2,K,X) = P(r,t,T_1) \int_{-\infty}^{s*} \left[P(s,T_1,T_2) - K \right] n(s,f_1,v_1) ds$$

The only difference between the rational option in Chapter 6 and the irrationally exercised option is that the holder of the irrationally exercised option exercises it only when the short rate of interest on date T_1 reaches a critical level $s*$ such that

$$P(s*,T_1,T_2) = K + X$$

The option will only be exercised if it is "in the money" by X dollars more than the strike price K. If X is 0, it's a rationally exercised option. The critical level of $s*$ is

$$s* = -\left[\frac{\ln(K + X) + G_{12}}{F_{12}} \right]$$

Substituting this value of $s*$ into the Jamshidian formulation and simplifying leads to a valuation formula for an irrationally exercised option that is nearly identical to that for a rationally exercised option, except the argument h (which we label $h*$ in the irrational case) differs slightly in that K is replaced by $K + X$:

$$V(r,t,T_1,T_2,K,X) = P(r,t,T_2)N(h*) - P(r,t,T_1)KN(h* - \sigma_P)$$

where

$$h* = \frac{1}{\sigma_P} \ln \left[\frac{P(r,t,T_2)}{(K + X)P(r,t,T_1)} \right] + \frac{\sigma_P}{2}$$

When X is 0, $h*$ reduces to h and the valuation formula is identical. If X is infinity, $h*$ is negative infinity, the option will never be exercised, and the option is worthless from the perspective of the holder. In Section 13.5, we illustrate the power of this formulation with a specific example.

13.5 VALUING A ZERO COUPON BOND WITH AN IRRATIONALLY EXERCISED EMBEDDED CALL OPTION

Consider the case of a 10-year zero coupon bond with an embedded European call option at 0.6 after 5 years that is exercised irrationally. We assume the Vasicek model parameters

$$\alpha = 0.08$$

$$\sigma = 0.015$$

$$\lambda = 0.01$$

$$\mu = 0.12$$

What is the value of this bond with the irrationally exercised embedded option? If the short-term rate of interest is 6 percent, the underlying 10-year zero coupon bond is worth 0.46238. If the option is exercised subject to a 4.5 percent transactions cost (0.6 + 0.045), the irrationally exercised option is worth 0.03994, and the package of the underlying bond less the embedded option is worth 0.42244.

The dynamics of irrational exercise can be very complex, allowing the user to model many forms of behavior that are quite common in the real world and a few, like negative convexity, that are fairly rare. Exhibit 13–1 shows the complex changes in the value of this bond (with the simplest possible embedded option) at short-term interest rates of 5.5 percent, 6 percent, 6.5 percent, and 7 percent for transactions costs ranging from 4.5 percent to 6.5 percent. The combination of interest rate levels and transactions costs results in the expected smooth transition from the price of a bond with a rationally exercised option to the price of a bond with no embedded option as the transactions cost rises to a level that effectively blocks exercise. What is surprising, however, is the fact that bond prices are not necessarily monotonically decreasing as rates (measured by the short rate r) rise, due to the irrationally exercised option. This is consistent with observable prices of mortgage securities, which, at certain times in the

EXHIBIT 13–1

Changes in Callable Zero Coupon Bond Price at Different Levels of Short Rate *r* and Transactions Cost

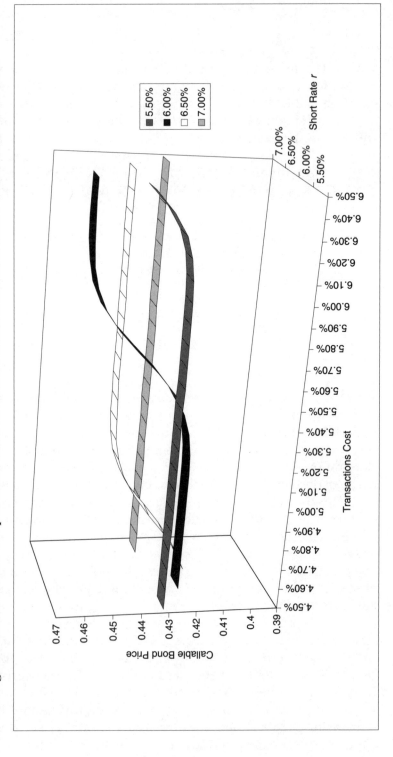

recent past, have fallen as rates have fallen because even irrational options holders had their threshold exceeded and began to refinance, reducing the value of the security to par.

The basic transactions cost approach is completely general and applies to all of the options-related securities in this book. We now turn briefly to securities with embedded American options to illustrate the full generality of the approach.

13.6 THE IRRATIONAL EXERCISE OF AMERICAN OPTIONS

In Chapter 12, we reviewed the fundamentals of the pricing of American fixed-income options. An American call option was valued on the premise of rational behavior throughout the life of the call, such that the holder of the call always acted so as to maximize the value of the call. In the case of a callable security, the holder of the call always acts so as to minimize the value of the security. Working backward, one period from maturity, the holder of the call is assumed to prepay if there is even a one-cent advantage of prepayment at par when compared to the present value of leaving the security outstanding at least one more period.

In the case of an irrationally exercised American call option, at every point (working backward from maturity) the holder of an option to call his bond or his loan will exercise that call option only if

$$\text{Value if prepayment option unexercised} > B(\tau) + X(\tau)$$

That is, exercise will take place only if the present value of the security if the call option is left unexercised exceeds the principal amount B by more than the transactions cost X prevailing at that instant in time. The fact that X varies over time will result in a rich array of realistic behavior in securities modeled in this way.

13.7 IMPLIED IRRATIONALITY AND HEDGING

When irrationality is modeled according to the transactions cost approach, the level of irrationality can be implied from observable market prices, just like "implied volatility" in the Black-Scholes model, achieving one of our primary objectives for a model of irrationality. Almost no observable security reflects the behavior of one consumer, so the best replication of the market price movement of a given security reflects a combination of irrational behavior by many consumers. Consider a security with value G and observable interest rate risk as measured by rDelta equal to G_r. We can model this security by breaking it into two pieces, using weights of w and $1 - w$. One piece consists of a rationally exercised security $V(r,t,0)$ with zero transactions costs. The other piece consists of an irrationally exercised security $V(r,t,X)$ with transactions costs of X. We solve this equation system for the weights w and transactions cost X such that both value and interest rate risk match the observable security's actual market behavior:

$$G = wV(r,t,0) + (1 - w)V(r,t,X)$$

$$G_r = wV_r(r,t,0) + (1 - w)V_r(r,t,X)$$

This results in a minimal need for historical research, efficient hedging of securities that contain irrationally exercised embedded options, and very fast calculation times instead of tedious Monte Carlo simulation in an attempt to use a historical prepayment function or prepayment table. We turn to the latter topic in Chapter 14.

EXERCISES

Use the term structure model parameters in the example on p. 251 and consider the case of a bank deposit that pays $30 in compounded interest at maturity, which is three years away. The original term to maturity was four years. The holder of this bank deposit has the right to receive his $100 principal plus 2 percent interest to the point of early withdrawal.

13.1 What is the value of this put option if exercised today?

13.2 What is the value of the put option if exercised in one year? What is the value if exercised in two years?

13.3 You are in charge of asset and liability management at the bank that originated this deposit. You know with certainty that the customer faces transactions costs of $5 and that the put option is exercisable in one year. Your only possible investment is three-year zero coupon bonds. How much should you buy?

13.4 Graph the value of the three-year deposit with embedded put from Exercise 13.3 as a function of the short rate r and transactions cost level. Describe the rate sensitivity and transactions cost sensitivity of value.

13.5 We define a new risk parameter as XDelta, the derivative of the value of an irrationally exercised option-related security with respect to the level of transactions costs. Derive the value of XDelta for the security in Exercise 13.3.

REFERENCES

Berk, J., and R. Roll. "Adjustable Rate Mortgages: Valuation." *Journal of Real Estate Finance and Economics* 1, June 1988, pp. 163–84.

Dunn, K. B., and C. Spatt. "Private Information and Incentives: Implications for Mortgage Contract Terms and Pricing." *Journal of Real Estate Finance and Economics* 1, April 1988, pp. 47–60.

Flannagan, C. T.; M. D. Herskovitz; and H. T. Loy. "Understanding and Modelling Cost of Funds ARMs Prepayments." Mortgage-Backed Securities Research, Merrill Lynch, February 1989, New York.

Green, J., and J. B. Shoven. "The Effect of Interest Rates on Mortgage Prepayments." *Journal of Money, Credit and Banking* XVIII, February 1986, pp. 41–59.

Jamshidian, Farshid. "An Exact Bond Option Formula." *Journal of Finance,* March 1989, pp. 205-9.

McConnell, John J., and Manoj Singh. "Rational Prepayments and the Valuation of Collateralized Mortgage Obligations." *Journal of Finance,* July 1994, pp. 891–922.

Quigley, J. M. "Interest Rate Variations, Mortgage Prepayments and Household Mobility." *The Review of Economics and Statistics* LXIX, November 1987, pp. 636–43.

Ramaswamy, K., and S. Sundaresan. "The Valuation of Floating Rate Instruments: Theory and Evidence." *Journal of Financial Economics* 17, December 1986, pp. 251–72.

Richard, S. F., and R. Roll. "Prepayments on Fixed-Rate Mortgage-Backed Securities." *Journal of Portfolio Management* 15, Spring 1989, pp. 73–82.
Schwartz, E., and W. Torous. "Prepayment and the Valuation of Mortgage-Backed Securities." *Journal of Finance* 44, June 1989, pp. 375–92.
Stanton, Richard. "Rational Prepayments and the Valuation of Mortgage-Backed Securities." *Review of Financial Studies*, Fall 1995, pp. 677–708.
van Deventer, Donald R. "The Valuation of Fixed and Floating Rate Mortgages." Kamakura Corporation research memorandum, December 1993.
Vasicek, Oldrich A. "An Equilibrium Characterization of the Term Structure." *Journal of Financial Economics* 5, November 1977, pp. 177–88.

CHAPTER 14

Mortgage-Backed Securities

14.1 INTRODUCTION TO THE ANALYSIS OF MORTGAGE-BACKED SECURITIES

The valuation and analysis of mortgages, both fixed and floating rate, is perhaps the most complex analytical problem in U.S. financial markets. Douglas Breeden (1991), one of the leading U.S. researchers in finance and the chief executive officer of mortgage fund manager Smith Breeden, commented about the problem as follows:

> Mortgages are viewed as far too complicated to value precisely and rigorously, even with the Black-Scholes model and the many improvements developed in the 18 subsequent years.

Mortgage analysis is a process of continuous improvement, a process that will continue indefinitely as researchers approach an unobtainable goal. The purpose of this chapter is to take a second look at mortgage-backed securities in the light of the implications of Chapter 13: that the transactions cost approach promises dramatic improvements in the speed and accuracy of securities that involve the irrational exercise of embedded options by consumers. Before looking at the implications of that approach, we look first at traditional industry practice.

14.2 PREPAYMENT SPEEDS AND THE VALUATION OF MORTGAGES

Until fairly recently, Wall Street analysis of mortgage-backed securities relied almost exclusively on "prepayment models" as a means of analyzing the embedded options in mortgage-backed securities. The prepayment models, in combination with Monte Carlo simulation, produce another number as output: the option-adjusted spread (OAS) on a mortgage-backed security. In the next few sections, we pose a number of questions and attempt to answer them:

- Do prepayment models have an options component?
- Are prepayment speeds predictable enough to use as an input for the option-adjusted valuation of mortgages?
- Is the truth about prepayment speeds obvious enough that very sophisticated market participants can reach a consensus about their levels?

Most prepayment models have objectives similar to ours in the rest of this book:

1. Security valuation.
2. Measurement of interest rate sensitivity.
3. Accurate hedges.
4. Guidance on "rich/cheap" analysis for security selection.

Prepayment speed models come in three basic varieties:

a. Models in which the prepayment speed is a function of time but not rate levels. Examples are the lifetime prepayment speed models of the Public Securities Association (PSA), conditional (or "constant") prepayment rate (CPR), and single monthly mortality (SMM).
b. Tables in which different prepayment speeds are assigned depending on the remaining maturity of the mortgage, the coupon level, and the current level of interest rates. We call this the prepayment table approach.

c. Prepayment functions, which are typically derived from historical data on prepayments and include more inputs than a prepayment table to provide the accurate prepayment speed.

Analytically, the constant prepayment speed models are the simplest. Prepayment tables, which are one step up in complexity, assume that you can accurately forecast prepayment speeds. Prepayment functions assume the future will be like the historical data set that produced the estimates used in the prepayment function. How well do these models work?

14.3 CONSTANT PREPAYMENT SPEEDS AS A PRINCIPAL AMORTIZATION ASSUMPTION

The most important point to make about the PSA, CPR, and SMM analysis is that these models have no options component at all. They represent an assumption about principal amortization and make it quite clear that the rate of principal amortization does not depend on the level of interest rates. As a result, no "rational" consumer response to lower rates is reflected in these three models at all.

Exhibit 14–1 shows how principal varies on a level-payment mortgage at different prepayment speeds. A higher prepayment speed lowers the level of principal outstanding. A higher prepayment speed also has the impact of increasing cash flow on the mortgage in the early years and decreasing it in later years, effectively shortening its duration. (See Exhibit 14–2.) These cash flows are not stochastic and don't depend on the level of interest rates.

We can illustrate the derivation of prepayment formulas for a mortgage model that assumes constant, continuous payments. Most analysis of level-payment mortgage loans is done on a discrete time basis, recognizing that mortgages are usually repaid in the form of equal payments paid to the lender monthly or, as in Canada, on a weekly or biweekly basis. The use of continuous time analysis results in simpler formulas that provide for faster computer solutions. The purpose of this section is to summarize these formulas.

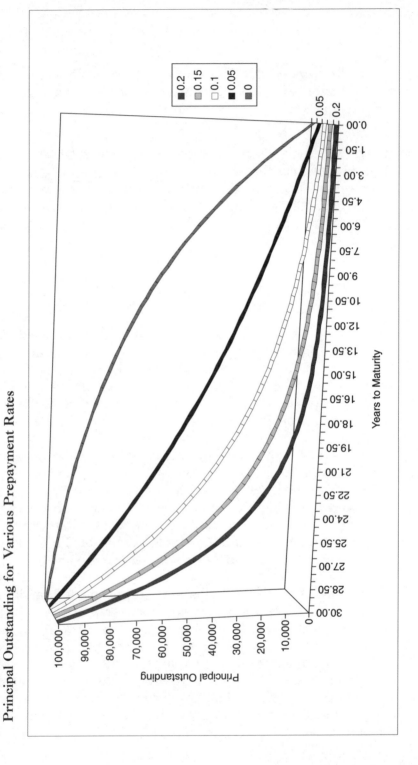

EXHIBIT 14-1

Principal Outstanding for Various Prepayment Rates

Total Annualized Cash Flow (Scheduled and Unscheduled) for Various Prepayment Rates

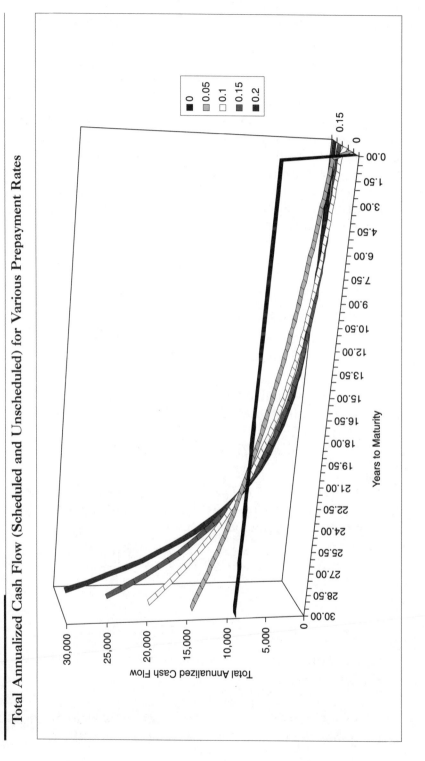

Mortgage Payments in Continuous Time

Let the initial principal on the loan be $L*$. The continuous level payment on the loan is c, and its continuous mortgage rate is y. We assume that the mortgage matures at time T and that it was originated at time 0. Its original term to maturity was $T = T - 0$, and its remaining term to maturity is $T - t = \tau$. The level payment c on the loan is the continuous constant amount such that the present value of c, discounted at the mortgage yield y, exactly equals the original principal amount $L*$:

$$L* = \int_0^T e^{-ys} c\, ds = \frac{c}{y}[1 - e^{-yT}]$$

Rearranging gives the formula for c:

$$c = \frac{yL*}{1 - e^{-yT}}$$

The remaining scheduled principal on the loan is a function of the remaining life of the loan $T - t = \tau$. We write this amount

$$L(\tau) = \frac{c}{y}[1 - e^{-y\tau}]$$

Note that $L(0) = 0$ and $L(T) = L*$. We can substitute the equation for c into this expression to get a formula that is independent of c for the remaining principal outstanding:

$$L(t,T) = L(\tau) = \frac{[1 - e^{-y\tau}]L*}{1 - e^{-yT}}$$

Interest-Only (IO) Cash Flows

The interest portion of the continuous cash flow is simply

$$i(\tau) = yL(\tau) = c[1 - e^{-y\tau}]$$

The interest-only (IO) piece is the continuous yield on the mortgage y times the principal outstanding at that instant.

Principal-Only (PO) Cash Flows

The principal-only (PO) portion of cash flows is the portion of the continuous cash flow c that is *not* interest:

$$p(\tau) = c - yL(\tau) = c - c[1 - e^{-y\tau}] = ce^{-y\tau}$$

Put another way, the principal portion is the negative of the instantaneous change in principal outstanding:

$$p(\tau) = \frac{\partial L(\tau)}{\partial \tau} = ce^{-y\tau}$$

Mortgage Valuation: No Prepayment

The value of the mortgage with no prepayment is its simple present value:

$$\text{Value} = c\int_t^T P(r,s,T)ds$$

In the Vasicek and extended Vasicek models, the interest rate sensitivity of value is

$$\frac{\partial \text{Value}}{\partial r} = c\int_t^T P_r(r,s,T)ds = c\int_t^T -\frac{1}{\alpha}\left[1 - e^{\alpha(T-s)}\right]P(r,s,T)ds$$

Mortgage Cash Flows with Prepayment

Many mortgages contain the right to pay all or some of the outstanding mortgage principal early. A typical simple assumption is that the amount repaid is a constant ratio k of the principal outstanding at that time. We denote the principal outstanding on such a mortgage by M. The continuous prepayment amount is

$$\text{Prepayment} = kM(t,T) = kM(\tau)$$

If mortgages are prepaid early at the rate k, what will be the continuous cash flow on the mortgage at any given time to maturity? To answer this question, we must determine the value of principal outstanding at any given time to maturity $T - t = \tau$. We know the following about a mortgage with early prepayment:

- The continuous scheduled payment on the mortgage will be continually reset such that

$$c(\tau) = \frac{yM(\tau)}{1 - e^{-y\tau}}$$

- The total payment will be the continuous scheduled payment plus the early prepayment of principal

$$\text{Total payment} = c(\tau) + kM(\tau) = \frac{yM(\tau)}{1 - e^{-y\tau}} + kM(\tau)$$

- The interest portion of the continuous payment is

$$i(\tau) = yM(\tau)$$

- The principal portion of total payment is

$$p(\tau) = \text{Total payment} - i(\tau) = \frac{yM(\tau)}{1 - e^{-y\tau}} + kM(\tau) - yM(\tau)$$

- Total principal due over the remaining life of the mortgage should equal total principal outstanding:

$$M(t,T) = \int_t^T \left[\frac{yM(s,T)}{1 - e^{-y(T-s)}} + kM(s,T) - yM(s,T) \right] ds$$

We can convert this into a partial differential equation by differentiating both sides with respect to t. This leads to the equation

$$M_t(t,T) = -\left[\frac{y}{1 - e^{-y(T-t)}} - y + k \right] M(t,T)$$

which must be solved subject to three boundary conditions:

a. $M(0,T) = L*$, the original principal amount on the loan.

b. $M(T,T) = 0$, the principal that remains outstanding at maturity.

c. $M(t,T) = L(t,T)$ when $k = 0$, since the loan in this case is identical to the no-prepayment example on p. 262.

The solution is

$$M(t,T) = \left[\frac{1 - e^{-y\tau}}{1 - e^{-yT}}\right]\frac{e^{k\tau}}{e^{kT}}L*$$

Given this solution, the total payment on the mortgage, including interest and both scheduled and unscheduled principal payments, is calculated as follows:

$$\text{Total payment} = Z(\tau) = \left[\frac{y}{1 - e^{-y\tau}} + k\right]\left(\frac{1 - e^{-y\tau}}{1 - e^{-yT}}\right)\frac{e^{k\tau}}{e^{kT}}L*$$

The value of the mortgage with early prepayment is the normal present value of these cash flows, which takes the form of an integral since payments are continuous rather than discrete:

$$\text{Value} = \int_0^\tau P(r,s)Z(s)ds$$

and rate sensitivity is

$$r\text{Delta} = \frac{\partial \text{Value}}{\partial r} = \int_0^\tau P_r(r,s)Z(s)ds$$

We get back to the fundamental question: How well will such a model work in practice? One problem is clear before we start: there is only one unknown, the prepayment speed k. If we have a Government National Mortgage Association (GNMA) mortgage-backed security whose price and interest rate risk are observable, can we match both price and risk with a single prepayment speed model? The answer is no, since we are trying to fit two equations (the known value and the known rate risk) with only one unknown, k. Only by accident will one k value solve both equations. Still, it is interesting to see how well such a simple model works in practice.

14.4 FITTING ACTUAL GNMA DATA WITH A SINGLE PREPAYMENT SPEED MODEL

In order to determine the relative effectiveness of the single prepayment speed model, we took 1,347 daily price quotations for a GNMA 8 percent mortgage-backed security. We assumed that the prepayment model was true, that is, that no matter what happens to interest rates the prepayment speed will stay constant over the life of the mortgage. We then compared the rate sensitivity in the real world with the prepayment model.[1] We calculated the present value of the GNMA using our model and compared it to actual GNMA prices. Actual GNMA prices over the November 28, 1988, to April 15, 1994, sample period showed a very smooth curve with a slight bend downward on the left-hand side of the graph at low rates, a plateau over a broad range of rates near a price of 105 or so, and then a decline in price as rates rise. (See Exhibit 14–3.)

We then solved for the prepayment rate k that provided the best fit to these data over all 1,347 days and plotted predicted versus actuals of the best case for any analyst, a model that on average had the right input variables. As shown in Exhibit 14–4, at first glance, the fit was surprisingly good for a one variable model.

When we overlaid the fitted prices versus interest rates, however, we could see systematic mispricing in the single prepayment model (Exhibit 14–5).

When we plotted the mispricing errors, our model was consistently too high in price when rates were very low or very high, and we were too low in price in the midrange. Our errors in the slope of the curve, the rDelta, were substantial except at very high rates. (See Exhibit 14–6.)

Why such serious errors? Because our simple model has no option component at all and ignores the fact that some consumer borrowers are eminently sensible. More people prepay their loans when rates are low than when they are high. Can we salvage the prepayment model approach by changing prepayment rates as interest rates change?

---

1. On each day, we took the actual 30-year U.S. government bond yield, and we assumed the credit spread was constant over the sample period (a rough first approximation).

GNMA 8% Market Price versus 30-Year U.S. Treasury Yield
November 28, 1988, to April 15, 1994

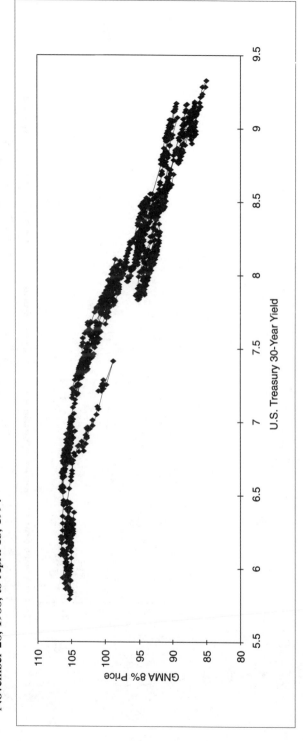

Actual GNMA 8% Prices Plotted versus Estimated GNMA 8% Prices Using Best-Fitting Constant Prepayment Speed
November 28, 1988, to April 15, 1994

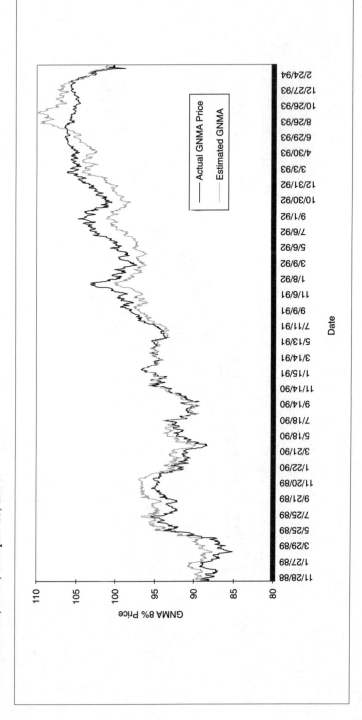

E X H I B I T   14–5

Actual GNMA 8% Prices Compared to Best-Fitting Prepayment
Speed Estimated Prices
November 28, 1988, to April 15, 1994

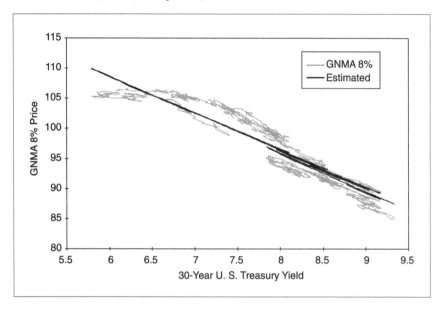

14.5 CAN WE FORECAST PREPAYMENT RATES?

The implication of the first sections of this chapter is that the single-speed approach to prepayment analysis doesn't work very well. We somehow need to do a better job of recognizing at least partially rational behavior to accurately meet our objectives:

- Correct market valuation.
- Correct interest rate sensitivity analysis.
- Correct hedging.

One way many market participants seek to account for rational behavior is to create a prepayment table that specifies what the prepayment rates will be at different times in different interest rate environments. Typically, a prepayment table will contain at least two dimensions, one for each payment and another for various levels of "refinancing advantage," the spread between the

EXHIBIT 14-6

Errors in Pricing Using Best-Fitting Prepayment Speed to Price GNMA 8%
November 28, 1988, to April 15, 1994

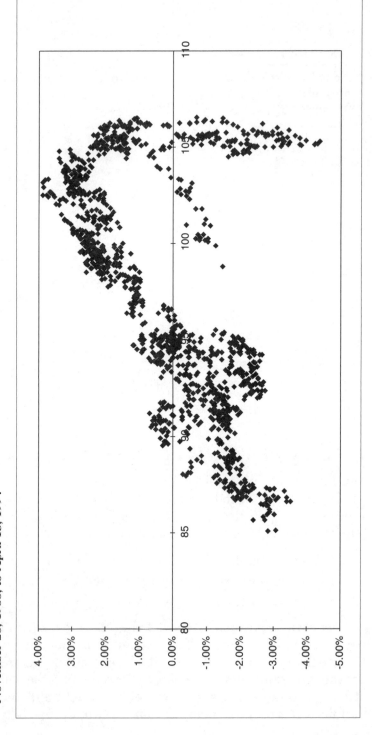

rate on the mortgage loan being analyzed and the current coupon rate on new mortgages. If there are five interest rate tiers and 360 payments, 1,800 input numbers will be required to get the three numbers we care about: value, rDelta, and the hedge amount for a given interest rate. Clearly, the prepayment table approach is expensive in terms of data input to output: a ratio of 600 numbers input for every 1 number output. Nonetheless, does it work?

When we ask "Does it work?" we are really asking whether forecasts of prepayment speeds are accurate, since, if they are not, the prepayment table will be filled with inaccurate numbers and the output from analysis that relies on those numbers will be highly inaccurate. Douglas Breeden (1994) takes a very interesting look at Wall Street's ability to forecast prepayment speeds, and we use data from his study liberally in this section. First, Breeden shows that Wall Street typically lacks consensus on the best constant lifetime prepayment speed for a given security. Exhibit 14–7 shows that the estimates on a 10 percent FNMA mortgage-backed security maturing in 2018 ranged from 20 percent to 40 percent.

When we go back to our GNMA 8 percent data set of 1,347 numbers and solve for the prepayment rate k that would cause the predicted price to equal the actual price, we see that the historical prepayment rates even under the simplest of models have jumped in a way that appears almost totally random (Exhibit 14–8).

Breeden also shows that the conditional prepayment rates as a function of the coupon on the mortgage-backed security and the refinancing incentive have been very unstable and have been inconsistent with rationality in many cases: Prepayment speeds for high-coupon mortgages have often been lower than prepayment speeds for high-coupon mortgages. (This phenomenon is often called *burnout,* shorthand for the fact that the most interest-rate-sensitive borrowers in a pool of loans leave the pool first via refinancing, reducing the interest rate sensitivity of the pool over time.) As Exhibit 14–9 shows, it is one thing to understand what burnout is and why it happens, and another thing to predict the degree to which it will occur.

In fact, it is easier to guess the value of an embedded option directly than it is to guess the prepayment rates needed as inputs to a formula to calculate option values. (See Exhibit 14–10.)

EXHIBIT 14-7

Estimates of FNMA Lifetime PSA Prepayment Rates
December 31, 1992 for 10% Coupon Due 2018

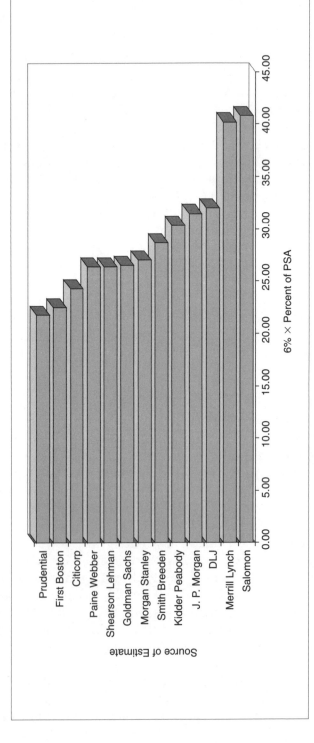

Source: Douglas Breeden, "Complexities of Hedging Mortgages," *Journal of Fixed Income*, December 1994.

EXHIBIT 14-8

Perfectly Fitting Prepayment Rates for Actual GNMA 8% Prices
November 28, 1988, to April 15, 1994

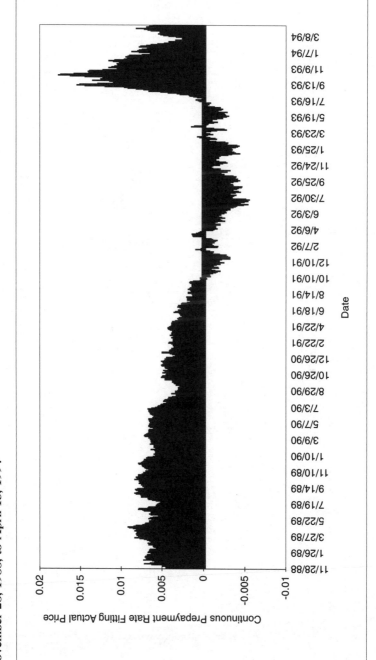

EXHIBIT 14-9

Conditional Prepayment Rate versus Par Coupon Level and Refinancing Incentive

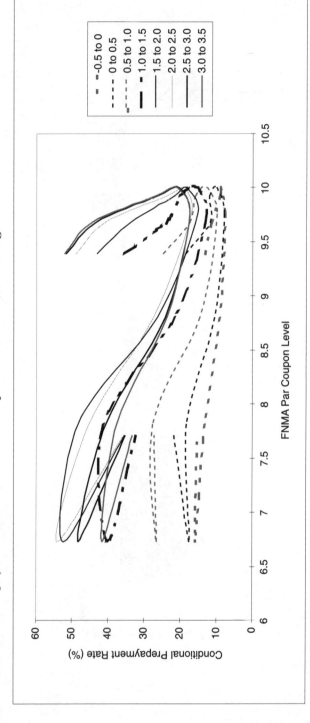

Source: Douglas Breeden, "Complexities of Hedging Mortgages," *Journal of Fixed Income*, December 1994.

Conditional Prepayment Rates on FNMAs, Sorted by Refinancing Incentive

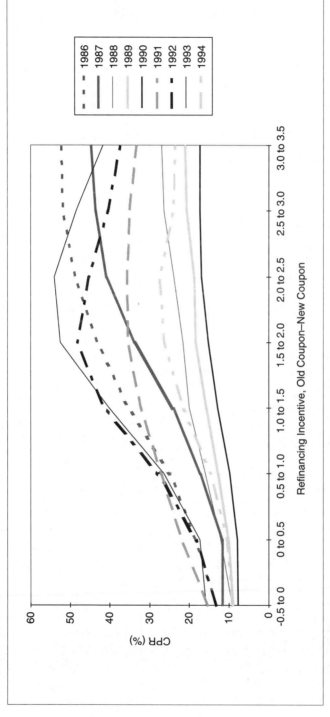

Source: Douglas Breeden, "Complexities of Hedging Mortgages," *Journal of Fixed Income,* December 1994.

14.6 OPTION-ADJUSTED SPREAD

Given the difficulties with prepayment models in general, what are the implications for the option-adjusted spread quotations common on Wall Street? First of all, we should summarize the option-adjusted spread (OAS) procedures, for the term *OAS* refers more to the procedures used than it does to the true concept of the risky spread on mortgages. Typically, analysts do the following:

- They assume that a prepayment function or prepayment table is true.
- They assume that Monte Carlo simulation is a good method for valuing an option, contrary to the observations in Chapter 12.
- They solve for the spread over a risk-free interest rate that provides a calculated value for the mortgage-backed security that matches the observable value.

In addition to the fundamental problems with the use of Monte Carlo simulation in the valuation of option-related securities, discussed in Chapter 12, OAS analysis typically incorporates the following errors:

1. *The refinancing incentive is not measured on a matched maturity basis.* Within the prepayment table, the refinancing incentive in the current market is measured in order to choose the correct prepayment rate from the prepayment table or prepayment function. This is measured as the difference between the rate on the mortgage being analyzed and the rate on a new 30-year fixed-rate mortgage. This sounds good at first glance, but a closer look gives cause for serious concern. If there are 5 years remaining on the mortgage, we are comparing its 5-year rate with the 30-year loan and assuming that refinancing is done on the basis of this apples-to-oranges comparison. In a swap trading unit or an investment management firm, anyone who said "30-year bonds are better than 5-year bonds because their yield is higher" would lose his or her job. Just this sort of comparison, however, is embedded in almost all OAS analysis. Why? Historical data on mortgage rates include only rates of new issue maturities (typically 15 and 30 years in the United States) and the analysts have no other data to measure refinancing spread. The reason for the choice of measure is clear, but it's an important source of inaccuracy.

2. *The refinancing incentive is measured on the basis of a 30-year mortgage rate, which does not include a premium for the call provisions of the loan.* Within the Monte Carlo simulation routine, there is no capability to calculate how much the premium should be on a new mortgage that's callable compared to a hypothetical "noncall" mortgage. Why? You have a chicken-and-egg problem: Using Monte Carlo and a prepayment table, we need to know what the option is worth in order to calculate what the option is worth! All of the refinancing incentives measured within the Monte Carlo routine are normally done assuming the mortgage is noncallable, introducing another source of error.

3. *The prepayment table should be path-dependent, but it's not.* If rates start at 6 percent, jump to 12 percent for 10 years, and then drop to 4 percent, the prepayment function and prepayment tables will produce the same prepayment speed prediction as if rates started at 6 percent, dropped to 3 percent for 10 years, and then jumped to 4 percent. Clearly, that should not be the case. Monte Carlo is often relied upon on the rationale that prepayments are path-dependent. We discuss that comment in more detail below, but it's clear that Monte Carlo replaces a path-dependence problem in the prepayment rates themselves with a path-dependence problem in the prepayment table.

4. *The OAS will match the market value of the observable security, but not its interest rate risk.* Why? For the same reason that the single prepayment speed model didn't work. We have two equations (value and rate sensitivity) we want to solve simultaneously, but only one variable (OAS) to adjust in order to do this. We can match both only by accident.

OAS is the "plug" or balancing number that offsets all of the errors inherent in Monte Carlo analysis and the four problems above. It's not surprising, given the lack of consensus on Wall Street about prepayment rates, that median broker estimates of OAS show very strange patterns when plotted by coupon level. Breeden (1994) cites data for the third quarter of 1989 and the fourth quarter of 1992 that show investors could double their spread by simply buying an MBS with a different coupon level, even though this discrepancy is public information widely disseminated by Wall Street firms.

One can only conclude that investors agree that the OAS consensus estimates of Wall Street firms contain enough errors that prices did not correct to erase the perceived spread differential.

Even more significant, Wall Street didn't bid up the price of the MBS with the widest reported OAS relative to the MBS with the lowest MBS. Clearly, OAS numbers are taken with a grain of salt by market participants. Gregg Patruno (1994) of Goldman, Sachs summarizes a common view by saying that as "the standard measure of mortgage relative value . . . OAS does not account for the complete nature of prepayment risk. Rather, it adjusts for the optionality due to interest rate fluctuations under the presumption that prepayment rates are a known, permanent function of interest rates."[2]

14.7 THE TRANSACTIONS COST APPROACH TO PREPAYMENTS

Patruno (1994) suggests both the reason for the problems with OAS and a potential solution to the problem:

> Homeowners are "willing" to refinance if the financial incentive is high enough to meet their requirements. We use the measure of refinancing incentive actually considered by typical homeowners and their bankers — not an abstract interest differential or ad hoc statistical artifact, but the real dollar savings expected on an after-tax basis, taking into account an appropriate mix of available mortgage rates and points.[3]

In other words, the only way to model consumer prepayment behavior effectively is to consider the rational value of the option to prepay. Patruno concludes that "the levels of current mortgage rates and transactions costs determine what fraction of the homeowners in the distribution should be considered willing to refinance."[4]

For these reasons, the authors believe that the transactions cost approach of Chapter 13, as analyzed by McConnell and Singh (1994) and Stanton (1995), is the only way to overcome the problems encountered in the full spectrum of prepayment and OAS analysis. How should the transactions cost approach be used?

The answer depends on the objective. If the objective is to match *both* the value and the rate sensitivity of an observable mortgage-backed security (something OAS analysis cannot do), then the procedure is straightforward. We use the American op-

---

2. Patruno (1994), p. 53.
3. Ibid., p. 47.
4. Ibid.

tion version of the transactions cost approach in Chapter 13. We have two equations and only two variables that can be determined by this process. We split the mortgage-backed security into two pieces, exactly as we did in Chapter 13, and we assume that transactions costs are constant over the life of the loan.[5] We have three potential variables to solve for:

1. Transactions cost level of mortgage pool 1, which we call m_1.
2. Transactions cost level of mortgage pool 2, which we call m_2.
3. Weight w of mortgage pool 1.

We match value and rate risk by solving the equations

$$\text{Value} = w\text{Value}[m_1] + (1 - w)\text{Value}[m_2]$$

$$\frac{\partial\text{Value}}{\partial r} = w\text{Value}_r[m_1] + (1 - w)\text{Value}_r[m_2]$$

for two of the three variables w, m_1, and m_2 where the ms represent the constant transactions cost of each of the two pieces of the mortgage-backed security we are trying to value. The value and rDelta of each of these pieces is calculated by using the trinomial lattice in Chapter 12 according to the transactions cost–based valuation of an American option in Chapter 13. We can do the calculation in two ways:

1. Set $w = 0.5$ (or any other number) and solve for the two variables m_1 and m_2.
2. Set $m_1 = 0$ (or any other number) and solve for m_2 and w.

14.8 IMPLICATIONS FOR OAV SPREAD, CMOs, AND ARMs

The approach in Section 14.7 is so brutally straightforward that the power of the transactions cost approach is easy to overlook. Consider some of the following implications.

---

5. This is for expositional purposes only. We can make the transactions cost function reflect seasonal factors, coupon on the loan, remaining life, etc.

Replace OAS with OAV Spread

The primary reason for the lack of OAS consensus among Wall Street firms is that all of the assumptions being made are assumptions about the borrower. It is no wonder that consensus is impossible. Instead, we recommend the option-adjusted value (OAV) spread. Consider a corporate treasurer who has to choose between issuing a 7-year noncall bond or a 10-year bond that is noncallable for 7 years. He makes the decision in a straightforward way. First, he asks for the rate on a comparable Treasury seven-year noncall bond and calculates his spread over Treasuries. Second, he calculates (since no observable Treasury is 10 years non-call 7) what the coupon would be on a 10-year noncall 7 Treasury bond that trades at par value. His "spread" on the 10-year noncall 7 issue is the difference between his coupon and the Treasury's coupon. He issues the bond with the lowest spread.

The spread on retail-oriented securities should be measured by answering the question of spread, not by making assumptions about the borrower (since the question is unanswerable with any level of consensus). The question should be asked (in the context of a fixed-rate MBS with a 7 percent coupon trading at 96 with level monthly payments and a maturity in 2017) in two parts:

1. What coupon would the U.S. Treasury pay on a security with level monthly payments, a maturity in 2017, and a value of 96?
2. Subtract the answer in (1) from 7. That is the OAV spread.

The odds of consensus in this calculation are much higher than in OAS. It requires only the techniques of Chapter 12 applied to the U.S. Treasury. No assumptions about the consumer borrowers are necessary, and the only lack of consensus will be due to disagreements about which term structure model and lattice design to use.

The analysis can be refined still further by requiring the Treasury issue to have two components that match the two pieces of the mortgage-backed security (see the previous section) that produce matching interest rate risk and value.

CMOs and ARMs

Collateralized mortgage obligations (CMOs) and adjustable rate mortgages (ARMs) can be analyzed in exactly the way we have outlined in Section 14.7, with McConnell and Singh (1994) providing a concrete example of that approach. ARMs, because of the path dependence of the security, are more complex, but even so the transactions cost approach provides substantial value relative to the traditional prepayment approach.

EXERCISES

14.1 Using the prepayment table approach, is the analysis of mortgage-backed securities path-dependent?

14.2 Instead of using the prepayment table approach, assume that you use the transactions cost approach and you model the security by breaking it into 10 pieces, each of which has a different level of transactions costs reflecting the different layers of rate sensitivity among consumers. If you simulated the prepayment behavior of this transactions cost–based portfolio, would the prepayment experience be path-dependent?

14.3 Would the financial analysis required to model the portfolio in Exercise 14.2 require a technique that deals with path dependence?

14.4 Write the formula for value of the portfolio in Exercise 14.2, assuming you have solved for the value of each piece using the techniques in Chapters 12 and 13.

14.5 Write the formula for rDelta of the portfolio in Exercise 14.2, assuming you know the rDelta of each piece from the techniques in Chapters 12 and 13.

14.6 Assume one MBS pool has been broken into three CMO tranches: the A, B, and C tranches. The A tranche gets all principal payments until 30 percent of original principal is retired. The B tranche gets all subsequent principal payments until another 32 percent of principal has been retired. The C tranche

gets the rest. Assume you can observe in the market
the value and rDelta of the original pool and the A,
B, and C CMO tranches. Using the transactions cost
approach, into how many pieces do you need to
break each CMO tranche? Write down the system of
equations that need to be solved to identify the
relevant transactions costs.

REFERENCES

Berk, J., and R. Roll. "Adjustable Rate Mortgages: Valuation." *Journal of Real Estate Finance and Economics* 1 (June 1988), pp. 163–84.

Breeden, Douglas T. "Complexities of Hedging Mortgages." *Journal of Fixed Income,* December 1994, pp. 6–42.

Dunn, K. B., and C. Spatt. "Private Information and Incentives: Implications for Mortgage Contract Terms and Pricing." *Journal of Real Estate Finance and Economics* 1 (April 1988), pp. 47–60.

Flannagan, C. T.; M. D. Herskovitz; and H. T. Loy. "Understanding and Modelling Cost of Funds ARMs Prepayments." Mortgage-Backed Securities Research, Merrill Lynch (February 1989).

Green, J., and J. B. Shoven. "The Effect of Interest Rates on Mortgage Prepayments." *Journal of Money, Credit and Banking* XVIII (February 1986), pp. 41–59.

Jamshidian, Farshid. "An Exact Bond Option Formula." *Journal of Finance,* March 1989, pp. 205–9.

McConnell, John J., and Manoj Singh. "Rational Prepayments and the Valuation of Collateralized Mortgage Obligations." *Journal of Finance,* July 1994, pp. 891–922.

Patruno, Gregg N. "Mortgage Prepayments: A New Model for a New Era." *Journal of Fixed Income,* December 1994, pp. 42–57.

Quigley, J. M. "Interest Rate Variations, Mortgage Prepayments and Household Mobility." *The Review of Economics and Statistics* LXIX (November 1987), pp. 636–43

Ramaswamy, K., and S. Sundaresan. "The Valuation of Floating Rate Instruments: Theory and Evidence." *Journal of Financial Economics* 17 (December 1986), pp. 251–72.

Richard, S. F., and R. Roll. "Prepayments on Fixed-Rate Mortgage-Backed Securities." *Journal of Portfolio Management* 15 (Spring 1989), pp. 73–82.

Schwartz, E., and W. Torous. "Prepayment and the Valuation of Mortgage-Backed Securities." *Journal of Finance* 44 (June 1989), pp. 375–92.

Stanton, Richard. "Rational Prepayments and the Valuation of Mortgage-Backed Securities." *Review of Financial Studies,* Fall 1995, pp. 677–708.

van Deventer, Donald R. "The Valuation of Fixed and Floating Rate Mortgages." Kamakura Corporation research memorandum, December 1993.

Vasicek, Oldrich A. "An Equilibrium Characterization of the Term Structure." *Journal of Financial Economics* 5 (November 1977), pp. 177–88.

CHAPTER 15

Nonmaturity Deposits

15.1 AN INTRODUCTION TO NONMATURITY DEPOSITS

The bulk of bank deposits and insurance liabilities are made up of "securities" with explicit maturities, although they are often putable by the consumer who supplied the funds, whether they come in the form of a time deposit or life insurance policy. These liabilities can be analyzed with the techniques of Chapters 12 and 13, even if the consumer's right to put the security back to the financial institution is exercised irrationally. A substantial portion, however, of the liabilities of major banks worldwide consists of "nonmaturity deposits." Similarly, the funds supplied to mutual fund managers of fixed-income funds also have no specific maturities. This chapter is relevant to both types of liabilities, but from here on we will refer to them as nonmaturity deposits within a banking industry context. These deposits have no specific maturity, and individual depositors can freely add or subtract balances as they wish. The interest rate on these deposits is usually, but not always, a function of open-market interest rates. Similarly, the level of deposit balances in aggregate often moves in sympathy with open-market interest rates. With the strong trend in mark-to-market-based risk management in banking, all bankers are faced with the difficult task of calculating the mark-to-market "value" of these nonmaturity deposits. This chapter provides an introduction to that difficult topic.

In September 1993, the Federal Reserve Board published proposed regulations for interest rate risk and capital adequacy. In its regulations, the Federal Reserve Board noted "the inherent difficulties in determining the appropriate treatment of nonmaturity deposits." In this chapter, we present a number of techniques for measuring the mark-to-market value of deposits that are theoretically rigorous yet easy to apply in practice. Most of the arguments applied here to the valuation of nonmaturity deposits can be applied equally well to the valuation of charge card loans, where again the balance as well as the rate on the loan fluctuates in response to market rate movements. For more on both deposit and charge card valuation, see Jarrow and van Deventer (1996a, 1996b).

15.2 THE "VALUE" OF THE DEPOSIT FRANCHISE

When we measure the "value" of deposits, what exactly are we trying to measure? If the bank had issued a bond to finance its assets, the value of the bond is its present value: the present value of future payments that the bank must make on the security it has issued. *Value* is the present value of future costs.

In the case of nonmaturity deposits, the value of the deposit could also mean the premium that a third party would be willing to pay above the face value of the deposits to assume ownership of the bank's deposit "franchise."[1] In this case, *value* means the net present value benefit of owning the deposit franchise: the value of cash provided by depositors less the present value cost of the deposit franchise.

In what follows, we use the word *value* to refer to the present value of the cost of the deposit franchise, exactly in keeping with

---

1. The average premium paid by purchasers of failed bank deposit franchises was 2.32 percent in 1,225 auctions run through October 28, 1994, by the Resolution Trust Corporation in the United States. The highest premium paid was 25.33 percent. Most of the deposits auctioned (more than 70 percent on average) were time deposits that would be expected to have very low premiums.

the analogy of the bank as bond issuer. The net present value benefit of having the deposit franchise can be calculated from the valuation formulas presented below by subtracting the "values" we calculate from the face value of the deposit. For example, the present value cost of $100 face value of savings deposits might be $65. The net present value benefit of the deposit franchise is $100 – $65, or $35. All references to value below refer to the present value of the cost of the franchise: $65.

We also assume that the deposit franchise is guaranteed by a riskless third party, which is the case in the United States and many other countries. This allows us to avoid dealing with the complexities of bankruptcy risk.

15.3 TOTAL CASH FLOW OF NONMATURITY DEPOSITS

The first step in valuing nonmaturity deposits is to isolate the total cash flows from the deposit franchise. Total costs consist of the following elements:

Total deposit cost cash flows in a given time period
= Interest paid on the deposit
+ Non-interest expense of servicing the deposit
– Non-interest revenue from the deposit franchise
– **Net increase in deposit balances**

Many readers will be surprised to see the net increase in deposit balances subtracted from costs in the equation above. The net change in deposit balances on many deposit products is the single most important cash flow in the valuation process, yet many analysts ignore this important determinant of value.

In the valuation of any security, total cash flow is the basic building block of valuation. For most securities, the maturity date is fixed and cash flow from "principal" stems from a predetermined payment schedule associated with that security. In the case of the nonmaturity deposit, however, the security is a perpetual one and principal is never "returned." Instead, changes in deposit balances are simply another source of cash flow. A simple example illustrates the point.

Consider a deposit category with balances of $100 where the sum of interest expense and processing costs is 2 percent of balances annually. Let's assume that this cash flow occurs at the end of every year. Let's also assume that the balances on this account grow at 2 percent a year, and that balances also increase in a one-time jump at the end of each year. What is the net cash flow associated with this account? On December 31 of each year, 2 percent of the deposit amount flows out in the form of interest expense and processing costs, and it flows back in on the same day in the form of increased deposit balances. The net cash flow from the deposit franchise is zero every year forever.

The present value cost of this deposit is zero, since there is never net cash inflow or outflow. Since the present value cost is zero, the "net present value" or premium that would be paid to gain this deposit franchise is $100, calculated as above: The deposit balance $100 − The present value of deposit costs ($0) = $100.

This example is deceptively simple: It is consistent with common sense, yet it will lead us to some surprising conclusions about the value of nonmaturity deposits. We will analyze the value of nonmaturity deposits in what follows using a series of progressively more realistic assumptions about deposit rate and balance behavior. We start by assuming that deposit balances are constant to derive a valuation formula for deposits. We then assume that interest rates are constant and balances are random. We derive deposit values for four different types of deposit variation. Finally, we provide a brief introduction to the most realistic case where both deposit balances and deposit rates are random, which is covered in more detail in Jarrow and van Deventer (1996a, 1996b).

15.4 DEPOSIT VALUATION WITH CONSTANT BALANCES OR KNOWN VARIATION IN BALANCES

In this section, we want to lay a foundation for random movements in deposit balance analysis by reviewing the case in which either deposit balances are constant or their future variation is known with certainty. The arguments we make can be classified as no-arbitrage arguments in this sense: Bankers are constantly comparing the cost of nonmaturity deposits to other sources of funds, and the present value of the nonmaturity deposit is calculated by reference to these alternative sources of funds; the present value of the nonmaturity deposit is the cost of replicating the cash flows of the deposit franchise from other funding sources.

Case 15.4.1: Constant Deposit Amount with Constant Fixed Rate on Deposits

Consider the case where the amount of the deposit is constant and the yield and processing costs associated with the deposit are both fixed percentages of the amount of the deposit D. In order to avoid the minutia of compounding calculations, let's assume that the interest expense and processing costs associated with the deposit franchise are paid continuously. Let the continuously paid deposit rate be y and the continuously paid processing costs be c. If both the interest and processing costs are paid continuously, the value V of the deposit is

$$V = \frac{(y + c)D}{R_c}$$

R_c is the rate on a continuously paid consol (perpetual fixed-rate bond) consistent with the risk-free yield curve. The present value of the cost of the deposit franchise is exactly the same as the value of a perpetual bond paying the identical amount of interest. The duration of the deposit is calculated as follows:

$$\text{Duration} = \frac{-\dfrac{\partial V}{\partial R_c}}{V} = \frac{\dfrac{(y + c)D}{R_c^2}}{V} = \frac{1}{R_c}$$

Example 15.4.1
The bank has a $100 nonmaturity deposit that costs 4 percent continuously, 3 percent in interest, and 1 percent in processing costs. The open-market interest rate for a perpetual fixed-rate bond is 10 percent. The present value of the cost of the deposit is interest cost of the deposit (4 percent times $100, or $4) capitalized at the 10 percent rate: $40 ($4/.1). The duration of the deposit

is [$4/(0.1)^2]/$40 = 10 years. The long duration is no surprise, since this is the equivalent of a perpetual fixed-rate bond.

Case 15.4.2: Constant Deposit Amount with Floating Rate at Proportional Spread

There is another form of deposit that leads to simple results if the amount of the deposit is constant. We assume the rate on the deposit is a continuously paid floating rate that is a constant proportion of the short-term risk-free market rate r. For purposes of this example, we could call this short rate Libor.[2] We let this proportion be k. In general, the market value of a perpetual floating-rate security that continuously pays at the riskless instantaneous rate of interest is its par value.[3] Note that the cash flows on the deposit exactly equal k times the cash flows on a perpetual floater at the short-term riskless rate with a par value of kD. To avoid riskless arbitrage, this means that the value of the deposit on a payment date must be exactly k times the value of the perpetual floater:

$$V = kD$$

Note that the duration of the continuously paid deposit is 0 since no interest rate r appears in the valuation formula.

Example 15.4.2

Assume that a $100 deposit account pays 60 percent of Libor forever, since the deposit is a nonmaturity deposit account. The cash flows on the account are $0.6 \times$ Libor $\times $100 =$ Libor $\times $60. The cash cost of the account is identical to the cash cost of a perpetual floater with a par value of $60 that pays Libor. The present value cost of a perpetual bond paying Libor is its par value. Therefore, the present value cost of the deposit must be $60. The present value does not change as rates change,[4] so the duration of the cost of the deposit is 0.

---

2. The discrete payment on one-month Libor or three-month Libor changes some of the formulas that follow in a minor way. We ignore these minor differences in what follows.
3. For proof of this proposition, see Cox, Ingersoll, and Ross (1980).
4. We ignore the impact on present value of an initial coupon rate that may have already been set.

Case 15.4.3: Constant Deposit Amount with Floating Rate and Linear Spread

If the deposit amount is constant and the deposit rate is a linear function of a floating market rate, then deposit pricing is a combination of Cases 15.4.1 and 15.4.2. In this case, we assume the deposit rate y is a simple function of short-term rates of the form $y = a + bR_f$, where R_f is the floating market rate (such as Libor) and R_c is the yield on a perpetual fixed-rate bond or consol. The cash flow on this deposit can be broken into two pieces: (1) a constant payment that can be valued as in Case 15.4.1 assuming $y = a$, and (2) a proportional payment, with a solution as in Case 15.4.2 using $y = bR_f$.

Once we have solved for the value of each component, the value of the total must equal the sum of each piece, or arbitrage will result.

The value is

$$V = \frac{aD}{R_c} + bD$$

The duration of the deposit is

$$\text{Duration} = \frac{-\dfrac{\partial V}{\partial R_c}}{V} = \frac{\dfrac{aD}{R_c^2}}{V} = \frac{a}{R_c(a + bR_c)}$$

Example 15.4.3
The bank has a $100 nonmaturity deposit that pays a rate equal to 4 percent plus 20 percent of Libor. These parameters of nonmaturity deposit rate behavior are determined by linear regression analysis on the historical movement of deposit rates. We assume that the rate on a perpetual fixed-rate bond is 10 percent. The cash flows on this deposit can be broken into two pieces. The first piece is fixed: 4 percent times $100 = $4 annually. The value of this piece is $4/0.1 = $40, as in the example above. The second piece depends on the level of Libor. The amount paid is 20 percent times Libor times $100, which is the same as the cash flow on a $20 security (20 percent times $100) paying Libor. The value of the second piece is $20, since we assume that a Libor floater always trades at a market value equal to par value. The sum of the fixed and floating pieces is

$60, the present value cost of the deposit. The duration of this deposit is [$4/(0.1)^2]/$60, or 6.67 years.

Case 15.4.4: Known Future Variation in Deposit Balances

Another simple case is the one where future variations in deposit balances are known with certainty, as are the interest rate and processing costs associated with deposits. The value of the deposit is simply the present value of the future known cash flows (the change in deposit amount, interest on the deposits, processing costs, etc.). We denote the present value of a dollar t years in advance as $P(t)$. The deposit value, assuming the cash flow at time t_i is given by X_i, is

$$V = \sum_{i=1}^{n} P[t_i] X_i$$

Unless this is true, there would be riskless arbitrage available, since the bank would fund itself using regular bond or time deposit issues instead of getting into the nonmaturity deposit business. Using continuous time notation, the relation between these discount factors and their continuously compounded yield to maturities y_i and maturities t_i is

$$P[t_i] = e^{-y_i t_i}$$

The duration of this deposit is a direct application of Macaulay's original duration formula in continuous time terms. We assume each y_i shifts by an amount z to $y_i* = y_i + z$. Duration[5] is

$$\text{Duration} = \frac{-\dfrac{\partial V}{\partial z}}{V} = \frac{\sum_{i=1}^{n} t_i P[t_i] X_i}{V}$$

---

5. Rate sensitivity with respect to the short-term rate of interest in a term structure model like those of Vasicek (1977) or Heath, Jarrow, and Morton (1992) can be calculated as well. The exact nature of the formula would depend on the term structure model chosen.

Example 15.4.4

Consider a bank with $110 in deposits. We assume that the net cash outflow from the bank's deposit business (interest expense less net increase in deposit balances) follows the schedule below:

Years	Present Value Factor	Cash Flow
1	0.95	50
2	0.90	33
3	0.85	23
4	0.79	11

After year 4 cash flow, the deposit balance reaches 0 and the bank exits from the deposit business. The present value cost of this deposit franchise is $105.44 (0.95 * 50 + 0.9 * 33 + 0.85 * 23 + 0.79 * 11). The duration of deposit costs is 1.9.

15.5 RANDOM DEPOSIT BALANCES WITH CONSTANT INTEREST RATES

A more realistic assumption about deposits is that deposit-related cash outflows are random. One reasonable assumption along these lines is that net deposit cash flows X (Interest costs + Processing costs − Net deposit inflow) is a random walk that drifts over time, subject to random shocks. Another possible assumption is that this random cash flow reverts to some mean or average level, subject to random shocks. We look at each of these assumptions and the resulting valuations in turn, under the assumption that interest rates are constant at a level r for all maturities, the same assumption at the heart of the Black-Scholes option model.

Even though these assumptions sound like they will lead to complex answers, the solutions we get are surprisingly simple if we are willing to make one powerful (but realistic) simplifying assumption: that there is no risk premium attached by bank shareholders to the risk of deposit balance variation. We assume that shareholders are risk neutral with respect to the volatility in deposit balances. This is a good working approximation to reality if the primary reason for deposit balance variation at a given bank is its battle with competing banks for market share. For example, the Federal Reserve may well target the money supply so that the aggregate growth in demand deposit balances nationally is 3 percent annually. If this assumption is true, then individual banks will grow faster than 3 percent only by taking deposits from another bank; on average, demand deposits at all banks will grow by 3 percent. If shareholders don't like the risk of deposit balance variation, they can "diversify away" this risk by owning, say, 1 percent of the stock of all banks in the United States. In this sense, we are assuming that shareholders care only about the average expected level of deposits, not the volatility of deposit balances. This useful assumption will give answers that are both simple and realistic for many practical purposes.

Case 15.5.1: The Change in Deposit Cash Outflows Is Normally Distributed

We start by defining X as the net deposit cash outflows that determine the net cost of the deposit: interest expense and processing cost less deposit balance inflows. We assume that these cash flows occur continuously and that X changes continuously. We assume that changes in X are normally distributed:[6]

$$dX = \alpha dt + \sigma dz$$

where dX denotes the change in net deposit cash flows X. The α is the drift in net deposit cash flows; in the second term, σ denotes the volatility of net deposit cash flows. The term dz is a shorthand reference to the "noise" generator, which triggers jumps in deposit balances.[7] We supplement this assumption about the variation in net deposit cash flows by the assumption above that bank shareholders are risk neutral with respect to variations in deposit cash flows.

The valuation of a security that fits these assumptions is given by Shimko (1992), with details of the calculation given in the appendix to this chapter. The value of deposits is

---

6. This stochastic process is a random walk. Readers who would like an extremely
   well-written introduction to stochastic processes should refer to Shimko (1992).
   His introduction to the subject is perhaps the most popular book on financial
   mathematics in the American financial services industry.
7. The dz term is the same standard Wiener process with a mean of 0 and standard
   deviation of 1 that we began using in Chapters 4 and 5 in the term structure
   model context.

$$V = \frac{X}{r} + \frac{\alpha}{r^2}$$

The duration of deposits in this case is

$$\text{Duration} = \frac{-\dfrac{\partial V}{\partial r}}{V} = \frac{\dfrac{X}{r^2} + \dfrac{2\alpha}{r^3}}{V} = \frac{1}{r}\left[\frac{rX + 2\alpha}{rX + \alpha}\right]$$

These valuation formulas are surprisingly simple, given the complexity of movements in deposit cash flows that we have assumed. Note that the volatility of deposit flows σ does not appear in the formula because shareholders are risk neutral regarding deposit flows. Likewise, the absolute amount of deposits D does not appear in the valuation formula. Only the net deposit cash flows, not the accounting value of deposits D, determine the value of deposits.

Example 15.5.1
Net deposit franchise cash costs (X) have recently been $50 per year, consisting of $90 in interest and processing expenses, less $40 annual increase in deposit balances. The change in net deposit costs (dX) is on average $10 per year (i.e., α is 10). The level of interest rates is 10 percent. The present value cost of this deposit franchise is $50/0.1 + 10/(0.1)^2 = $1,500. Duration is (0.1 * $50 + 2 * $10)/[(0.1 * $50 + $10) * 0.1] or $25/($15 * 0.1) = 16.7.

Case 15.5.2: Net Deposit Cash Outflows Change Randomly around a Long-Run Mean Level

Another possible assumption about the net deposit cost cash outflows is that they jump randomly around the same long-run average level. The volatility of net deposit cost cash outflows may or may not depend on the level of net deposit cash flows. We could use any number of specifications for the way that net deposit cash flows change:

$$dX = k(\mu - X)dt + \sigma dt$$

$$dX = k(\mu - X)dt + \sqrt{X}\sigma dz$$

$$dX = k(\mu - X)dt + X\sigma dz$$

In each of these three cases, k is the speed of mean reversion (the speed of the deposit "cycles" around the long-run average level) of net deposit cash outflows X around a long-run level, μ. In the first case, the level of X doesn't affect the size of the random jumps in X. In the second and third cases, the size of the random jumps in X depend on X; the jumps are proportional to the square root of X or the level of X itself.

Shimko (1992) gives the valuation for the second case. For all three of these cases, the value of deposits is

$$V = \frac{rX + k\mu}{r(r + k)}$$

The true duration of deposits is calculated as follows:

$$\text{Duration} = \frac{-\dfrac{\partial V}{\partial r}}{V} = \frac{\dfrac{-X}{r(r+k)} + \dfrac{(rX + k\mu)(2r + k)}{r^2(r+k)^2}}{V}$$

$$= \frac{-X}{rX + k\mu} + \frac{2r + k}{r(r + k)}$$

See the appendix to this chapter for the derivation.

Example 15.5.2
Let's assume that deposits bounce around an average level in a deposit balance cycle that lasts one year. We set $k = 1/L$, where L is the number of years the cycle lasts. In this case, both L and k are 1. If the current net cash deposit outflow (interest and processing costs less deposit inflow) is at a $10 per year annual rate, then X is 10. We assume the long-run average level μ is 20. We assume the interest rate r is 10 percent. Then the mark-to-market present value of the cost of the deposit franchise is $(0.1 * 10 + 1 * 20)/(0.1 * 1.1) =$ 190.9. Using the same assumptions, duration is 10.4.

Case 15.5.3: The Percentage Change in Deposits Is Normally Distributed

Another reasonable assumption about deposits is that the percentage change in the amount of deposits, not the absolute change in deposit cash outflows X, jumps about randomly. A common assumption is that the percentage change in deposits is normally distributed.[8] In that case, the percentage change in the deposit balance can be written

$$\frac{dD}{D} = \alpha dt + \sigma dz$$

Assuming that the interest rate and processing costs on the deposit are y and c, respectively, the total cash cost to the owner of the deposit franchise is $(y + c)D$ less the change in deposit levels, dD. In this case, the present value of cost of the deposits is

$$V = \frac{(y + c - \alpha)D}{r - \alpha}$$

The duration of deposits is calculated as follows:

$$\text{Duration} = \frac{-\dfrac{\partial V}{\partial r}}{V} = \frac{1}{r - \alpha}$$

See the appendix to this chapter for details of the derivation.

Example 15.5.3
Let's assume that the rate on deposits is 4 percent and processing costs are 2 percent annually. We also assume that the average annual growth rate in deposit balances α is 3 percent. If deposit balances are \$100 and the interest rate r is 9 percent, then the calculation has the following steps. The net cash outflow on the deposits $(y + c - \alpha)D$ is $(4\% + 2\% - 3\%)100 = \$3$. This is divided by $9\% - 3\% = 6\%$, so the present value cost of the deposit is \$50. The duration of the deposit is $1/(9\% - 3\%) = 16.7$ years.

Case 15.5.4: The Level of Deposits Changes Randomly around a Long-Run Mean Level

Another reasonable assumption about the absolute level of deposits is that the amount of deposits D itself changes randomly around a stable long-run level μ with deposit interest rate y and

---

8. This is equivalent to assuming that the gross amount of deposits is lognormally distributed, the same assumption used for stock prices in the Black-Scholes options model.

processing costs c. In that case, we can write the shorthand notation for the change in deposits as

$$dD = k(\mu - D)dt + \sigma dz$$

The valuation of deposits is again derived from calculating the present value cost of interest costs $(y + c)D$ less net deposit inflows. The present value cost in this case is

$$V = \frac{k}{r}\left[\frac{(y+c)-r}{r+k}\right]\mu + \left[\frac{k+y+c}{r+k}\right]D$$

Duration is calculated as follows:

$$\text{Duration} = \frac{-\dfrac{\partial V}{\partial r}}{V} = \frac{Br^2 + 2Ar + kA}{Br^3 + (A + kB)r^2 + kAr}$$

where

$$A = k\mu(y + c)$$

$$B = (k + y + c)D - k\mu$$

Example 15.5.4
Assume the long-run average level of deposits μ is 100 and that the current level of deposits D is 80. We assume that the interest rate r is 10 percent and that the length of the deposit balance fluctuation cycle L is one year. Then $k = 1/L = 1$. We assume that the interest cost on the deposit y is 4 percent and processing costs c are 2 percent. Therefore, the value of the deposit, using the formula above, is 40.7. The duration of the deposit is 14.3.

15.6 THE VALUATION OF DEPOSITS WHOSE RATES AND BALANCES VARY WITH OPEN-MARKET RATES

In Section 15.4, we assumed that deposit balances were constant and interest rates were random. In Section 15.5, we assumed that interest rates were constant and deposit balances were random. Using the same basic approach as Sections 15.4 and 15.5, we can value nonmaturity deposits in the most realistic case: where deposit rates and deposit balances vary randomly in response to changes in open-market interest rates. Jarrow and van Deventer

(1996a, 1996b) discuss the derivation of the valuation formula for nonmaturity deposits in detail. These more realistic valuation assumptions are critical for the correct measurement of the interest rate risk of nonmaturity deposits.

There are literally an endless number of ways to specify the complex lags that link nonmaturity deposit rates and balances with open-market rates. Selvaggio (1996), for example, presents an elegant money-demand-based relationship involving complex lags to relate deposit balances to open-market interest rates. In this section, we focus on more straightforward linear relationships to illustrate the van Deventer–Jarrow approach. These relationships can be generalized in a number of ways, although some specifications have no analytical solution and have to be estimated using numerical methods.

Jarrow and van Deventer assume that deposit balances are a linear function of the short rate r in the Vasicek model

$$D = a_0 + a_1 r$$

and the risk-neutral short rate has the same specification as in previous chapters:

$$dr = \alpha(\tilde{\mu} - r)dt + \sigma dz$$

Jarrow and van Deventer also assume that the deposit rate is a linear function of interest rates:

$$i = -b + nr$$

Normally, we would expect b to be positive and n to be between 0 and 1.[9] If b is not positive, banks will lose money on the nonmaturity deposit franchise at low interest rate levels. The implications of this formulation are that the dollar interest expense on nonmaturity deposits will be a quadratic function of the short rate r, a point to which we return later. Multiplying the balance relationship times the rate relationship gives

$$\text{Interest expense} = -a_0 b + (na_0 - a_1 b)r + a_1 nr^2$$

---

9. In practical implementation, we have often found the quantity $-b$ to be positive, suggesting that at least in the short term there is an effective floor on consumer deposit rates.

Jarrow and van Deventer show that the present value cost of the deposit franchise under these assumptions is

$$V = D(0) - \left[a_0 b + a_1(1-n)\alpha\tilde{\mu}\right]\int_0^\tau P(t)dt$$

$$- \left[a_0(1-n) + a_1 b - a_1(1-n)\alpha\right](1 - P(\tau)) - a_1(1-n)\left[r - f(\tau)P(\tau)\right]$$

where $D(0)$ is the initial amount of deposits and f and P are the τ-maturity forward rate and zero coupon bond price prevailing at time 0. This valuation formula is easy to apply because it involves only the parameters of the deposit balance and rate formulas and the Vasicek model parameters we have used throughout this book. The formula above assumes that the deposit franchise ends at time τ, but if we let τ reach infinity, we can rewrite the present value of deposit cost as

$$V = H_0 V_0 + H_1 V_1 + H_2 V_2$$

where the quantities V_i represent the value of securities paying r^i on principal of \$1 in perpetuity. These "primitive securities" have values

$$V_0 = \int_0^\infty P(t)dt$$

$$V_1 = 1$$

$$V_2 = r - \alpha + \alpha\tilde{\mu}\int_0^\infty P(t)dt$$

and the weights H_i are

$$H_0 = -a_0 b$$

$$H_1 = D(0) - \left[a_0(1-n) + a_1 b\right]$$

$$H_2 = -a_1(1-n)$$

Since these weights do not depend on r, f, or P, they are independent of the level of interest rates. Accordingly, the hedge of nonmaturity deposits is one of the rare cases where one can use a "buy-and-hold" hedge to manage interest rate exposure as long as one hedges with the primitive securities that pay r^i. The security paying r^0 is a perpetual bond paying $1 forever. The security paying r^1 is a perpetual floating-rate bond, and the security paying r^2 is a "power" bond paying r to the second power.

Example 15.6.1

Exhibit 15–1 shows the valuation of $100 in nonmaturity deposits when interest rates vary from a base-case level of 5 percent. We assume that the interest rate on the deposit is 2 percent plus 0.4 times the level of short-term interest rates (say, Libor). We show changes in the mark-to-market present value cost of deposits for various assumptions about the response of deposit balances to changes in Libor, ranging from a –$4 change for a 1 percent rate increase to a +$4 change for a 1 percent rate increase. As shown below, the valuation of deposits depends dramatically on the response of deposit balances to changes in interest rate levels.

If the response of deposit balances to rates is 0, then the valuation reduces to the simple valuation in Case 15.4.3. In general, a low level of market rates increases the present value cost

E X H I B I T   15–1

Present Value of Cost of Nonmaturity Deposits Using Jarrow–van Deventer Approach for Various Assumptions on Changes in Deposit Balances in Response to Rate Changes

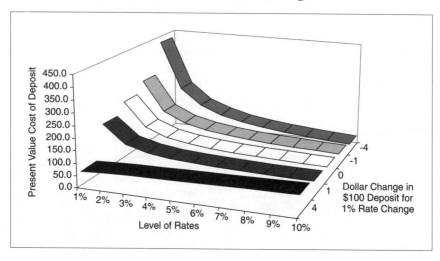

of deposits because of the effective floor on the deposit rate of 2 percent. The duration, or slope of the valuation curve with respect to rates, changes fairly dramatically with the assumption about the responsiveness of deposit balances to changes in rates. For an accurate valuation of nonmaturity deposits, it is essential to take this sensitivity into account.

15.7 USING THE JARROW–VAN DEVENTER FORMULA IN PRACTICE

The use of "implied" parameters in the Jarrow–van Deventer formula is essential for accurate use in practice. There are two reasons for this. The first reason is simply political: logical arguments alone cannot prove the "truth" of deposit pricing formulas.[10] The second reason that implied parameters are essential is that the market's view of the deposit franchise can be based on substantially different expectations about the sensitivity of rate and balance behavior than historical regression analysis would predict for the parameters a_0, a_1, b, and n. Consider Exhibit 15–2, which shows a graph of consumer deposit rates in the United States. There are three distinct pricing regimes: a long period of constant rates at a 5.65 percent level, a nearly one-to-one reduction as Libor fell, and then a very shallow rate of increase in the deposit rate as Libor returned to prior levels. Regression coefficients of the variable n, for example, could range from 0 to 1 depending on what period was used for the regression analysis. Again, only empirical data can properly capture market expectations.

One available set of data is the auction results of deposit franchises by the Resolution Trust Corporation mentioned ear-

---

10. Within almost every banking institution, there are two polarized schools of thought on the present value cost of deposits. The first school of thought says, "Deposits are putable to the bank at par at any time by consumers; therefore, they are worth par and we can only invest deposit proceeds in floating-rate instruments if we want zero interest rate risk." The other school of thought argues, "Deposits at this bank have been X or greater for 20 years, so we have a perpetual liability with principal amount X. Because of its long maturity, we can invest those funds in long-term fixed-rate assets with zero interest rate risk." Only empirical data can resolve this kind of debate.

ABC Bank Savings Rate versus Three-Month Libor

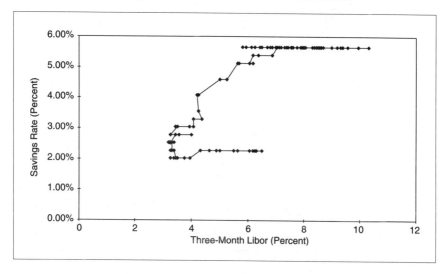

lier in this chapter. Unfortunately, these data are of no value to non-American readers and their increasing age makes them less and less relevant to American banks. Moreover, the task is complicated in that the auctions were typically auctions of a mixed bag of time deposits and various nonmaturity deposit categories; a large number of auctions would have to be analyzed to extract results for separate deposit categories.

Jarrow and Levin (1996) suggest a more practical approach that takes advantage of the techniques in the other chapters of this book. We want to find the assumptions that best reflect the market's view of the present value cost of the deposit franchise. We *need* to know the market's view since historical data show management's behavior has not stayed constant and regression coefficients haven't been stable. The steps in this "back-testing" analysis are as follows:

1. Select the appropriate data set of peer banks for analysis. (Depending on the application of the analysis, this could be made up of one bank, regional peers, or a larger data set.)

2. Exclude any bank whose stock price is clearly distorted by events such as mergers or other significant one-time events (such as the impact of the Procter & Gamble incident on Bankers Trust Company).

3. Select the longest relevant time frame for analysis.

4. Using the techniques elsewhere in this book, mark to market all assets and liabilities except nonmaturity deposits.

5. Calculate the implied market value of nonmaturity deposits as follows:

Implied cost of nonmaturity deposits =

$$\Sigma V_{assets} - \Sigma V_{other\ liabilities} - \text{Stock price(number of shares)}$$

In making this calculation, we have found it very effective to use the loan loss reserve as a proxy for losses embedded in the loan portfolio.

6. Using nonlinear regression analysis, solve for the coefficients a_0, a_1, b, and n that best fit the historical data.

In using this method, we have reached a number of conclusions:

1. In general, it has been a very, very effective means of basing nonmaturity deposit interest rate risk calculations on market reality rather than arbitrary assumptions.

2. Market estimates of deposit interest rate relationships implicitly assume that banks will "bid up" direct and indirect deposit costs if the spread between deposit costs and open-market rates gets too wide. Typically, the implied values of the parameter n are much closer to 1 than simple regression analysis would indicate.

3. Bankers who argue that the market isn't right on average clearly have never done the analysis we recommend.

The second conclusion is an important one that is consistent both with the authors' experience in setting bank retail deposit rates and marketing strategies and with simple logic. Banks add branches, improve staff, and advertise more when the spread on retail deposits is very wide. The market knows this, even though it's not reflected in simple regressions of deposit rates on open-market rates. This result means that the school of thought that argues deposits have present value costs closer to par is usually closer to being right than the school that argues deposits are a long-maturity perpetuity.

There are a number of refinements that can be made to this analysis. Perhaps the most important is to recognize that banks have the option to withdraw from the retail deposit-gathering business, which Bankers Trust did in the 1970s. This option keeps the market value loss on nonmaturity deposits in extremely low-rate environments from getting too large.

E X E R C I S E S

Assume in what follows that α is 0.08, the long-run expected value of the risk-neutral interest rate is 0.12, that the value of a security that pays $1 continuously forever is $10, and that the short rate r is 6 percent. Use the Jarrow–van Deventer deposit pricing formula to answer the following questions.

15.1 The supersaver nonmaturity deposit product has a current balance of $100. The rate on the deposit category follows the formula Rate = 2% + 0.4 Fed funds rate.[11] Deposit balances are intermediated when rates rise, according to the formula for deposit balances D = 112 – 2 Fed funds rate. What is the current rate on the supersaver account? Is the historical regression analysis on deposit balances consistent with the current account balance? If not, change the regression analysis (known in the scientific community as applying a "fudge factor") so that there is consistency.

15.2 What is the present value cost of this deposit product?

---

11. For simplicity, ignore any adjustment for actual/360-day interest.

15.3 What is the present value of profits on this deposit product?

15.4 Write down the formula for the rDelta of the Jarrow–van Deventer valuation formula.

15.5 What is the amount of each of three primitive securities (a consol paying $1 forever, a floater paying r forever, and a power bond paying r^2) necessary for a buy-and-hold hedge of the present value cost of the account?

15.6 How would your answers to Exercises 15.2 and 15.3 change if the coefficients measured on the deposit rate relationship were incorrect? Do a sensitivity analysis on the coefficient of 0.4, incremented from 0 to 1 by movements of 0.1.

15.7 As a practical banker, what would you do if you were uncertain whether the value of 0.4 were accurate or not? Recently your predecessor couldn't answer the question and got fired for doing nothing. Assume, therefore, that "Do nothing" is not the option you'd choose.

REFERENCES

Adams, Kenneth J., and Donald R. van Deventer. "Fitting Yield Curves and Forward Rate Curves with Maximum Smoothness." *Journal of Fixed Income*, June 1994, pp. 52–61.

Cox, John C.; Jonathan E. Ingersoll, Jr.; and Stephen A. Ross. "An Analysis of Variable Rate Loan Contracts." *Journal of Finance*, May 1980, pp. 389–403.

———. "A Theory of the Term Structure of Interest Rates." *Econometrica*, March 1985, pp. 385–407.

Federal Reserve System. *Risk-Based Capital Standards: Interest Rate Risk*. Notice of Proposed Rulemaking. Washington, D.C.: Federal Reserve Board, September 14, 1993.

Heath, David; Robert Jarrow; and Andrew Morton. "Bond Pricing and the Term Structure of Interest Rates: A Discrete Time Approach." *Journal of Financial and Quantitative Analysis*, December 1990, pp. 419–40.

Hull, John, and Alan White. "Pricing Interest Rate Derivative Securities." *Review of Financial Studies*, Winter 1990, pp. 573–92.

———. "One-Factor Interest-Rate Models and the Valuation of Interest-Rate Derivative Securities." *Journal of Financial and Quantitative Analysis* 28 (June 1993), pp. 235–54.

Hutchinson, D., and G. Pennacchi. "Measuring Rents and Interest Rate Risk in Imperfect Financial Markets: The Case of Retail Bank Deposits." Unpublished manuscript, University of Illinois, 1994.

Jamshidian, Farshid. "An Exact Bond Option Formula." *Journal of Finance,* March 1989, pp. 205–9.

Jarrow, Robert A., and Jonathan W. Levin. "The Pricing of Non-Maturity Deposits." *American Banker,* March 8, 1996.

Jarrow, Robert A., and Donald R. van Deventer. "The Arbitrage-Free Valuation and Hedging of Demand Deposits and Credit Card Loans." Kamakura Corporation working paper, 1996a.

———. "Power Swaps: Disease or Cure?" *Risk,* February 1996b.

Macaulay, Frederick R. *Some Theoretical Problems Suggested by Movements of Interest Rates, Bond Yields, and Stock Prices in the United States since 1856.* New York: Columbia University Press, 1938.

McCulloch, J. Huston. "The Tax Adjusted Yield Curve." *Journal of Finance* 30 (June 1975), pp. 811–29.

Marcus, Alan J., and Israel Shaked. "The Valuation of FDIC Deposit Insurance Using Option-Pricing Estimates." *Journal of Money, Credit, and Banking* 16 (September 1984), pp. 446–60.

Merton, Robert C. "Theory of Rational Option Pricing." *Bell Journal of Economics and Management Science* 4 (Spring 1973), pp. 141–83.

———. "On the Pricing of Corporate Debt: The Risk Structure of Interest Rates." *Journal of Finance,* May 1974, pp. 449–70.

———. "An Analytic Derivation of the Cost of Deposit Insurance and Loan Guarantees: An Application of Modern Option Pricing Theory." *Journal of Banking and Finance,* June 1977, pp. 3–11.

———. "On the Cost of Deposit Insurance When There Are Surveillance Costs." *Journal of Business,* July 1978, pp. 439–52.

Modigliani, F., and M. H. Miller. "The Cost of Capital, Corporation Finance, and the Theory of Investment." *American Economic Review,* June 1958, pp. 261–97.

Pennacchi, George G. "Alternative Forms of Deposit Insurance: Pricing and Bank Incentive Issues." *Journal of Banking and Finance* 11 (June 1987a), pp. 291–312.

———. "A Reexamination of the Over- (or Under-) Pricing of Deposit Insurance." *Journal of Money, Credit, and Banking* 19 (August 1987b), pp. 341–60.

Selvaggio, Robert D. "Using the OAS Methodology to Value and Hedge Commercial Bank Retail Demand Deposit Premiums." In *Handbook of Asset and Liability Management,* rev. ed., eds. F. Fabozzi and A. Konishi, 1996.

Shimko, David C. *Finance in Continuous Time: A Primer.* Miami: Kolb, 1992.

Vasicek, Oldrich A. "An Equilibrium Characterization of the Term Structure." *Journal of Financial Economics* 5 (November 1977), pp. 177–88.

APPENDIX
_____

Derivation of Valuation Formulas in Section 15.5

Case 15.5.1: The Change in Deposit Cash Outflows Is Normally Distributed

The change in deposit cash outflows is X. We assume that X is a random walk, which means that changes in X are normally distributed. The changes in X are given by the formula

$$dX = \alpha dt + \sigma dz$$

The change in the value of deposits V is given by Ito's lemma (see Shimko, 1992, for an explanation of Ito's lemma):

$$dV = V_X dX + \frac{1}{2} V_{XX} (dX)^2 + V_t$$

$$= V_X [\alpha dt + \sigma dz] + \frac{1}{2} V_{XX} \sigma^2 dt + V_t$$

$$= \left[\alpha V_X + \frac{1}{2} V_{XX} \sigma^2 \right] dt + V_X \sigma dz + V_t$$

Since the deposits have no maturity and no time-based coefficients, the derivative with respect to time t is 0. Since investors are assumed to be risk neutral, we can analyze the value on the basis of its expected "capital gain," noting that $E[dz] = 0$, plus its cash flow X, the change in deposits. The expected return must be equal to an equivalent amount of money invested at the short rate r to avoid arbitrage.

$$rV = \alpha V_X + \frac{1}{2} V_{XX} \sigma^2 + X$$

We must solve this equation for X. Guess $V = AX + B$. In that case, the equation becomes

$$rAX + rB = \alpha A + X$$

$$\text{so } A = \frac{1}{r}$$

$$B = \frac{\alpha A}{r} = \frac{\alpha}{r^2}$$

When X and α are both 0, the value of the deposit franchise should be 0, and it is under this valuation formula.

Case 15.5.2: Net Deposit Cash Outflows Change Randomly around a Long-Run Mean Level

In this case, we allow the change in deposit cash outflows, X, to be described by one of three common assumptions that allow for X to move around a long-run mean μ:

$$dX = k(\mu - X)dt + \sigma dz$$

$$dX = k(\mu - X)dt + \sqrt{X}\sigma dz$$

$$dX = k(\mu - X)dt + X\sigma dz$$

The movement in the value of deposits is described by Ito's lemma:

$$dV = V_X dX + \frac{1}{2}V_{XX}(dX)^2 + V_t$$

By assumption, the cash outflow on the deposit is X. The expected capital gain on the value of the deposit is

$$E(dV) = V_X k(\mu - X) + \frac{1}{2}V_{XX}(dX)^2$$

where $(dX)^2$ depends on which of the three processes we have selected for X. We note that V_t is 0 due to the perpetual nature of the claim and the fact that we have assumed constant coefficients for the process that describes movements in X. The solution for V comes from the partial differential equation, which requires that the total return on V must equal the riskless rate times V:

$$V_X k(\mu - X) + \frac{1}{2}V_{XX}(dX)^2 + X = rV$$

We guess that the solution is of the form

$$V = AX + B\mu$$

In that case, the partial differential equation reduces to

$$Ak(\mu - X) + X = rAX + rB\mu$$

Solving for A and B gives

$$A = \frac{1}{r + k}$$

$$B = \frac{k}{r(r + k)}$$

Rearranging allows us to express V as

$$V = \frac{rX + k\mu}{r(r + k)}$$

When X and μ are both 0, the present value cost of the deposit franchise should be and is 0.

Case 15.5.3: The Percentage Change in Deposits Is Normally Distributed

The change in deposit levels is assumed to be

$$\frac{dD}{D} = \alpha dt + \sigma dz$$

The change in the value of deposits is given again by Ito's lemma:

$$dV = V_D dD + \frac{1}{2}V_{DD}\sigma^2 D^2 + V_t$$

The expected value of the change in value is

$$E(dV) = V_D \alpha D + \frac{1}{2}V_{DD}\sigma^2 D^2$$

The expected net cash flow is the interest cost of deposits and processing cost of deposits less the expected change in deposit balances:

$$E[\text{Cash flow}] = (y + c)D - \alpha D$$

To avoid arbitrage, the expected total cost of the deposits (interest and processing costs less deposit inflows) must be equal to the risk-free rate r times the value of deposits:

$$V_D \alpha D + \frac{1}{2} V_{DD} \sigma^2 D^2 - \alpha D + (y + c)D = rV$$

We guess a solution of the form $V = AD$. The equation above then becomes

$$\alpha AD + (y + c - \alpha)D = rAD$$

Solving this for A leads to the solution for deposit value

$$V = \frac{(y + c - \alpha)D}{r - \alpha}$$

When the deposit balance D is 0, the present value cost of deposits should be and is 0 under this valuation formula.

Case 15.5.4: The Level of Deposits Changes Randomly around a Long-Run Mean Level

The change in deposits is given by

$$dD = k(\mu - D)dt + \sigma dz$$

As in Case 15.5.2, we could have selected a number of other alternatives that allow the variation of deposits to be a function of the level of deposits. Two alternatives are

$$dD = k(\mu - D)dt + \sqrt{D}\sigma dz$$

$$dD = k(\mu - D)dt + D\sigma dz$$

These alternative formulations lead to the same solution. The expected cash cost of deposits is composed of interest and processing costs less the expected change in deposit balances:

$$E[\text{Cash flow}] = (y + c)D - k(\mu - D)$$

Adding this to the expected change in deposit value V leads to the valuation equation that constrains the total cost of deposits to equal the risk-free rate times V:

$$V_D k(\mu - D) + \frac{1}{2}V_{DD}(dD)^2 - k(\mu - D) + (y + c)D = rV$$

We guess a solution of the form

$$V = AD + B\mu$$

Substituting this expression and the derivatives $V_D = A$ and $V_{DD} = 0$ and solving for A and B leads to the valuation formula for V:

$$V = \frac{k}{r}\left[\frac{(y + c) - r}{r + k}\right]\mu + \left[\frac{k + y + c}{r + k}\right]D$$

When μ and D are 0, V is 0, as it should be.

CHAPTER 16

The Valuation of Risky Debt

16.1 INTRODUCTION TO THE VALUE OF RISKY DEBT

All of the analysis in this book up until this chapter has explicitly or implicitly assumed that the term structure of interest rates was a risk-free term structure. In Chapter 6, the derivation of the value of options on zero coupon and coupon-bearing bonds was based on the assumption that the underlying bond is riskless and the writer of the option is a risk-free entity. In this chapter, we begin to relax these assumptions. The valuation of risky debt lies at the heart of the theory of finance. As of this writing, the valuation of risky debt and its implications for the pricing of derivatives on risky debt or derivatives traded by risky entities is still in its early days. We expect that, in the second edition of this book, this chapter will undergo the most revision!

Models of risky debt fall into two categories. The first, pioneered by Merton (1974), looks through the risky debt issue to the underlying assets of the firm as a stochastic variable. The second class of models takes either the credit spread itself or the firm's debt ratings as a stochastic variable. This chapter concentrates on the former approach, but we believe that the second approach offers considerable promise as a practical risk management tool.

While the material in this chapter may be new to many market participants, more than 50 banks are now using these and related techniques, including most of the largest banks in the United States and the principal European countries. We expect that the number of financial institutions devoting considerable resources to these techniques will dramatically increase in the future.

16.2 THE MERTON MODEL OF RISKY DEBT

Merton's (1974) model of risky debt was one of the first powerful implications to stem from the Black-Scholes options model. We follow Shimko, Tejima, and van Deventer's (1993) exposition in this section. Consider a firm whose assets have a market value currently equal to V. The assets are risky because of interest rate risk, foreign exchange risk, commodity price risk, and other basic business risks. Merton assumes that the firm's assets have a lognormal distribution such that the random percentage changes in the value of the firm's assets are lognormally distributed:

$$\frac{dV}{V} = \alpha dt + \sigma_v dz_1$$

where α and σ_v are the constant drift and the volatility of the asset's value.[1] The lognormal assumption is an attractive one, given that the firm's assets can never have negative value. The constant volatility assumption may be a good one for some asset classes, but it is not consistent with assets such as bonds, whose volatility tends toward zero as the bonds approach maturity. Merton assumes that risk-free interest rates are constant at a level r. (We relax this assumption in Section 16.3.) Merton assumes that the company finances its business with the issue of a single zero coupon bond with principal amount B maturing at time T. Given these assumptions, what should be the pricing on this risky debt? What should be the spread over Treasuries, in U.S. bond trader's parlance?

Merton makes the standard perfect-market assumptions, including the absence of taxes, transactions costs, bankruptcy costs, and so on. He assumes a Modigliani and Miller (1958) environment where the market value of the firm is independent of the firm's capital structure. At time T, it is assumed that the firm's

---

1. Note the change in notation from previous chapters. We make the change for
     consistency with Shimko, Tejima, and van Deventer (1993).

assets can be converted to cash with no transactions costs at their true value. Given these assumptions, if the value of the firm's assets V is greater than B, the bonds will be paid off without a loss. If not, the debt holders will receive the assets of the firm or their cash value. At maturity of the debt, then, the value of the firm's assets is

$$E = \text{Max}[V_T - B, 0]$$

Merton concludes that the equity in the firm is in reality a call option on the assets of the firm with a strike price of B and a maturity of T.

If the assets of the firm are a tradable asset, then we can apply the Black-Scholes options pricing formula directly to calculate the value of the firm's equity:

$$\text{Equity value} = V N(d_1) - B e^{-r\tau} N(d_2)$$

where

$$d_1 = \frac{\ln\left(\dfrac{V}{B}\right) + \left(r + \dfrac{1}{2}\sigma_v^2\right)\tau}{\sigma_v\sqrt{\tau}}$$

$$d_2 = d_1 - \sigma_v\sqrt{\tau}$$

$\tau = T - t$ is the time to maturity on the debt, and $N(z)$ represents the cumulative normal distribution function evaluated at z. The value of the risky debt of the firm, given the Modigliani and Miller assumptions, is

$$D = V - E = V N(h_1) + B e^{-r\tau} N(h_2)$$

where

$$h_1 = \frac{\ln\left(\dfrac{B e^{-r\tau}}{V}\right) - \dfrac{1}{2}\sigma^2\tau}{\sigma\sqrt{\tau}}$$

$$h_2 = -h_1 - \sigma\sqrt{\tau}$$

The yield on risky debt is

$$r_D = -\frac{1}{\tau}\ln\left(\frac{D}{B}\right)$$

The spread on risky debt compared to the risk-free rate of interest is

$$\text{Spread} = r_D - r$$

See Ingersoll (1987) or Uyemura and van Deventer (1992) for more on the Merton approach.

16.3 RISKY DEBT WITH STOCHASTIC INTEREST RATES

Shimko, Tejima, and van Deventer (1993) extend the Merton model to the case of stochastic interest rates. Merton's (1973) model for the pricing of options when interest rates are stochastic is directly relevant to the problem of risky debt valuation. Merton's stochastic interest rate model for option valuation is applicable only to those term structure models where the instantaneous variance of a zero coupon bond's return is independent of the level of interest rates and is nonstochastic. This assumption is consistent with the Vasicek (1977) term structure model; its close relatives described in Chapter 5; and the single-factor Gaussian implementation of the Heath, Jarrow, and Morton (1992) term structure model. At this point, we assume that the short-term risk-free interest rate r is consistent with the Vasicek model and follows the same stochastic process[2] as in Chapters 5–15:

$$dr = k(\gamma - r)dt + \sigma_r dz_2$$

The constant k is the speed of mean reversion, γ is the long-run expected value of the short rate, σ_r is the volatility of the riskless instantaneous interest rate r, and dz_2 represents the stochastic shocks to interest rates from the Wiener process driving interest rates. We assume that the stochastic variables driving movements in both interest rates and the firm's assets are instantaneously correlated and have correlation coefficient ρ:

$$dz_1 dz_2 = \rho dt$$

---

2. Note the change in notation to maintain consistency with Shimko, Tejima, and van
   Deventer (1993).

It is a direct application of Merton's stochastic interest rate options model to find the formula for the value of risky debt $H(r,t,T,B,V)$ when interest rates are stochastic:

$$H(r,t,T,B,V) = VN(-h_1) + BP(\tau)N(h_2)$$

and we use the definitions

$$\delta(s) = -\frac{1 - e^{-ks}}{k}\sigma_r$$

$$v^2(s) = \sigma_v^2 + \delta(s)^2 - 2\rho\sigma_v\delta(s)$$

$$T = \int_0^\tau v(s)^2 ds$$

$$= \tau\left(\sigma_v^2 + \frac{\sigma_r^2}{k^2} + \frac{2\rho\sigma_v\sigma_r}{k}\right) + \left(e^{-k\tau} - 1\right)\left(\frac{2\sigma_r^2}{k^3} + \frac{2\rho\sigma_r\sigma_v}{k^2}\right) - \frac{\sigma_r^2}{2k^3}\left(e^{-2k\tau} - 1\right)$$

and

$$h_1 = \frac{\ln\left(\dfrac{V}{P(\tau)B}\right) + .5T}{\sqrt{T}}$$

$$h_2 = h_1 - \sqrt{T}$$

Using the Shimko, Tejima, and van Deventer (1993) notation, $N(z)$ is the standard cumulative normal distribution function; $\delta(s)^2$ is the instantaneous variance of the Vasicek model risk-free zero coupon bond with maturity s; $v(s)^2$ is the instantaneous variance of the risky debt function H; and T is the integrated instantaneous variance of the risky debt function H over the life of the risky bond consistent with Merton's (1973) options model, which shows the need to incorporate the integrated time-dependent variance in a formula strongly resembling the Black-Scholes formulation. Shimko, Tejima, and van Deventer show how this solution can be obtained by solving a stochastic partial differential equation with two random variables (V and r) for H subject to the boundary condition that the debt at maturity is equal to the minimum of par value or the value of the firm's assets V.

This formula contains an important number of implications for practical financial management, which we cover briefly in the next section and in more detail in later chapters.

16.4 IMPLICATIONS OF THE VALUATION OF RISKY DEBT

Shimko, Tejima, and van Deventer (1993) explore a number of implications of this basic valuation formula for risky debt. The first important implication stems from the correlation between "credit risk" (as measured by the market value of the assets being financed) and interest rate risk.

Is "Matched Maturity" Funding the Best Strategy?

When this correlation is nonzero, the zero-risk funding strategy for this asset is impacted by the degree of correlation and will not simply be the "matching maturity" associated with the underlying assets. If we define the zero interest rate risk funding strategy to be the one that eliminates any interest rate volatility from equity returns, we can solve for the combination of face value of debt B and maturity T such that the sensitivity of both the underlying asset value and the debt financing the asset are equal. Shimko, Tejima, and van Deventer show that this occurs for the maturity T such that

$$B = \frac{[1 - N(h_1)]\sigma_v \rho k V}{P \sigma_r N(h_2)(1 - e^{-k\tau})}$$

Impact of Correlation between Interest Rate Risk and Asset Values

Another implication is the strong spread and valuation impact of the correlation between interest rate risk and asset values. Credit spread is dramatically affected by the level of correlation. We work from a base case that assumes the following standard parameter values:

$$k = 0.1$$

$$\sigma_r = 0.015$$

$$\gamma = 0.11$$

$$\text{Market price of risk} = 0.01$$

$$V = 100$$

$$\sigma_v = 0.1$$

$$\rho = 0$$

In analyzing relative spread movements, we assume that the assets, which are worth 100, will always be financed by risky debt with a market value of 90. This means, of course, that the face value of the debt B will be adjusted upward by maturity to assure that we are making this apples-to-apples comparison.

When we shift the correlation of rates and asset values between −1 and 1, a dramatic variation in credit spreads results, as shown in Exhibit 16–1. If nothing else, the graph in this exhibit

E X H I B I T   16–1

Impact of Interest Rate and Asset Value Correlation on Credit Spread on Risky Debt

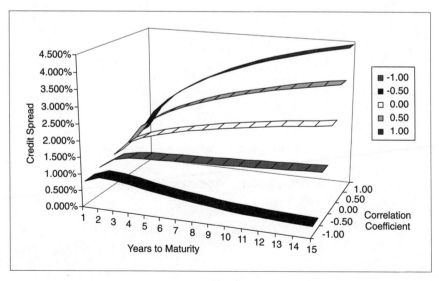

should serve to alert financial market participants to the critical importance of incorporating correlation in fixed-income security pricing. When pricing mortgages, the correlation of home prices with the level of interest rates should be one of the most important determinants of the right spread over U.S. Treasuries of a callable home mortgage loan.

Impact of Asset Volatility on Credit Spreads

Most large banks and insurance companies long ago insured that the "loan-to-value" ratio is a standard component in their loan-pricing formulas. Increasingly, it is the volatility of the underlying asset that is getting the attention of lenders worldwide. Exhibit 16–2 shows that asset volatility is one of the major drivers of credit spreads, as one would expect. With historical data on home price volatility, for example, the formula on p. 315 provides guidance on the size of spread needed over the matching-maturity risk-free rate needed at any loan-to-value ratio.

E X H I B I T   16–2

Impact of Underlying Asset Value Volatility on Credit Spread on Risky Debt

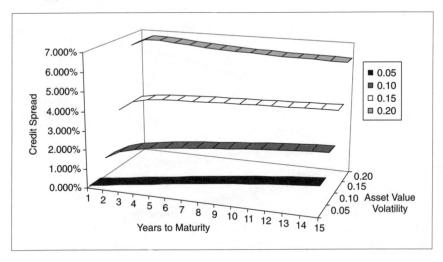

16.5 OTHER APPROACHES TO THE VALUATION OF RISKY DEBT

Longstaff and Schwartz (1995) extend the approach of Shimko, Tejima, and van Deventer (1993) to allow for the valuation of risky coupon debt on the assumption that the firm avoids financial distress as long as asset values remain above a critical level K. The authors also present a complete survey of recent work, most of it unpublished, on risky debt. Jarrow and Turnbull (1995) price a wide array of securities on the assumption that a risk-free term structure and a risky term structure are observable. Securities valued include options on risky debt, vulnerable options, and equity derivatives. The future promises dramatic developments in credit risk analysis with great implications for financial institutions worldwide.

EXERCISES

For the following exercises, use the assumed base-case parameter assumptions. Use common spreadsheet software to get the solutions.

16.1 Holding the principal amount B constant, how do spreads over the risk-free matching-maturity yield change as maturities lengthen in annual increments from 1 year to 10 years?

16.2 Redo the calculation in Exercise 16.1, holding the market value of the risky debt issued at each maturity equal to 90 by changing B to a different value at each maturity. (Use the "solver" capability, available in most spreadsheet packages, to do this.)

16.3 How do the results in Exercise 16.2 change if you change the loan-to-value ratio to 95 percent and 85 percent instead of 90 percent?

16.4 How do credit spreads change as interest rates (i.e., the short rate r) change? Why?

16.5 Calculate the Greeks for risky debt: first derivatives with respect to r (rDelta), V (VDelta), the volatility of the risk-free rate (rVega), the volatility of asset value (VVega), and the correlation of rates and value (ρ in its true meaning, not the Black-Scholes Greek incarnation).

16.6 Can you hedge risky debt with a position in V and riskless bonds? What is the formula for the appropriate hedge ratios?

16.7 The risky debt formula is a two-random-factor term structure model (r and V). What are other choices for the two factors to drive a two-factor term structure model? In your opinion, which of the choices are best suited to the credit risk problem? Why?

REFERENCES

Cox, John C.; Jonathan E. Ingersoll, Jr.; and Stephen A. Ross. "A Theory of the Term Structure of Interest Rates." *Econometrica* 53 (March 1985), pp. 385–407.

Dothan, L. Uri. "On the Term Structure of Interest Rates." *Journal of Financial Economics* 6 (March 1978), pp. 59–69.

Heath, D.; R. Jarrow; and A. Morton. "Bond Pricing and the Term Structure of Interest Rates: A New Methodology for Contingent Claims Valuation." *Econometrica* 60 (1992), pp. 77–105.

Ingersoll, Jonathan. *Theory of Modern Financial Decision Making.* New York: Rowman & Littlefield, 1987.

Jarrow, Robert A., and Stuart M. Turnbull. "Pricing Derivatives on Financial Securities Subject to Credit Risk." *Journal of Finance* (March 1995), pp. 53–85.

Longstaff, Francis A., and Eduardo S. Schwartz. "A Simple Approach to Valuing Risky Fixed and Floating Rate Debt." *Journal of Finance* (July 1995), pp. 789–819.

Merton, Robert C. "Theory of Rational Option Pricing." *Bell Journal of Economics and Management Science* 4 (Spring 1973), pp. 141–83.

———. "On the Pricing of Corporate Debt: The Risk Structure of Interest Rates." *Journal of Finance* 29 (May 1974), pp. 449–70.

———. "An Analytic Derivation of the Cost of Deposit Insurance and Loan Guarantees: An Application of Modern Option Pricing Theory." *Journal of Banking and Finance* 1 (June 1977), pp. 3–11.

———. "On the Cost of Deposit Insurance When There Are Surveillance Costs." *Journal of Business* 51 (July 1978), pp. 439–52.

———. *Continuous Time Finance.* Cambridge, MA: Basil Blackwell, 1990.

Shimko, David C. "The Equilibrium Valuation of Risky Discrete Cash Flows in Continuous Time." *Journal of Finance*, (December 1989), pp. 1373–83.

Shimko, David C.; Naohiko Tejima; and Donald R. van Deventer. "The Pricing of Risky Debt When Interest Rates Are Stochastic." *Journal of Fixed Income* (September 1993), pp. 58–66.

Uyemura, Dennis G., and Donald R. van Deventer. *Financial Risk Management in Banking*. Chicago: Probus, 1992.

van Deventer, Donald R. "Overcoming Inadequacy." *Balance Sheet* (Summer 1993).

Vasicek, Oldrich A. "An Equilibrium Characterization of the Term Structure." *Journal of Financial Economics* 5 (November 1977), pp. 177–88.

CHAPTER 17

Foreign Exchange Markets: A Term Structure Model Approach

17.1 INTRODUCTION TO FOREIGN EXCHANGE FORWARDS AND OPTIONS

The term structure model approach that we have taken in earlier chapters provides a sound foundation from which to approach foreign-currency-denominated securities and derivatives. The variety of foreign exchange (FX)–related securities is great, but we limit ourselves to an introductory view of the term structure model approach's implications for FX analysis. In this chapter, we concentrate solely on foreign exchange forward contracts and European options on the spot foreign exchange rate. Foreign exchange futures contracts and options on FX futures involve a combination of the techniques in this chapter and those in Chapters 6 and 7, but we leave such analysis as advanced exercises for interested readers.

We assume that the domestic market is country 1 and the foreign market is country 2. The spot rate of foreign exchange S represents the cost in country 1 currency of one unit of country 2 currency. In countries 1 and 2, we assume that the domestic bond markets behave according to the Vasicek model, and that short rates move in accordance with the mean-reverting stochastic process of that model:

$$dr_i = \alpha_i[\mu_i - r_i]dt + \sigma_i dz_i$$

Note the addition of a subscript to denote each country. In the foreign exchange market, the spot rate of foreign exchange follows a stochastic process such that the spot rate is lognormal with a drift term that can depend on other economic variables:

$$\frac{dS}{S} = \mu_s(r_1, r_2, t)dt + \sigma_s dz_s$$

The volatility of the spot foreign exchange process is assumed to be a constant. We denote the foreign exchange process parameters by the subscript s. We further assume that the random shocks to domestic interest rates, foreign interest rates, and the spot foreign exchange rate are instantaneously correlated in accordance with the following correlation coefficients:

$$(dr_1 dr_2) = \rho_{12}\sigma_1\sigma_2$$

$$(dr_1 dS) = \rho_{1s}\sigma_1\sigma_s S$$

$$(dr_2 dS) = \rho_{2s}\sigma_2\sigma_s S$$

This sets the analytical stage for looking at foreign exchange futures and options.

17.2 FOREIGN EXCHANGE FORWARDS

The pricing of foreign exchange forwards can be set by an arbitrage argument that doesn't rely on any of the assumptions above. Assume that it's time t and the observable forward price of country 2 currency at time T as a function of the spot rate S and interest rates in the two countries is $H(t, T, S, r_1, r_2)$. Let's assume we want to invest, from the perspective of our position in country 1, in country 2 currency for T years and maximize our currency 2 holdings at time T. We define $P_1 = P_1(r_1, t, T)$ as the T maturity country 1 zero coupon bond and $P_2 = P_2(r_2, t, T)$ as the country 2 T maturity zero coupon bond. Assume that country 1 is the United States and country 2 is Japan. S and H both represent the dollar cost of one yen. There are two investment strategies:

STRATEGY 1

1. Borrow P_1 dollars, which will become \$1 at time T.
2. Sell \$1 forward at current time t for yen deliverable at time T, which will generate yen proceeds of $1/H$.

STRATEGY 2

1. Borrow P_1 dollars.
2. At current time t, convert the dollars to P_1/S yen at the spot exchange rate S.
3. Invest $P_1 1/S$ yen in a zero coupon yen bond maturing at time T, resulting in time T yen proceeds of $P_1/(SP_2)$.

To avoid arbitrage, the results of these two strategies must be equal, so the forward rate H must equal

$$H(t,T,S,r_1,r_2) = \frac{SP_2}{P_1}$$

In Section 17.3, we take advantage of this relationship to find the value of a European option on foreign exchange.

17.3 FOREIGN EXCHANGE OPTIONS

Hilliard, Madura, and Tucker (HMT, 1991) assume that bond prices in country 1 and country 2 follow the Vasicek stochastic process and that the spot rate follows a lognormal process with the form given in Section 17.1. Prior to the HMT work, the most popular model of foreign exchange options was the Garman-Kohlhagen (1983) model, a variation on the Black-Scholes model that assumes the interest rates in country 1 and country 2 are constant at levels r_1 and r_2. Garman and Kohlhagen show that the value of a European call option maturing at time T from the perspective of time t to purchase one unit of country 2's currency at a strike price of K is

$$V(t,T,S,r_1,r_2) = Se^{-r_2\tau}N(h) - Ke^{-r_1\tau}N(h - \sigma_s\sqrt{\tau})$$

where

$$\tau = T - t$$

and

$$h = \frac{\ln\left(\dfrac{S}{K}\right) + \tau\left[r_1 - r_2 + \dfrac{\sigma_s^2}{2}\right]}{\sigma_s\sqrt{\tau}}$$

When interest rates change, the volatility used in the option calculation must change to reflect the impact that interest rates in both countries and their instantaneous correlation with the spot rate have on the variance in the price of forward foreign exchange for delivery at time T. HMT show that the value of the call option under the stochastic interest rate case is

$$V(t,T,S,r_1,r_2,K) = P_1(r_1,t,T)[H(t,T,S,r_1,r_2)N(h*) - KN(h* - v_h)]$$

$$= S P_2(r_2,t,T)N(h*) - P_1(r_1,t,T)KN(h* - v_h)$$

where

$$h* = \frac{\ln\left(\dfrac{H(t,T,S,r_1,r_2)}{K}\right) + \dfrac{1}{2}v_h^2}{v_h}$$

and v_h is the standard deviation of the price of the forward foreign exchange rate H at time T from the perspective of time t.

Using our standard notation for the volatility of interest rates in each country as of time T from the perspective of time t

$$v_i^2(t,T) = \frac{\sigma_i^2}{2\alpha_i}\left[1 - e^{-2\alpha_i\tau}\right]$$

and

$$F_i = \frac{1}{\alpha_i}\left[1 - e^{-\alpha_i\tau}\right]$$

allows us to write v_h as in HMT as follows:

$$v_h^2 = \sigma_s^2\tau + M_2 + M_5 + 2(\rho_{s1}\sigma_s M_1 - \rho_{s2}\sigma_s M_4 - \rho_{12}M_3)$$

where HMT use the notation

$$M_1 = \frac{\sigma_1}{\alpha_1}[\tau - F_1]$$

$$M_2 = \frac{\sigma_1^2}{\alpha_1^2}[\tau - 2F_1] + \frac{v_1^2}{\alpha_1^2}$$

$$M_3 = \frac{\sigma_1 \sigma_2}{\alpha_1 \alpha_2}\left[\tau - F_1 - F_2 + \frac{1}{\alpha_1 + \alpha_2}\left(1 - e^{-(\alpha_1 + \alpha_2)\tau}\right)\right]$$

$$M_4 = \frac{\sigma_2}{\alpha_2}\left[\tau - F_2\right]$$

$$M_5 = \frac{\sigma_2^2}{\alpha_2^2}\left[\tau - 2F_2\right] + \frac{v_2^2}{\alpha_2^2}$$

17.4 IMPLICATIONS OF A TERM STRUCTURE MODEL–BASED FX OPTIONS FORMULA

In an environment where the correlation between risk exposures, as popularized by the value-at-risk approach we discuss in later chapters, is a very high priority, the term structure model approach to FX option valuation provides an immense improvement over the constant interest rate–based Garman-Kohlhagen approach, despite the latter's proven usefulness to date. In the term structure model approach:

- Correlation between country 1 interest rates, country 2 interest rates, and the spot rate is explicitly recognized.
- The option valuation can be stress-tested for changes in correlation, with a range of new Greeks, first derivatives with respect to these correlation parameters.
- The formula explicitly recognizes that the volatility of the spot rate at time T, the option exercise date, is directly affected by the volatility of interest rates in the two countries. The more traditional approach ignores this source of volatility.
- Interest rate–related hedges stemming from FX options and forward positions can be done using the rDelta approach, which we discuss in more detail in later chapters, in a way fully consistent with all other fixed-income and interest rate derivative hedging. Hedges using maturities other than the maturity of the FX option can be calculated and put into place. Like its relative the Black-Scholes model, the Garman-Kohlhagen

model's fixed interest rate assumption makes this impossible without some additional (and contradictory) assumptions about the way the world is.

All of these benefits are powerful ones, and they come with no additional cost. The other wings of the trading floor most likely have been using the term structure model approach already, so bringing it to the FX desk is both desirable and probably overdue. The HMT model will bring greater accuracy in both pricing and hedging. Section 17.5 contains the evidence.

17.5 IMPROVED ACCURACY OF THE STOCHASTIC INTEREST RATE FX MODEL

HMT tested a simplified version of the stochastic interest rate model, with the speed of mean reversion α set to 0, on 2,702 European[1] currency options from the PHLX currency options database. The authors tested out-of-sample European call options prices produced by both the stochastic interest rate model and by the constant interest rate Garman-Kohlhagen model and compared theoretical prices to actual prices from September 1987 to April 1989. Even handicapped by the assumption that α is 0, the model's performance was very good, as shown in Exhibit 17–1.

The stochastic interest rate model substantially outperformed the constant interest rate model for every currency, with success rates ranging from 89 percent to 96 percent. Better pricing translates into better hedging, so the model offers substantial benefits in practical use.

17.6 EXTENSIONS OF THE STOCHASTIC INTEREST RATE APPROACH TO FOREIGN CURRENCY–RELATED SECURITIES PRICING

The same basic approach to valuation can be taken to a wide variety of foreign currency–related securities pricing. For practical use, the extension to foreign currency futures and foreign currency futures options is essential to accurately price popular exchange-traded contracts. Since most foreign currency options that are

---

1. HMT report that European currency option trading represented about 6 percent of the volume for American foreign currency options over the same time period.

E X H I B I T   17–1

Comparison of Mean Absolute Pricing Errors
Stochastic Interest Rate and Constant Interest Rate Foreign Exchange
Option Models

Currency	Number of Observations	Percent of Sample in Which Model Forecast Was Most Accurate	
		Constant Rates	Stochastic Rates
Australian dollar	1,149	5.31%	94.69%
British pound	251	8.37%	91.63%
Canadian dollar	173	3.47%	96.53%
Deutsche mark	76	10.53%	89.47%
Japanese yen	83	7.23%	92.77%
Swiss franc	970	5.26%	94.74%

Source: Hilliard, Madura, and Tucker (1991).

exchange traded are American options, numerical methods are
necessary since the interim cash flow (interest payments on
bonds in each country) makes early exercise of American foreign
currency options a possibility. Amin and Jarrow (1991) have used
the Heath, Jarrow, and Morton (1992) framework to price foreign
currency options, again explicitly modeling the correlation between interest rates in the two countries. Both the HMT approach
and the Amin and Jarrow approach seem certain to gain increased
popularity among market participants in the years ahead.

E X E R C I S E S

Assume the following parameters in these exercises:

	Country 1	Country 2
α	0.08	0.2
σ	0.015	0.02
Long-run level of r (μ)	0.09	0.13
Market price of risk	0.01	0.02
ρ_{12}	0.4	
ρ_{1s}	0.2	
ρ_{2s}	−0.5	
σ_s (spot rate)	0.1	

17.1 The currency country 1 price (in domestic "baloneys") for one unit of country 2's currency ("salamis") is 0.5; that is, you get only 0.5 baloneys for each salami. What is the one-year forward baloney–salami exchange rate?

17.2 What is the price of a six-month European call option on the salami exchange rate at a strike price of 0.45?

17.3 How does the option price change if the correlation between country 1 interest rates and the exchange rate changes from 0.2 to 0.7?

17.4 What is the price of a six-month European put option on the salami exchange rate at a strike price of 0.45?

17.5 What Greeks should a sophisticated trader use when hedging his or her portfolio using the constant interest rate model? Write the formula for each Greek for a European call option.

17.6 How many securities are needed to hedge a position in the call option in Exercise 17.2?

17.7 What hedge would you recommend to a trader who is long on the call option in Exercise 17.2 and doesn't want to be? Assume that the easiest hedge (closing out the position) isn't a possibility.

REFERENCES

Amin, Kaushik I., and Robert A. Jarrow. "Pricing Foreign Currency Options Under Stochastic Interest Rates." *Journal of International Money and Finance*, June 1991, pp. 310–29.

Garman, Mark B., and Steven W. Kohlhagen. "Foreign Currency Option Values." *Journal of International Money and Finance*, December 1983, pp. 231–37.

Heath, D.; R. Jarrow; and A. Morton. "Bond Pricing and the Term Structure of Interest Rates: A New Methodology for Contingent Claims Valuation." *Econometrica* 60 (January 1992), pp. 77–105.

Hilliard, Jimmy E.; Jeff Madura; and Alan L. Tucker. "Currency Option Pricing with Stochastic Domestic and Foreign Interest Rates." *Journal of Financial and Quantitative Analysis*, June 1991, pp. 139–51.

Ingersoll, Jonathan. *Theory of Modern Financial Decision Making.* New York: Rowman & Littlefield, 1987.

Merton, Robert C. "Theory of Rational Option Pricing." *Bell Journal of Economics and Management Science* 4 (Spring 1973), pp. 141–83.

Vasicek, Oldrich A. "An Equilibrium Characterization of the Term Structure." *Journal of Financial Economics* 5 (November 1977), pp. 177–88.

CHAPTER 18

Alternative Term Structure Models

18.1 INTRODUCTION TO ALTERNATIVE TERM STRUCTURE MODELS

In Chapter 16, we presented a two-factor term structure model in the guise of a discussion of the valuation of risky debt. The two risky variables were the short rate of interest r, which drives the risk-free yield curve's movements, and the value of the underlying assets being financed. There is a wide variety of alternative term structure models to the basic Vasicek model (and its close relative, the extended Vasicek or Hull and White model) that we have used to illustrate the basic term structure approach to risk management. Each of the alternative models has distinct advantages and disadvantages, which we survey briefly here. The Vasicek family of models has tractability as its greatest strength. The Gaussian nature of interest movements means that a wide range of analytical solutions to the valuation of fixed-income securities and derivatives is available, as we have seen in previous chapters. Its strength is also its weakness: the model allows for negative interest rates, and historical interest rates in almost all major markets show evidence of a dependence on more than one factor. These weaknesses of the model vary in importance, depending on the state of the economy. As this book is being written, the yen Libor rate is near ⅜ of 1 percent. The standard levels of interest volatility we have been using throughout this book have ranged from 0.005 to 0.02, and anything in that range would imply a very high probability of negative rates in the Japanese market. While observable floor prices in yen have a small positive price for a floor at zero, Black's (1995) argument that market participants will use their "option" to hold cash in order to avoid negative interest rates is a persuasive one. In today's yen market, a model that does not allow for negative interest rates has significant attractions.

Similarly, the explanatory power of a one-factor model varies with the economy. We show in Chapter 19 that the one-factor extended Vasicek model has a very good ability to explain 54 simultaneous U.S.-dollar swaption prices at a wide variety of strike prices and maturities. Similarly, except for the low level of yen rates, yen yield curve movements have been very well-behaved over a long period of time, and a single-factor model has great power to model historical movements. Canadian and Australian experience, however, has featured complex yield curve movements where two or more factors would add realism to a term structure model.

Section 18.2 reviews alternative one-factor interest rate models, most of which allow avoidance of negative interest rates. Section 18.3 provides an introduction to two-factor models. Section 18.4 briefly reviews the Heath, Jarrow, and Morton approach, and Section 18.5 summarizes the considerations in term structure model selection.

18.2 ALTERNATIVE ONE-FACTOR INTEREST RATE MODELS

The Cox, Ingersoll, and Ross (CIR, 1985) model, which the authors derive in a general equilibrium framework, has been as popular in the academic community as the Vasicek model has been among financial market participants. It is therefore appropriate that we begin our discussion of one-factor model alternatives to the Vasicek model with a review of the CIR approach.

The CIR Model

The Cox, Ingersoll, and Ross (1985) model has been particularly influential because the original version of the paper was in circulation in the academic community at least since 1977, even though the paper wasn't formally published until 1985. CIR assume that the short-term interest rate is the single stochastic factor driving interest rate movements, and that the variance of the short rate of interest is proportional to the level of interest rates. This has the highly desirable property of preventing negative short rates of interest, and it means that interest rate volatility is higher in periods of high interest rates than it is in periods of low interest rates. The realism of this assumption depends on which financial market is being studied, but casual empiricism would lead one to believe that it's a more desirable property when modeling the United States (1978–85), Brazil, or Mexico than it would perhaps be for Swiss financial markets.

The authors assume that stochastic movements in the short rate take the form

$$dr = k(\mu - r)dt + \sigma\sqrt{r}dz$$

Following Ingersoll (1987) and imposing the usual no-arbitrage conditions on the bond market, the partial differential equation defining the pricing of zero coupon bonds can be derived subject to the boundary condition that a zero coupon bond must have a value equal to 1 at maturity. CIR show that the value of a zero coupon bond with maturity $\tau = T - t$ takes the form

$$P(r,\tau) = A(\tau)e^{-B(\tau)r}$$

where

$$A(\tau) = \left[\frac{2\gamma\, e^{(\gamma+\lambda+k)\frac{\tau}{2}}}{g(\tau)}\right]^{\frac{2k\mu}{\sigma^2}}$$

$$B(\tau) = \frac{-2(1 - e^{-\gamma\tau})}{g(\tau)}$$

$$g(\tau) = 2\gamma + (k + \lambda + \gamma)(e^{\gamma\tau} - 1)$$

$$\gamma = \sqrt{(k + \lambda)^2 + 2\sigma^2}$$

The authors also derive an analytical solution for the price of a European call option on a zero coupon bond.

In practical application, the CIR model has met with mixed results in spite of the strong theoretical attractiveness of the no-negative-interest-rates feature of the model. Hull and White (1990) note that the extended version of the model, which would exactly fit an observable yield curve, may not fit some yield curve shapes where instantaneous forward rates turn negative. For the reasons noted by Black (1995), this problem normally can be corrected by using the maximum smoothness forward rate technique of Chapter 2, instead of linear smoothing or cubic spline smoothing, which can frequently result in negative forward rates.

Flesaker (1993) notes a more serious constraint on practical use: the difficulty of estimating parameters for the CIR model because of the existence of many local optimums. We discuss this topic at some length in Chapter 19. Finally, Pearson and Sun (1994) test a two-factor version of the CIR model for nominal interest rates and conclude that the extended CIR model fails to provide a good description of the Treasury market. The empirical work on term structure models in general is still in its early stages, and we feel that the CIR model deserves to remain a strong candidate for practical use pending testing of the extended version of the model in a wide variety of economic environments.

The Dothan Model

Dothan (1978) provides a model of short rate movements where the short riskless rate of interest r follows a geometric Wiener process. The short rate has a lognormal distribution and will therefore always be positive:

$$dr = \sigma r dz$$

The resulting analytical solution for zero coupon bond prices is quite complex. The Dothan model, while sharing one of the attractive properties of the CIR model, lacks the "mean reversion" term

$$k(\mu - r)$$

which has been so important to the success of the CIR and Vasicek models in producing realistic interest rate cycles.

The Longstaff Model

Longstaff (1989) proposes a model in which the variance of the short rate is proportional to the level of the short rate, like the CIR model, and the mean version of the short rate is a function of its square root:

$$dr = k(\mu - \sqrt{r})dt + \sigma\sqrt{r}dz$$

The resulting pricing equation for zero coupon bonds is unique in comparison to other term structure models in that the implied yield to maturity on zero coupon bonds is a nonlinear function of the short rate of interest:

$$P(r,\tau) = A(\tau)e^{B(\tau)r + C(\tau)\sqrt{r}}$$

A, B, and C are complex functions of the term structure model parameters and are described in Longstaff (1989).

In empirical tests, Longstaff concludes that the nonlinearity of yields does bring additional explanatory power to the model but that "the actual pricing of even intermediate term discount bonds may be more complex than can be accommodated within the context of a single-state-variable model."[1]

The Black, Derman, and Toy Model

Black, Derman, and Toy (1990) suggest another model that avoids the problem of negative interest rates and allows for time-dependent parameters. The stochastic process specifies the percentage change in the short-term rate of interest:

$$d[\ln(r)] = [\theta(t) - \phi(t)\ln(r)]dt + \sigma(t)dz$$

The model has many virtues from the perspective of financial market participants. It combines the ability to fit the observable yield curve (like the Ho and Lee and extended Vasicek models) with the nonnegative restriction on interest rates and the ability to model the volatility curve observable in the market. The model's liability is the lack of tractable analytical solutions, which

---

1. Longstaff (1989), p. 222.

are very useful in (*a*) confirming the accuracy of numerical techniques and (*b*) valuing large portfolios where speed is essential.

The Black and Karasinski Model

Black and Karasinski (1991) further refine the Black, Derman, and Toy (1990) approach with the explicit incorporation of time-dependent mean reversion:

$$d[\ln(r)] = \phi(t)\big[\ln[\mu(t)] - \ln(r)\big]dt + \sigma(t)dz$$

This modification allows the model to fit observable cap prices, one of the richest sources of observable market data incorporating interest rate volatility information. The authors describe in detail how to model bond prices and interest derivatives using a lattice approach. The model, like its predecessor, the Black, Derman, and Toy model, is quite popular among financial market participants.

18.3 TWO-FACTOR INTEREST RATE MODELS

As we discuss below, one of the challenges in specifying a two-factor model is selecting which two factors are the most appropriate. Given Chapter 16's focus on credit risk, the two factors of the risky debt term structure model in that chapter were the riskless short rate of interest and the value of the asset being financed. In this section, we review a number of two-factor models that are based on various assumptions about the two risky factors.

The Brennan and Schwartz Model

Brennan and Schwartz (1979) introduced a two-factor model where both a long-term rate and a short-term rate follow a joint Gauss-Markov process. The long-term rate is defined as the yield on a consol (perpetual) bond. Brennan and Schwartz assume that the log of the short rate has the following stochastic process:

$$d[\ln(r)] = \alpha[\ln(l) - \ln(p) - \ln(r)]dt + \sigma_1 dz_1$$

The short rate r moves in response to the level of the consol rate l and a parameter p relating the "target value" of $\ln(r)$ to the level of $\ln(l)$. Brennan and Schwartz show that the stochastic process for the consol rate can be written

$$dl = l[l - r + \sigma_2^2 + \lambda_2\sigma_2]dt + l\sigma_2 dz_2$$

In this expression, λ is the market price of long-term interest rate risk. Longstaff and Schwartz proceed to test the model on Canadian government bond data, with good results.

The Two-Factor CIR Model

Chen and Scott (1992) derive a two-factor model in which the nominal rate of interest i is the sum of two independent variables y_1 and y_2, both of which follow the stochastic process specified by CIR:

$$dy_i = k_i(\theta_i - y_i)dt + \sigma_i\sqrt{y_i}\,dz_i$$

Chen and Scott show that the price of a discount bond in this model is

$$P(y_1,y_2,t,T) = A_1 A_2 e^{-B_1 y_1 - B_2 y_2}$$

where A and B have the same definition as in the CIR model, with the addition of the appropriate subscripts. The authors go on to value a wide range of interest rate derivatives using this model. The end result is a powerful model with highly desirable properties and a wealth of analytical solutions.

The Two-Factor Vasicek Model

Hull and White (1993) show that there is a similar extension for the Vasicek model when the nominal interest rate i is the sum of two factors r_1 and r_2. The value of a zero coupon bond with maturity τ is simply the product of two factors P_1 and P_2, which have exactly the same functional form as the single-factor Vasicek model, except that one is driven by r_1 and the other by r_2:

$$V(r_1,r_2,\tau) = P_1(r_1,\tau)P_2(r_2,\tau)$$

Both stochastic factors are assumed to follow stochastic processes identical to the normal Vasicek model:

$$dr_i = \alpha_i(\mu_i - r_i)dt + \sigma_i dz_i$$

This model, as yet largely unexplored by financial market participants, seems to offer a great deal of potential.

The Longstaff and Schwartz Stochastic Volatility Model

Longstaff and Schwartz (1992) propose a model in which two stochastic factors, assumed to be uncorrelated, drive interest rate movements. The factors x and y are assumed to follow the stochastic processes

$$dx = (\gamma - \delta x)dt + \sqrt{x}dz_1$$

$$dy = (\eta - vy)dt + \sqrt{y}dz_2$$

The authors demonstrate that both the short-term interest rate r and the variance of changes in the short rate V are linear functions of x and y:

$$r = \alpha x + \beta y$$

$$V = \alpha^2 x + \beta^2 y$$

Longstaff and Schwartz derive the value of a discount bond in this economy to be

$$V(x,y,\tau) = E_1(\tau)e^{E_2(\tau)x + E_3(\tau)y}$$

where

$$E_1(\tau) = A^{2\gamma}(\tau)B^{2\eta}(\tau)e^{k\tau}$$
$$E_2(\tau) = (\delta - \phi)[1 - A(\tau)]$$
$$E_3(\tau) = (v - \psi)[1 - B(\tau)]$$

$$A(\tau) = \frac{2\phi}{(\delta + \phi)[e^{\phi\tau} - 1] + 2\phi}$$

$$B(\tau) = \frac{2\psi}{(v + \psi)[e^{\psi\tau} - 1] + 2\psi}$$

$$\phi = \sqrt{2\alpha + \delta^2}$$

$$\psi = \sqrt{2\beta + v^2}$$

$$k = \gamma(\delta + \phi) + \eta(v + \psi)$$

Longstaff and Schwartz describe procedures for valuing interest rate–related derivatives under this framework in great detail.

In short, there is a rich array of choices for financial market participants who require the additional explanatory power of a two-factor model and who are willing to incur the costs, which we discuss below, of such models. Perhaps the richest approach to multifactor risk management, however, is that of Heath, Jarrow, and Morton (1992), to which we now turn.

18.4 THE HEATH, JARROW, AND MORTON APPROACH

Heath, Jarrow, and Morton (1992) take a dramatically different approach to the selection of the stochastic "state variables." Most of the models discussed both in this chapter and in previous chapters focus on the short rate of interest as a state variable. In the case of the two-factor models in the previous section, the selection of what the two variables actually should be is part of the art of practical application. The HJM approach is dramatically different. The current term structure in its entirety, much as Ho and Lee assumed in our discussions in Chapter 5, is the state variable. We know from Chapters 1 and 2 that the term structure can be described analytically by the entire range of zero coupon bond yields, zero coupon bond prices, or continuous forward rates. HJM focus their analysis on forward rates because of the ease of exposition that results. The single-factor version of the HJM model says that the change in forward rates as of current time t with maturity at time u can be described by a volatility function, a drift function, and one Wiener process supplying shocks to the term structure:

$$f(t + dt, u) - f(t, u) = \sigma(x, y, z)dz + \text{Drift}(x, y, z)dt$$

The variables x, y, and z represent arbitrary arguments in the volatility and drift functions.

Constant Single-Factor Volatility

If the volatility function is a constant, then HJM show that the model reduces to the continuous time limit of the Ho and Lee (extended Merton) model, which we discussed in Chapter 5.

Exponentially Declining Volatility

If the volatility function is chosen such that

$$\sigma(u - t) = \sigma_0 e^{-\alpha(u-t)}$$

then the single-factor version of HJM reduces to the single-factor extended Vasicek model of Hull and White, and the two parameters in the equation above have the same volatility and speed of mean reversion implications as in the extended Vasicek discussion in Chapter 5.

CIR Version of HJM

The Cox, Ingersoll, and Ross (1985) model is shown to be a special case of the HJM approach if the volatility function is a deterministic function g times the square root of spot rate (the forward rate as of time t with maturity t):

$$\sigma(x, y, z) = g(u - t)\sqrt{f(t,t)}$$

Other Volatility Structures

The richness of the HJM approach stems from the fact that a wide variety of other volatility structures can be chosen to more precisely match either historical or observable volatility of the term structure.

Two-Factor HJM Modeling

When there is more than one stochastic factor driving evolution of the term structure, the first equation in this section is written instead

$$f(t + dt, u) - f(t, u)$$

$$= \sigma_1(x, y, z) dz_1 + \sigma_2(x, y, z) dz_2 + \text{Drift}(x, y, z) dt$$

As in the single-factor case, the kind of specifications that can be made are almost limitless.

Most of the time (although there are exceptions) the evolution of the term structure in the HJM model is path-dependent; that is, it depends on the exact history of term structure evolution because in general an upward move in rates followed by a downward move in rates does not lead to the same yield curve as the down-up evolution. This means that the bushy tree or Monte Carlo approaches, which we discussed in Chapter 12, must be used. As HJM point out, though, there are a number of path-independent variations of HJM as well.

The HJM approach is rapidly becoming the standard method for term structure modeling on Wall Street because of the generality of its application, the realism offered by matching yield curve and volatility structures, and the relatively good speed of numerical solutions based on this approach. For a thorough, readable discussion of the implementation of this approach, see Jarrow (1996).

18.5 TERM STRUCTURE MODEL SELECTION

The selection of a term structure model is more than a model choice. Choosing the number of factors and a specific model almost inevitably implies a given degree of accuracy in parameter estimation and restricts the user to a specific numerical technique for security valuation. For example,

- Selecting a two-factor HJM model usually restricts the user to a bushy tree solution of American option valuation and will produce parameters with less individual statistical significance than the parameters in a single-factor model.
- Selecting the Black-Karasinski model means that no analytical solutions are available and that both parameter estimation and hedging will depend on a binomial or trinomial tree.

- Selecting the single-factor extended Vasicek model maximizes speed and the availability of analytical solutions, at some cost in realism of term structure movements.

The choice of a model, then, can't be unbundled from the resulting requirements for parameter estimation and the requisite numerical solutions. *For this reason, it is not necessarily true that more stochastic factors will improve the quality of the valuation and hedging of a particular security. Back-testing and out-of-sample testing are necessary to compare the joint hypothesis of Model A/Parameter Estimation Approach A/Numerical Technique A with Model B/Parameter Estimation Approach B/Numerical Technique B.*

In general, we can make the following observations regarding the practical use of alternative term structure models:

- Models with mean reversion work better in practice than models without mean reversion.
- Numerical techniques produce "deltas" and "gammas" of much lower quality than analytical techniques. The rDeltas that result from numerical techniques have a stair-step nature that can't be avoided except by dramatically increasing the number of time steps used.
- Models with few analytical solutions require more processing time. While they may have theoretical attractions, some of the net "theory benefits" will be offset by the inaccuracy of a user who summarizes transaction data to reduce run time. Net-net, the lower-quality theory applied to each record individually can produce a better answer in many circumstances than higher-quality theory applied to aggregated data. Consider two 5-year caps, one at a 9 percent strike and the other at an 11 percent strike. An analyst who adds them together and uses an average strike of 10 percent to reduce the high-powered term structure model's calculation time will get a much lower-quality answer than one who doesn't.[2]

---

2. Such averaging happens every day in every major bank around the world.

- Reducing the number of time steps when evaluating an American option to improve calculation time results in dramatic errors. A 30-year callable mortgage with 360 possible "call dates" has a much different value than a 30-year mortgage with 20 call dates. A three-factor model using a bushy tree approach with 20 time steps will produce a less accurate answer than a one-factor model assuming 100 time steps.
- Historical parameter estimation produces lower-quality parameter estimates if there are a lot of parameters because of multicolinearity. For example, the Brennan and Schwartz two-factor model, which is based on a long rate and a short rate, is very inaccurate in the yen market in practical use, not because of problems with the theory but because multicolinearity in the regression analysis can render the parameter estimates statistically insignificant.
- Models that contain true economic meaning outperform models that are based on purely historical data with no underlying meaning, all other things being equal. For example, a model that explains term structure movements on the basis of movements in the real rate of interest, inflation, and the value of the underlying risky asset being financed will almost always outperform a model based on changes in the level, slope, and bend in the yield curve.

Which Two Factors?

Focusing on two-factor models with true economic meaning begs the question of which two factors are the most important. A list of possible factors would normally include the following:

- The short real rate of interest.
- The long real rate of interest.
- The instantaneous rate of inflation.
- The long-run expected level of inflation.
- The instantaneous credit spread.

- The long-run expected credit spread.
- The value of the asset being financed.
- The parallel shift in the yield curve.
- The spread between the "short" rate and the "long" rate.

The best choice of factors will depend on the problem at hand, and the proof of which choice is "best" will have to be based on more than logic alone.

As market participants ourselves, the authors believe that a competition between two alternative joint choices of models/parameters/numerical techniques can only be resolved by extensive historical and out-of-sample testing of hedging accuracy, since almost all models can fit observable data well.

EXERCISES

For purposes of Exercises 18.1–18.4, assume the Cox, Ingersoll, and Ross term structure model parameters are as follows:

$$\text{mu } (\mu) = 0.12$$

$$\text{kappa } (k) = 0.08$$

$$\text{sigma } (\sigma) = 0.015$$

$$\text{lambda } (\lambda) = 0.01$$

18.1 What is the price of zero coupon bonds with maturities of 1, 2, and 3 years in the CIR model?

18.2 How different are these prices from the prices that would prevail in the Vasicek model if all of the parameters had the same values?

18.3 What is the rDelta in the CIR model?

18.4 Assume you own two-year zero coupon bonds with a face amount of $100. You are concerned about "model risk," so you want to hedge your exposure with a hedge that involves equal market values of the one-year zero coupon bond and the three-year zero coupon bond (assume that there is no liquidity in the two-year maturity). Using the CIR model, what should the proper hedge amount be in the one-year and three-year bonds to eliminate the interest rate risk of your position?

For purposes of Exercises 18.5–18.10, assume that the two-factor Vasicek model applies. We assume that risk factor 1 is the riskless rate of interest and that risk factor 2 is the credit spread on bonds issued by the major New Jersey investment banking firm Golden, Spats & Co. We assume parameter values for risk factor 1 are as follows:

$$\text{mu } (\mu) = 0.09$$

$$\text{kappa } (k) = 0.1$$

$$\text{sigma } (\sigma) = 0.015$$

$$\text{lambda } (\lambda) = 0.01$$

We assume the parameters for risk factor 2, the credit spread,[3] are as follows

$$\text{mu } (\mu) = 0.02$$

$$\text{kappa } (k) = 0.05$$

$$\text{sigma } (\sigma) = 0.002$$

$$\text{lambda } (\lambda) = 0.001$$

18.5 What would zero coupon bond prices be for Golden, Spats at 1 year and 1.5 years?

18.6 What would be the price of a one-year forward contract on an 18-month GS&Co. zero coupon bond?

18.7 What are the *r*Deltas in this specification of a two-factor Vasicek model for (*a*) the riskless rate of interest and (*b*) the credit spread?

18.8 Assume that GS&Co. has issued you, Metropolis Life Insurance Company, $100 principal amount of the one-year forward on the 18-month GS&Co. zero coupon bond at an exercise price of $90. You can hedge this position only with a one-year maturity bond and a two-year maturity bond, the only

---

3. These parameter estimates are hypothetical and are not based on actual data.

maturities where there is liquidity in GS&Co. zero coupon bonds. How much of each bond should you use to hedge?

18.9 What concerns would you have in using this specification of a risky debt model?

18.10 (Advanced.) Assume the model as specified exactly matches the observable GS&Co. zero coupon bond prices for 1 year, 5 years, and 10 years. Fit the risky debt model of Chapter 16 to these observable prices by assuming the parameters for the risk-free yield curve are correct and solving for the underlying asset value, asset volatility, and correlation that result in exactly matching zero prices using common spreadsheet software.

18.11 How would you solve the problem in Exercise 18.8 using this specification of the model? What are your answers?

REFERENCES

Black, Fischer. "Interest Rates as Options." *Journal of Finance,* December 1995, pp. 1371–77.

Black, Fischer; E. Derman; and W. Toy. "A One-Factor Model of Interest Rates and Its Application to Treasury Bond Options." *Financial Analysts Journal,* Spring 1990, pp. 33–39.

Black, Fischer, and Piotr Karasinski. "Bond and Option Pricing when Short Rates Are Lognormal." *Financial Analysts Journal,* July-August 1991, pp. 52–59.

Brennan, Michael J., and Eduardo Schwartz. "A Continuous Time Approach to the Pricing of Bonds." *Journal of Banking and Finance,* July 1979, pp. 133–55.

Chan, K. C.; G. Andrew Karolyi; Francis A. Longstaff; and Anthony B. Sanders. "An Empirical Comparison of Models of the Short Term Interest Rate." *Journal of Finance,* July 1992, pp. 1209–28.

Chen, Ren-Raw, and Louis Scott. "Pricing Interest Rate Options in a Two-Factor Cox-Ingersoll-Ross Model of the Term Structure." *Review of Financial Studies,* Winter 1992, pp. 613–36.

Cox, John C.; Jonathan E. Ingersoll, Jr.; and Stephen A. Ross. "A Theory of the Term Structure of Interest Rates." *Econometrica* 53 (March 1985), pp. 385–407.

Dothan, L. Uri. "On the Term Structure of Interest Rates." *Journal of Financial Economics* 6 (March 1978), pp. 59–69.

Flesaker, Bjorn. "Testing the Heath-Jarrow-Morton/Ho-Lee Model of Interest Rate Contingent Claims Pricing." *Journal of Financial and Quantitative Analysis,* December 1993, pp. 483–96.

Heath, D.; R. Jarrow; and A. Morton. "Bond Pricing and the Term Structure of Interest Rates: A New Methodology for Contingent Claims Valuation." *Econometrica* 60 (January 1992), pp. 77–105.

———. "Easier Done than Said." *Risk,* October 1992.

Ho, Thomas S. Y., and Sang-bin Lee. "Term Structure Movements and Pricing Interest Rate Contingent Claims." *Journal of Finance,* December 1986, pp. 1011–29.

Hull, J., and A. White. "Pricing Interest Rate Derivative Securities." *Review of Financial Studies,* 1990, pp. 573–92.

———. "Efficient Procedures for Valuing European and American Path-Dependent Derivatives." *Journal of Derivatives,* Fall 1993, pp. 21–31.

———. "Numerical Procedures for Implementing Term Structure Models I: Single-Factor Models." *Journal of Derivatives,* Fall 1994a, pp. 7–16.

———. "Numerical Procedures for Implementing Term Structure Models II: Two-Factor Models." *Journal of Derivatives,* Fall 1994b, pp. 37–48.

———. "A Note on the Models of Hull and White for Pricing Options on the Term Structure: Response." *Journal of Fixed Income,* September 1995, pp. 97–102.

Ingersoll, Jonathan. *Theory of Modern Financial Decision Making.* New York: Rowman & Littlefield, 1987.

Jarrow, Robert A. *Modelling Fixed Income Securities and Interest Rate Options.* New York: McGraw-Hill, 1996.

Longstaff, Francis A. "A Nonlinear General Equilibrium Model of the Term Structure of Interest Rates." *Journal of Financial Economics,* August 1989, pp. 195–224.

Longstaff, Francis A., and Eduardo S. Schwartz. "Interest Rate Volatility and the Term Structure: A Two-Factor General Equilibrium Model." *Journal of Finance,* September 1992, pp. 1259–82.

———. "A Two-Factor Interest Rate Model and Contingent Claims Valuation." *Journal of Fixed Income,* December 1992, pp. 16–23.

———. "A Simple Approach to Valuing Risky Fixed and Floating Rate Debt." *Journal of Finance,* July 1995, pp. 789–819.

Merton, Robert C. "Theory of Rational Option Pricing." *Bell Journal of Economics and Management Science* 4 (Spring 1973), pp. 141–83.

———. "On the Pricing of Corporate Debt: The Risk Structure of Interest Rates." *Journal of Finance* 29 (May 1974), pp. 449–70.

Pearson, Neil D., and Tong-sheng Sun. "Exploiting the Conditional Density in Estimating the Term Structure: An Application to the Cox, Ingersoll and Ross Model." *Journal of Finance,* September 1994, pp. 1279–1304.

Shimko, David C.; Naohiko Tejima; and Donald R. van Deventer. "The Pricing of Risky Debt When Interest Rates Are Stochastic." *Journal of Fixed Income,* September 1993, pp. 58–66.

Vasicek, Oldrich A. "An Equilibrium Characterization of the Term Structure." *Journal of Financial Economics* 5 (November 1977), pp. 177–88.

Estimating the Parameters of Term Structure Models

19.1 INTRODUCTION TO THE ESTIMATION OF TERM STRUCTURE MODEL PARAMETERS

Many discussions of the use of term structure models in risk management overlook the very real difficulties of estimating the parameters for use in such models. Market participants have gotten used to the idea of estimating parameters from observable market data thanks to the popularity of the Black-Scholes option pricing model and the accepted market practice of estimating "volatility" for use in the model from market option prices. "Implied volatility" is the value of volatility in the Black-Scholes model that makes the theoretical price equal to the observable market price. The same basic concepts are just as necessary but harder to do in a term structure model context for reasons we explain in this chapter. In this section and Sections 19.2–19.5, we base our comments on a data set that includes 2,320 days of Canadian government bond data provided by a major Canadian financial institution (Exhibit 19–1). The data spanned the time period January 2, 1987, to March 6, 1996. In Section 19.6, we turn to U.S. swaption data provided by one of the leading New York derivatives dealers.

Estimation procedures for term structure models have not progressed as rapidly as the theory of the term structure itself, and leading-edge practice is undergoing rapid change. In the view

Historical Movements in Canadian Government Bond Rates, 1987–1996

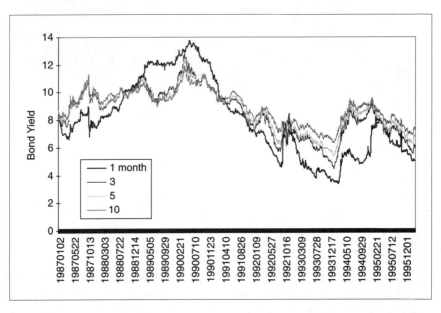

of the authors, there is a hierarchy of approaches of varying quality for determining the appropriate parameters. In this chapter, we follow a number of approaches:

1. *Traditional academic approach*, following theory precisely to estimate the "stochastic process" for the short-term riskless rate of interest, in this case the one-month Canadian government bill yield. This approach is generally not satisfactory in any market, and we found it to be unsatisfactory on Canadian data as well.

2. *Volatility curve approach*, matching parameters to the historical relative volatilities of bond yields at different maturities. This approach worked moderately well.

3. *Advanced volatility curve approach*, in which we used a two-step process to (*a*) fit relative yield changes on all 2,320 days based on the theoretical relationship between the short rate and longer-term yields by regression analysis, and then (*b*) fit term structure model parameters to the regression coefficients.

4. *Single-day yield curve fitting*, which is the yield curve equivalent of "implied volatility" using the Black-Scholes model.

5. *Option-based derivative price fitting*, which the authors feel is the most satisfactory method in markets that have a rich array of option-related derivatives prices.

We discuss each of these methods in turn.

19.2 TRADITIONAL ACADEMIC APPROACH

Almost all single-factor term structure models rest on the assumption that the sole random factor driving interest rates is the short-term rate of interest. They then assume a particular formula for these random movements. In the Vasicek model, this formula is

$$dr = \alpha(\mu - r)dt + \sigma dz$$

where α is the speed of mean reversion, μ is the long-run expected value of the short rate, and σ is interest rate volatility, as explained in previous chapters. The market price of risk, the fixed-income equivalent of the Sharpe ratio, is the fourth parameter in the Vasicek model. The traditional academic approach estimates these parameters by running the regression equation

$$\Delta r = A + Br + \varepsilon$$

using the shortest observable interest rate as a proxy for r (which is an instantaneous interest rate according to the theory). In the Vasicek model, the theoretical parameters can be related to the regression parameters since

$$\alpha = -B$$

and

$$\mu = -\frac{A}{B}$$

For an example of an elegantly done analysis of a number of theoretical models' parameters, see Chan, Karolyi, Longstaff, and Sanders (1992). This study, while carefully done, suffers from the typical outcome of such studies: In no case does the assumed stochastic process explain more than 3 percent of the variation in the short-term rate of interest. We find the same problem when

Change in One-Month Rate Canadian T-Bill Rate versus Level of
One-Month Rate, 1987–1996

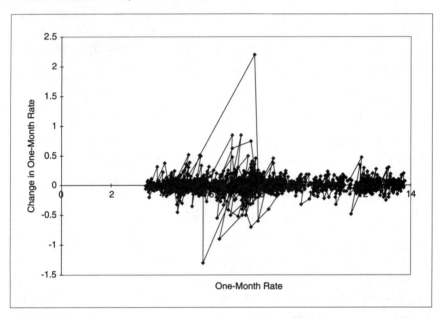

running the above regression on 2,320 days of data using the one-
month Canadian bill rate as the short rate proxy. The regression
equation has literally zero explanatory power (an R^2 of 0.0007)
and neither A nor B is statistically significant. Therefore, we conclude that this approach is not useful in the Canadian market. The
scatter diagram in Exhibit 19–2 informally confirms the lack of
correlation between the level of interest rates and the change in
the level of the short rate. The Vasicek model would have led one
to expect a negative correlation, since α is a positive number.

   In almost all major markets, this approach leads to similar
results. The short rate is often the control mechanism for monetary policy and thus reflects a much more complex set of variables than one equation can capture.

19.3 VOLATILITY CURVE APPROACH

Many market participants use parameter estimates that are consistent with the historical relative degree of volatility of longer-
term "yields" in relationship to the short rate. Under the Vasicek

and extended Vasicek models, the volatility of zero coupon bond yields is

$$\text{Var}[y(\tau)] = f(\tau)^2 \sigma^2$$

where

$$f(\tau) = \frac{1 - e^{-\alpha\tau}}{\alpha\tau}$$

since zero coupon yields in both versions of the model can be written as linear functions of the short rate r:

$$y(\tau) = f(\tau)r + g(\tau)$$

Therefore, market participants calculate observable variances for bond yields[1] and then choose values of σ and α that best fit historical "volatility." The authors' findings for the Canadian government bond market were based on the use of par bond coupon rates as proxies for zero coupon bond yields. The results of this analysis are summarized in Exhibit 19–3.

The best-fitting α value was 0.305. This is a fairly large speed of mean reversion and reflects the relatively large variation in short-term Canadian rates, relative to long rates, over the sample period. Interest rate volatility was also high at 0.0285. At the current low levels of Canadian interest rates, this volatility level would clearly be too high. Comparable figures for the U.S. swap market, based on a fit to 54 swaptions prices, which we discuss in Section 19.6, were a speed of mean reversion of 0.05379 and an interest rate volatility of 0.01369.

19.4 ADVANCED VOLATILITY CURVE APPROACH

A more sophisticated approach takes the linear relationship between the short rate and zero coupon bond yields

$$y(\tau) = f(\tau)r + g(\tau)$$

for any given maturity τ and fits a regression equation of the form

$$dy(\tau) = A(\tau) + B(\tau)dr$$

---

1. Market participants usually take the shortcut of approximating zero coupon yields by the par bond coupon levels at each maturity, the same approach we take here in the interest of brevity.

EXHIBIT 19-3

Variance in Canadian Government Interest Rates
January 2, 1987, to March 6, 1996

	Canadian Treasury Bills					Canadian Government Bond Years to Maturity						
	1 Month	2 Months	3 Months	6 Months	1 Year	2	3	4	5	7	10	25
Actual variance	7.677	8.346	7.433	6.842	6.529	3.880	3.044	2.623	2.237	1.909	1.471	0.996
Estimated variance	7.943	7.745	7.552	7.008	6.051	4.564	3.496	2.717	2.143	1.389	0.794	0.140
Error	−0.266	0.602	−0.119	−0.166	0.478	−0.684	−0.452	−0.095	0.094	0.520	0.677	0.856
Squared error	0.071	0.362	0.014	0.028	0.228	0.468	0.204	0.009	0.009	0.270	0.458	0.732
Best-fitting parameter values:												
α	0.305172											
σ	2.854318%											
Maturity τ	0.083333	0.166667	0.25	0.5	1	2	3	4	5	7	10	25

Note: Interest rates and variance are in percent.

to yields at a given maturity τ. Of course, A and B will be different for each maturity, as theory predicts. We know that

$$B(\tau) = f(\tau)$$

so after getting estimates of B for n different maturities over a historical data period, we can then find the values of α that produce the best fit to the observed values of B. For the Canadian market, we performed a regression of par bond coupon yields (as proxies for zero coupon bond yields) on the one-month Canadian government bill rate. The results of these regressions showed a higher implied mean reversion speed at shorter maturities:

Implied Speed of Mean Reversion
By Historical Sensitivity to Movements in the
Canadian Treasury Bill Rate, 1987–1996

Yield = m*short rate + b

	3-Year Bond Yield	10-Year Bond Yield	25-Year Bond Yield
Coefficient of short rate	0.31430	0.17709	0.13505
Standard error	0.01960	0.01573	0.01349
t-score	16.03177	11.26116	10.01270
$R2$	0.09985	0.05189	0.04422
Best-fitting α	1.00921	0.56275	0.29600

The best-fitting α at three years was a very high 1.00921. At 25 years, the α at 0.296 is much more consistent with the historical variances reported in Section 19.3. This chart provides a strong clue that a two-factor model would add value (assuming away other problems, like parameter estimation and the valuation of American options, which are strong disadvantages of two-factor models) in the Canadian market. This is true of most markets where recent interest rate fluctuations have been large and where current rate levels are near historical lows. The Australian market has had similar experiences.

19.5 IMPLIED PARAMETERS FROM AN OBSERVABLE YIELD CURVE

Most market participants feel more comfortable basing analysis on parameter values implied from observable securities prices than on historical data *when observable prices are sufficient for this task*. For example, if the only observable data are on the yield curve itself, we can still attempt to fit the actual data to the theory by maximizing the goodness of fit from the theoretical model. In many markets around the world, the yield curve itself *is* the only observable interest rate "derivative." In the Vasicek model, as explained in previous chapters, the price of a zero coupon bond is given by the relationship

$$P(\tau) = e^{-F(\tau)r - G(\tau)}$$

where

$$F(\tau) = \frac{1}{\alpha}\left[1 - e^{-\alpha\tau}\right]$$

$$D = \mu + \frac{\sigma\lambda}{\alpha} - \frac{\sigma^2}{2\alpha^2}$$

$$G(\tau) = D[\tau - F(\tau)] + \frac{\sigma^2}{4\alpha}F(\tau)^2$$

and μ is the long-run expected value of the short rate, λ is the market price of risk, and α and σ are the speed of mean reversion and the level of interest rate volatility. In the extended Vasicek (Hull and White) model, only α and σ are explicitly identified. Zero coupon bond prices have the form

$$P(\tau) = e^{-F(\tau)r - G(\tau) - H(\tau)}$$

where H is a "plug" that forces the theoretical model to fit the observable data correctly.

We want the model we estimate to have the maximum goodness of fit, which means that we want to minimize the "extension" in the extended Vasicek model; this is consistent with our stress on the underlying economic logic of the factors we could select in the multifactor term structure model discussion in Chapter 18. This prejudice means we want to minimize the value of the function H over the yield curve range we are fitting. We do this by creating the best-fitting Vasicek yield curve and calculating the function H at a later stage. We have four unknowns in the Vasicek model. To maximize goodness of fit, we can pull a large number of zero coupon bond prices from the observable yield curve and try to find the parameters that fit as well as possible.

In first-class derivatives software, the authors feel strongly that it is essential to have access to a sophisticated nonlinear regression package to estimate the parameters. For purposes of this section, we have used simple spreadsheet software to better illustrate the process of estimation. Because the simple spreadsheet software lacks the power of the approach used by the best nonlinear regression routines, we have arbitrarily set the market price of risk to 0 and the long-run expected value of the short rate $r\,(\mu)$ to equal the 10-year bond yield. We then find the best-fitting α and σ. The result is generally of marginal acceptability. This is a common conclusion, as pointed out by the former head of derivatives research at Merrill Lynch (see Flesaker, 1993), and one of the reasons why market participants often feel compelled to supplement current yield curve data with historical parameter data.

To illustrate the yield-curve-fitting approach, we took yield curve data for the beginning, middle, and end of the data set and picked the days for which the 10-year Canadian government bond yield reached its highest and lowest points. We used maturities at one month, six months, and 2, 3, 4, 5, 7, and 10 years so that we could use the same input data for all five of the dates chosen. The results of this analysis, using simple spreadsheet software to obtain parameters, were as follows:

Best-Fitting Parameters for Selected Yield Curves
Canadian Government Bond Market,
Extended Vasicek Model
Using Common Spreadsheet Nonlinear Equation Solver

Environment Date	Data Beginning January 2, 1987	Highest Rates April 19, 1990	Data Mid-Point August 1, 1991	Lowest Rates January 28, 1994	Data Ending March 6, 1996
Mean reversion	0.01462	0.25540	0.62661	0.70964	0.58000
Volatility	0.00000	0.05266	0.00000	0.00000	0.00100
Mark price of risk	0.00000	0.00000	0.00000	0.00000	0.00000
Long-run R	0.08730	0.11950	0.09885	0.06335	0.07600
Estimate quality	Low	Medium	Low	Low	Low

Note: Spreadsheet solver capabilities are limited. Market price of risk and long-run expected short rate were arbitrarily set to displayed values with optimization on speed of mean reversion and volatility.

The results were consistent with other approaches in generally showing a high degree of mean reversion. The lack of power in spreadsheet nonlinear equation solving is reflected in the low or zero values for interest rate volatility and illustrate the need for *other data* (caps, floors, swaptions, bond options prices, etc.) and more powerful techniques for obtaining these parameters. We found that common spreadsheet packages could not obtain a reasonable solution for March 6, 1996, with two unknowns due to the straightness of the yield curve. In the Cox, Ingersoll, and Ross (CIR) model, it is the authors' experience that the problem of local optimums is much more serious than it is with the Vasicek model. Even using a powerful nonlinear regression technique, we found that it was not possible to converge to a solution for CIR parameters on 40 percent of 848 observations in the yen swap market on which we tested the CIR model. In the Vasicek model, one must take care in modeling the situation in which α approaches 0. This is a frequent cause of failed parameter estimates, particularly when using common spreadsheet software.

19.6 THE BEST APPROACH

Given the results described in Section 19.5, we think it is essential to use parameters estimated from observable caps, floors, and swaptions data (or other option-related securities prices[2]) to the extent they are available. To illustrate the power of this approach, we turn now to U.S.-dollar data on European swaption prices observable in August 1995.[3] At the time the data were obtained, there were 54 observable swaption prices. A swaption, as discussed earlier, gives the holder the right to initiate a swap of predetermined maturity and fixed-rate level on an exercise date in the future. We estimated extended Vasicek model parameters by choosing the speed of mean reversion (α) and interest

---

2. In the U.S. market, there is a fairly large number of callable U.S. Treasury securities whose prices provide some guide to interest rate volatility. When rates are infinitely high, the value of the call option is 0; therefore, the power to extract parameter estimates is greatest when bond prices trade roughly in the range between 95 and par value. Also in the U.S. market there are more than 400 callable U.S. agency securities, which may actually provide the richest source of information on term structure model parameters for a nearly risk-free yield curve.

3. The data used in this section were provided by one of the largest U.S.-dollar swap dealers in the world.

EXHIBIT   19–4

Market European Swaption Prices versus Extended Vasicek
Estimated Prices, August 1995 (U.S. $)
Swaption Exercise Period: Six Months

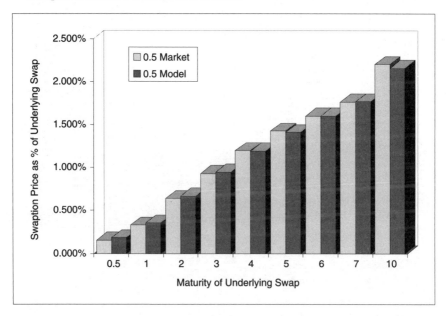

rate volatility (σ) that minimized the sum of the squared errors in
pricing these 54 swaptions.[4] The "price" of the swaption was
obtained by converting the Black-Scholes volatility quotation for
the swaption price to the percentage of notional principal that
the equivalent dollar swaption price represented. The exercise
periods on the swaptions were 0.5, 1, 2, 3, 4, and 5 years. The
underlying swap maturities were 0.5, 1, 2, 3, 4, 5, 6, 7, and 10
years. Exhibit 19–4 shows the relative pricing performance of
swaptions with a six-month exercise period for all nine observable maturities.

The largest absolute mispricing error of the six-month swaptions was five basis points. The market price of a 10-year swaption was 2.21 percent of notional principal, compared to a model

---

4. Note that another criterion could have been to select the parameters that minimized
the sum of the squared percentage error in pricing the swaptions.

EXHIBIT   19-5

Market European Swaption Prices versus Extended Vasicek
Estimated Prices, August 1995 (U.S. $)
Swaption Exercise Period: One Year

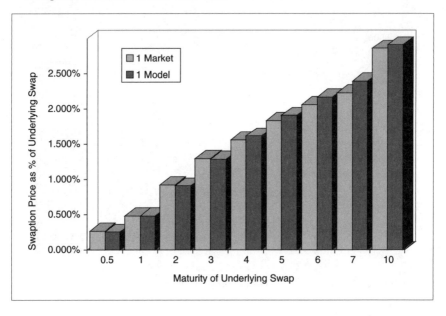

price of 2.16 percent. For swaptions with a one-year exercise period, the fit was also excellent, as shown in Exhibit 19–5.

The largest mispricing was at seven years, where the model
indicated 2.39 percent as the price versus an actual of 2.23 percent of notional principal. For swaptions of two years in exercise
price, the performance was still better (see Exhibit 19–6).

The largest mispricing for a two-year exercise period was 10
basis points of notional principal (a model price of 3.74 percent
versus true market price of 3.64 percent). As shown in Exhibit
19–7 on page 364, the three-year results indicated a maximum
error of only six basis points at seven years (model price of 3.42
percent, compared to 3.36 percent in reality).

For four-year swaptions (see Exhibit 19–8 on page 365), the
maximum error was 16 basis points at four years (3.03 percent
market price compared to a 2.87 percent model price).

EXHIBIT 19–6

Market European Swaption Prices versus Extended Vasicek
Estimated Prices, August 1995 (U.S. $)
Swaption Exercise Period: Two Years

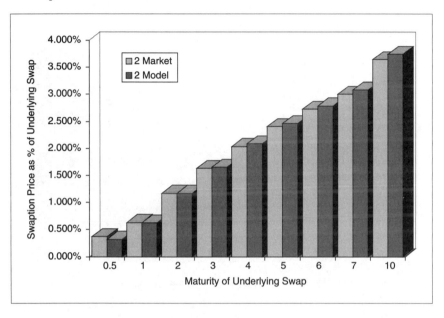

The five-year results (see Exhibit 19–9 on page 366) were also good, with a worst-case error of 15 basis points at seven years due to a model price of 3.63 percent compared to a true market value of 3.48 percent.

Overall, the extended Vasicek model's performance was extraordinary. The average model error was literally zero basis points with a mean absolute error of five basis points of notional principal, even though only two parameters (in addition to the current yield curve) were used to price 54 securities. Compare this to the Black model for commodity futures, which is often used for swaptions and caps and floors pricing. The Black model required 54 different implied volatility values to match actual market prices, even though the model in theory assumes that one volatility parameter should correctly price all 54 swaptions. Volatilities in the Black

EXHIBIT   19-7

Market European Swaption Prices versus Extended Vasicek Estimated Prices, August 1995 (U.S. $)
Swaption Exercise Period: Three Years

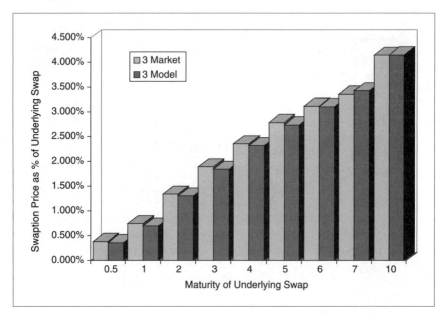

model ranged from 0.13 to 0.226, a very wide range that should indicate the need for caution to swaption market participants.

In summary, the extended version of the Vasicek model, when applied to swaption prices, proved two things:

- Swaptions provide a rich data set with very good convergence properties that allow market participants to use even common spreadsheet software to obtain high-quality term structure parameter estimates.
- The accuracy of the extended Vasicek model, using only two parameters held constant over 54 swaptions, is far superior to that of the Black commodity futures model in predicting actual market prices.

In estimating term structure parameters, the lesson is clear. A rich data set of current prices of securities with significant op-

E X H I B I T   19–8

Market European Swaption Prices versus Extended Vasicek
Estimated Prices, August 1995 (U.S. $)
Swaption Exercise Period: Four Years

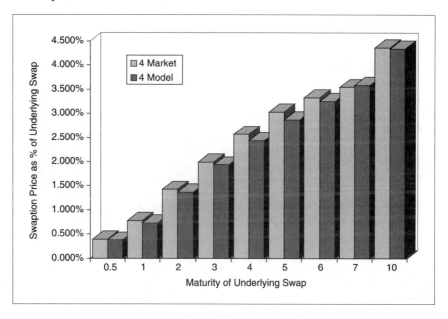

tionality is necessary to provide an easy-to-locate global opti-
mum for almost any popular term structure model.

EXERCISES

19.1 Assume that the historical zero coupon bond yield
variance (in percent) has been as follows:

1 year	4.25%
2 years	3.54%
3 years	3.23%
5 years	2.75%
7 years	2.13%
10 years	1.95%

EXHIBIT   19–9

Market European Swaption Prices versus Extended Vasicek
Estimated Prices, August 1995 (U.S. $)
Swaption Exercise Period: Five Years

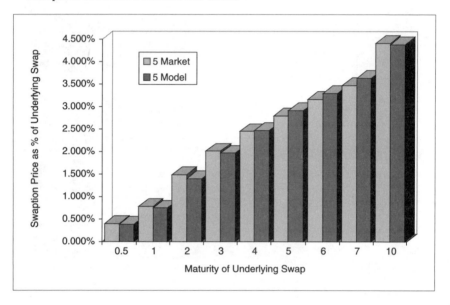

What are the best-fitting values of σ and α in the Vasicek model?

19.2 Assume that regressions of the zero coupon bond yield on the short-term rate of interest have produced the following values:

1 year	0.74
3 years	0.52
5 years	0.36
7 years	0.24
10 years	0.16

What are the best-fitting values of σ and α in the Vasicek model?

19.3 What are the best-fitting Vasicek parameters for the following zero coupon bond prices? Assume that the model will be "extended" to a perfect fit after the unextended Vasicek model is made to fit as well as possible.

1 year	0.92
2 years	0.83
3 years	0.74
5 years	0.58
7 years	0.47
10 years	0.35

19.4 (Advanced.) What form does the Vasicek model take as α approaches 0? What impact does this fact have on parameter estimation?

REFERENCES

Chan, K. C.; G. Andrew Karolyi; Francis A. Longstaff; and Anthony B. Sanders. "An Empirical Comparison of Models of the Short Term Interest Rate." *Journal of Finance*, July 1992, pp. 1209–28.

Flesaker, Bjorn. "Testing the Heath-Jarrow-Morton/Ho-Lee Model of Interest Rate Contingent Claims Pricing." *Journal of Financial and Quantitative Analysis*, December 1993, pp. 483–96.

CHAPTER 20

Hedging and
Risk Measurement

20.1 INTRODUCTION TO HEDGING AND
RISK MEASUREMENT

Valuation, hedging, and risk measurement are by-products of the same basic calculation. Throughout this book, we have described asset prices as functions of random variables and derived partial equilibrium prices for those assets, assuming that there is no arbitrage. Having done this, we measured risk by the first derivative of value with respect to the risky variable(s) (the rDelta) and discussed in detail how to "delta hedge" the asset's value. In this chapter, we step back from the leaves and trees of asset valuation to focus on the forest of risk management.

All financial institutions face basically the same hierarchy of everyday problems, whether the institution is a life insurance company, a fund manager, or a bank. Managers of industrial companies face a closely related set of problems:

- On a risk-adjusted basis, what assets should we sell and what assets should we buy to maximize the stock price of the organization?
- What level of risk should we have to maximize the stock price of the organization?
- How should the aggregate level of risk be measured?

- If the risk level of the organization is inconsistent with the desired level, which of all the instruments available should be used for hedging, and how much of each should be incorporated in the hedge?
- On a risk-adjusted basis, which members of management did well, and which members did poorly?
- On a risk-adjusted basis, did the company do better or worse than its peers?

From a management perspective, the answers to these questions are the primary concern of the most senior levels of management. From an academic point of view, the questions posed are either (a) trivially simple with an obvious answer, or (b) so incredibly complex that there is no known answer in the theory of finance. The purpose of this chapter is to bridge the grand canyon between the idealized assumptions used for valuation and the realities that must be reflected in management actions.

20.2 PORTFOLIO SELECTION: WHAT ASSETS SHOULD WE SELL AND WHAT ASSETS SHOULD WE BUY?

The answer to the difficult question of which assets to sell and which to buy is trivial in an academic sense: buy low and sell high. However, it is definitely not trivial in a practical sense. Of the hundreds of traded mortgage-backed securities available for purchase, which are the 10 best and which are the 10 worst? No firm on Wall Street and no financial theorist can answer this question with confidence. In Chapter 5, we discussed the Vasicek model parameter λ, the market price of risk, as the fixed-income equivalent of the Sharpe ratio, which measures the compensation that the holder of the security receives in compensation for the assumption of risk. In the Vasicek model, all fixed-income securities must conform to the pricing equation developed by Jamshidian in Chapter 6. For securities that have a nonzero cost and that have no cash flow before maturity, the market price of risk is related to the security's price and risk statistics by this equation:

$$\lambda = \frac{P_r \alpha [\tilde{\mu} - r] + \frac{1}{2} P_{rr} \sigma^2 + P_t - rP}{-\sigma P_r}$$

The Sharpe ratio, which measures "excess return" per unit of risk, is similar to the market price of risk calculation:

$$\text{Sharpe ratio} = \frac{\text{Expected return} - \text{Risk-free return}}{\text{Standard deviation of return}}$$

In the Vasicek model case, the numerator is made up of the drift in the bond's price

$$\text{Drift} = \text{Expected return} = P_r \alpha [\mu - r] + \frac{1}{2} P_{rr} \sigma^2 + P_t$$

less the riskless return on the same amount of money, rP. The denominator of the expression for λ is the instantaneous volatility of the security's price.

How do we do rich/cheap analysis in a one-factor model using the equivalent of the Sharpe ratio? We effectively calculate λ for each security, buy the "high λ" securities and sell the "low λ" securities.

All of the valuation techniques in this book provide us with enough information to do this, assuming that parameter values are estimated correctly. Still, this approach leaves out a number of important considerations where the theory of finance has yet to provide much guidance:

- In reality, there are multiple risk factors, not just one.
- The risk of the next asset purchased, from the portfolio point of view, is the incremental change in portfolio risk that results from the purchase, not the total risk of the security when viewed in isolation.
- The amount of incremental risk, particularly when bankruptcy costs are a realistic concern,[1] is unique to each institution, and these factors are not reflected to a sufficient degree in the available valuation formulas.
- The ideal degree of diversification, thanks to the insights of Harry Markowitz (1959), William Sharpe (1964), and John Lintner (1965), has been much studied in the context of equity portfolio management, but a great deal remains to be done in a fixed-income setting

---

1. The authors believe that bankruptcy costs, broadly defined, dictate implicitly much of the global risk management strategy of major financial institutions.

where securities are held "long" and "short" and
bankruptcy has a nonzero probability.

Given these considerations, the portfolio selection problem is
trivial only when the assumptions of the model are too simple.

20.3 WHAT LEVEL OF RISK MAXIMIZES SHAREHOLDER VALUE?

The risky debt model of Chapter 16 provides a substantial amount
of guidance regarding the pricing of risky debt and the amount of
capital required in the face of the value of the asset being financed,
the volatility of that asset's return, and the correlation of the asset
return with the level of interest rates. In two recent articles, van
Deventer (1993, 1994) shows how the Shimko, Tejima, and van
Deventer (1993) risky debt pricing formula can be used to calculate
the amount of capital necessary to finance assets of varying degrees
of risk and correlation in such a way that the cost of debt used to
finance each activity is the same. Capital allocation has to be done
with great care to avoid buying bad assets and promoting the wrong
managers, as we discuss below. Exhibit 20–1 shows how simple risk-
adjusted capital is related both to the correlation between asset
values and interest rates and to the level of volatility of asset values.

Using hypothetical volatilities and correlations, van Deventer
(1993) shows how capital ratios on typical U.S. bank and insurance
company assets would need to vary to equalize the one-year financing rate associated with each asset class. (See Exhibit 20–2.)

Still, even this approach leads to unsatisfactory answers
when we ask the critical question "What level of risk maximizes
shareholder value?" Why? Assume that the level of asset volatility in the risky debt model is something that management can
select. If management and shareholders are one and the same,
and if the cost of bankruptcy is zero, management will select the
highest risk asset available, since the value of equity in the risky
debt model (and in the Black-Scholes options model) increases
when asset volatility increases. Clearly, management that follows
this prescription in the real world will have a short tenure.

A theoretical model that explicitly answers the question in
this section has yet to be published. Experience, judgment, and
peer group comparisons — supplemented by clear measures of
risk described in this book — provide the only answers available.

E X H I B I T   20–1

Value of Capital Ratios for Varying Levels of Asset Volatility,
Interest Rate Volatility, and Correlation

Rate and Asset Value Correlation	Asset Volatility	Interest Rate Volatility			
		0.05	0.10	0.15	0.20
−1.00	0.05	1.81	1.08	2.22	3.89
−1.00	0.10	7.90	4.75	2.93	2.55
−1.00	0.15	15.14	11.03	7.66	5.29
−1.00	0.20	22.61	18.03	13.87	10.36
−0.50	0.05	3.51	4.00	5.31	7.08
−0.50	0.10	9.79	8.65	8.42	8.85
−0.50	0.15	17.03	14.99	13.62	12.89
−0.50	0.20	24.44	21.87	19.77	18.19
0.00	0.05	4.92	6.24	7.95	9.79
0.00	0.10	11.48	11.74	12.44	13.39
0.00	0.15	18.65	18.32	18.22	18.42
0.00	0.20	26.16	25.21	24.53	24.12
0.50	0.05	6.15	8.24	10.12	12.02
0.50	0.10	13.02	14.37	15.77	17.15
0.50	0.15	20.40	21.23	22.08	22.95
0.50	0.20	27.76	28.17	28.58	29.01
1.00	0.05	7.26	9.79	12.06	13.82
1.00	0.10	14.45	16.71	18.67	20.40
1.00	0.15	21.91	23.83	25.45	26.84
1.00	0.20	29.28	30.85	32.13	33.20

Source: Donald van Deventer, "Overcoming Inadequacy,"*Balance Sheet,* Summer 1993.

20.4 HOW SHOULD THE AGGREGATE LEVEL OF RISK BE MEASURED?

J. P. Morgan's "value-at-risk" concept and the associated data provided by J. P. Morgan have provided an invaluable boost to the importance of risk management worldwide. The limits of the value-at-risk measure, as it has been popularized, are well known.[2] Throughout this book, we have emphasized the *r*Delta

---

2. The major limitations are the lack of term structure model analytics for option valuation, the lack of a yield curve smoothing capability to interpolate between "on-the-run" maturities, the short time horizon, the assumption of normally distributed asset values, and the use of historical data for volatility and correlation values.

E X H I B I T   20–2

Sample Capital Allocation as a Function of Asset Volatility and Correlation

Asset Class	Hypothetical Asset Volatility	Correlation with Interest Rates	Capital as Percent of Asset Market Value
Three-month Treasury bills	0.05	−1.00	1.08
30-year Treasury bonds	0.10	−1.00	4.75
Floating-rate loan to foreign client	0.10	0.00	11.74
30-year fixed-rate mortgage	0.15	−0.50	14.99
Fixed-rate home construction loans	0.20	−0.50	21.87

Source: Donald van Deventer, "Overcoming Inadequacy," *Balance Sheet,* Summer 1993.

and the associated Greeks, or first derivatives, as the keys to both risk measurement and hedging. In this section, we want to further emphasize how the total valuation surface, not just an arbitrary worst-case scenario, is essential to the quantification of risk. For example, consider three portfolios whose values change as the short rate changes as in Exhibit 20–3.

Looking at the chart in Exhibit 20–4 (on page 376) summarizes the many dimensions of risk that must be controlled. If we tabulate the values of the three portfolios, we can see the dilemma most clearly.

There are three simple criteria for ranking the risk of these portfolios that illustrate the risk measurement dilemma nicely:

- Local risk, the change in value for small changes in rates.
- Value at risk, defined as the worst case with a maximum probability of 1 percent.
- Global risk, defined (for exposition's sake) as the standard deviation of the outcomes for the scenarios graphed.[3]

---

3. For exposition's sake, we take a simple standard deviation, not the proper probability-weighted variance.

Comparison of Various Portfolio Values

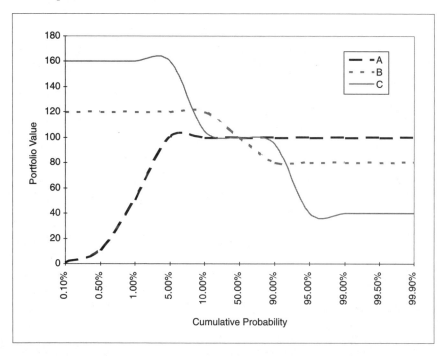

Unfortunately, the three risk measures give inconsistent rankings for the risk of the three portfolios:

	Local Risk	Value at Risk	Global Risk
Most risky	B	A	C
Medium risk	C	C	A
Least risky	A	B	B

There is only one risk measure that can be reduced to a single number: stock price. As mentioned above, finance theory fails us in translating the full range of possible valuations for a portfolio or for an institution into stock price. Nonetheless, it is clear that the full "valuation surface" (when there is more than one risk factor) has to be taken into account by management. Management does not have the luxury of being able to focus on a single risk measure, even one as elegant as value at risk.

E X H I B I T   20–4

Hypothetical Portfolio Values

Short rate mean	0.07
Short rate volatility	0.02

Level of Short-Term Interest Rate	Number of Sigmas from Mean	Cumulative Probability	Portfolio		
			A	B	C
1.26%	−2.87	0.10%	1	120	160
1.69%	−2.65	0.50%	10	120	160
2.35%	−2.32	1.00%	50	120	160
3.71%	−1.65	5.00%	100	120	160
4.44%	−1.28	10.00%	100	120	105
7.00%	0.00	50.00%	100	100	100
9.56%	1.28	90.00%	100	80	95
10.29%	1.65	95.00%	100	80	40
11.65%	2.32	99.00%	100	80	40
12.31%	2.65	99.50%	100	80	40
12.74%	2.87	99.90%	100	80	40
Simple standard deviation			39	20	54
Local rate sensitivity			0	20	5
1% worst-case outcome			99	20	60

20.5 THE BEST HEDGE

The purity of the assumptions behind the term structure models used in this book provides valuable guidance regarding the proper hedge for any complex portfolio. Given the *r*Delta of the portfolio (or multiple *r*Deltas for each of the risk factors) we can structure a hedging portfolio that *locally* eliminates all of these risks. The word *locally* emphasizes the gap between theory and the real world. For all of the assets valued in this book, with the exception of certain types of nonmaturity deposits, the ideal "delta hedge" is a function of the current date, current rates, and the time to maturity of the underlying portfolio. The hedging problem is straightforward in an academic sense for these reasons:

- There are only N risk factors in the model.
- Therefore, we can hedge the portfolio with any N assets.
- Which N assets are chosen doesn't matter; any N will work.
- When time passes or rates change, the hedge is costlessly rebalanced.

The reality of management responsibility is much different:

1. There are many, many risk factors that are not captured by the model.
2. Therefore, the model's prescription that only N securities are needed to hedge must be taken with a large grain of salt; a larger number of hedging securities must be employed.
3. Which assets are chosen is very important because rebalancing is expensive, and transactions costs will be incurred every time rebalancing takes place.
4. Independent of costs, sometimes rebalancing is literally impossible (as in the stock market crash of October 1987) because of rapid price movements and a lack of liquidity.

Consider the simplest case, where the term structure is driven by one risky factor, the short rate r, and the portfolio matures by time t. Assume that any one of N assets can be selected and that the rebalancing of a hedge ratio for each of these assets incurs the same cost, which is proportional to the variance of the hedge ratio over time and over various levels of interest rates. The objective is to select the asset i that minimizes rebalancing cost. The best hedging instrument is the security i that has a hedge ratio w with minimum variance:

$$\text{Minimize (Variance}[w_i]) =$$

$$\min\left[\int_0^\tau \int_{-\infty}^\infty [w(i,t,r) - \text{Mean}[w]]^2 n(r, \text{Mean } r, \sigma_r, t)\,dr\,dt \right]$$

where n represents the normal distribution function for r as of time t.

This is a nontrivial problem. Consider one asset: a fixed-rate level-pay mortgage with an embedded American call option. The perfect hedge is clearly a combination of a noncallable fixed-rate level-pay security and an American call option on such a security. Assume that the bank has 1 million of these mortgages maturing on 3,763 different maturity dates at 41 different coupon levels and that there are 54 on-the-run maturities[4] available for the only liquid American option available, American swaptions. How many swaption maturities should the bank use? How much of each maturity should be put in place?

Risk management practice in this area is rapidly evolving to deal with these very real concerns.

20.6 PERFORMANCE EVALUATION: WHICH MANAGERS DID WELL?

Every organization must reward its best performers and admonish those who don't perform well to improve rapidly. How should performance be measured? In a recent article, van Deventer and Levin (1995) summarize the key considerations:

- Performance should be measured on a market value, not a financial accounting, basis.
- Performance should be measured on a relative, not an absolute, basis. A 15 percent return on equity, for example, is meaningless in a 60 percent inflation environment.
- Performance should be relative to a naive strategy that could have been easily implemented if management had not been in place, to measure management's incremental value added. In the investment management business, performance relative to a broad-based market index ("Buy x percent of everything") is an appropriate base from which to measure value added. In the insurance business, life policies generated have to be judged relative to the cost of issuing bonds with the same risk characteristics as an alternative funding strategy. In the banking business, did the portfolio of three-year fixed-rate auto loans outperform a benchmark

---

4. That is, standard maturities.

portfolio of Treasury notes after considering processing costs, credit losses, and origination costs?
- Performance should be measured relative to the naive strategy of equivalent risk.

In every organization, there are large numbers of managers for which financial accounting data are the only data available. Even in this case, care should be taken to ensure that a focus on inaccurate and misleading financial accounting figures does not result in (*a*) subpar asset generation and (*b*) unfair and incorrect performance evaluation of managers.

20.7 RISK-ADJUSTED RETURN ON CAPITAL

Risk-adjusted return on capital has become just as popular a concept as value at risk, due to the openness of the Bankers Trust Company regarding the use of this technique.[5] As implemented by Bankers Trust, the major features of the risk-adjusted return on capital (RAROC) are as follows:

- Returns are measured on a market value basis, not a financial accounting basis.[6]
- The "worst case" is defined as the portfolio value that would be exceeded 99 percent of the time (the 1 percent worst case).
- Capital is measured as the amount of funds necessary to prevent bankruptcy of the portfolio in the event that the 1 percent worst case occurs.
- Risk-adjusted return on capital is the return on this hypothetical amount.
- Unit performance is measured on a relative, not an absolute, basis since the definition of the worst case can arbitrarily raise or lower RAROC returns.

Bankers Trust's use of the concept is consistent with the views expressed in Section 20.6. Unfortunately, many banks misuse the

---

5. The authors wish to thank Dr. Daniel Borge of Bankers Trust Company for his explanation of Bankers Trust's RAROC system. Dr. Borge is not responsible for any of the controversial views held by the authors.
6. Bankers Trust Company is in a fairly unique position to take this step, since it had only $12 billion in loans on a $110 billion balance sheet.

E X H I B I T   20–5

Measured Risk-Adjusted Return on Capital for $10 Return on $100 Asset

Definition of Worst-Case Scenario	Number of Standard Deviations	Asset Value Standard Deviation				
		0.1	1	5	10	20
0.01%	−5.00	2,000.0%	200.0%	40.0%	20.0%	10.0%
0.05%	−3.22	3,104.5%	310.5%	62.1%	31.0%	15.5%
0.10%	−3.11	3,213.0%	321.3%	64.3%	32.1%	16.1%
0.50%	−2.58	3,882.0%	388.2%	77.6%	38.8%	19.4%
1.00%	−2.33	4,297.8%	429.8%	86.0%	43.0%	21.5%
5.00%	−1.64	6,079.9%	608.0%	121.6%	60.8%	30.4%

concept by emphasizing absolute levels of performance (e.g., "Risk-adjusted return on capital must exceed 15 percent . . .") instead of relative performance. Others use accounting-based return measures instead of market value measures. Finally, many banks have not taken advantage of the relatively easy "benchmark portfolios" to measure management's value added. The table in Exhibit 20–5 shows how the absolute RAROC level can be moved up or down just by changing the definition of the worst case.

The risk-adjusted return on capital concept has become almost too popular. To avoid rewarding the wrong managers or providing an incentive to originate the wrong assets or liabilities, a number of steps are important:

- Capital should never be allocated to units that have assets but no liabilities or liabilities but no assets. Select a benchmark portfolio to measure management performance instead, often in the guise of a transfer pricing policy that helps translate between a true market value measure and standard internal financing accounting practices:
  a. Were term life policies cheaper than matching maturity bonds?
  b. Were savings deposits, after branch processing costs, cheaper than large certificates of deposit?

c. Did charge card loans after expenses and credit losses yield more than Libor?
- The worst-case bankruptcy probability should be selected so that the transfer price on the risky activity has the same yield as the organization's liabilities (i.e., set the probability of bankruptcy to that of the organization as a whole).
- Always emphasize the relative performance and true value-added.

20.8 SUMMING UP

The term structure model techniques solve a range of practical security valuation problems, ranging from risky debt to nonmaturity deposits to life insurance policy valuation. The term structure model approach provides a powerful set of tools that enable a dramatic improvement in the management of financial institutions and the financial activities of industrial firms. Mathematics is no substitute for good judgment, and the reverse is true as well.

REFERENCES

Levin, Jonathan, and Donald R. van Deventer. "Fund Managers Show Way to Gauge Risk." *American Banker,* November 3, 1995.

Lintner, John. "Security Prices, Risk, and Maximal Gains from Diversification." *Journal of Finance*, 1965, pp. 587–615.

Markowitz, Harry M. *Portfolio Selection: Efficient Diversification of Investments.* New Haven, CT: Cowles Foundation for Research in Economics at Yale University, 1959.

Sharpe, William F. "Capital Asset Prices: A Theory of Market Equilibrium under Conditions of Risk." *Journal of Finance*, September 1964, pp. 425–42.

Shimko, David C.; Naohiko Tejima; and Donald R. van Deventer. "The Valuation of Risky Debt When Interest Rates Are Stochastic." *Journal of Fixed Income,* September 1993, pp. 58–66.

van Deventer, Donald R. "Overcoming Inadequacy." *Balance Sheet,* Summer 1993.

———. "New Capital Ratio Gauge Takes Integrated Approach to Credit and Rate Risks." *American Banker*, January 6, 1994.

INDEX

FINANCIAL RISK MANAGEMENT IN BANKING

The Theory and Application of Asset & Liability Management

Dennis G. Uyemura and Donald R. van Deventer

Financial Risk Management in Banking provides a practical and comprehensive overview of aggressive asset and liability management (ALM) which highlights the nuances that set ALM apart from basic financial concepts and practices as they are taught even at the MBA level.
ISBN: 1-55738-353-7   447 pages

THE TREASURERS HANDBOOK OF FINANCIAL MANAGEMENT

Applying the Theories, Concepts and Quantitative Methods of Corporate Finance

Treasury Management Association

Treasury management encompasses a broad spectrum of corporate finance — from capital structure and working capital management to capital budgeting and risk management. Whether the treasury manager oversees one or many aspects of the company's finances or outsources them, this book is a critical tool to under-standing and managing short- and long-term financial issues.
ISBN: 1-55738-884-9   500 pages

INTEREST RATE SPREADS AND MARKET ANALYSIS

Tools for Managing and Reducing Rate Exposure in Global Markets

Seventh Edition
Citicorp

Although there has not been, and may never be, a formula to predict the future movement of interest rates and market volatility, financial managers must still con-tend with the pressures of investing and financing amidst global market uncertainty. *Interest Rate Spreads and Market Analysis* is designed to foster an understanding of key global market rates and prices, providing a 10-year historical database for long-term and short-term indices.
ISBN: 1-55738-862-8   300 pages

MANAGING FINANCIAL RISK

A Guide to Derivative Products, Financial Engineeriing and Value Maximization

Charles W. Smithson with Clifford W. Smith, Jr. & Wilford D. Sykes

Provides a system for evaluating a varied continuum of financial risks, and offers techniques and strategies for maximizing the value of a firm in the face of risk. Includes an in-depth evaluation of various risk management products, including forwards, futures, swaps, options, and hybrid securities — as well as a "building block" approach to implementating these products in your firm.
ISBN: 0-7863-0008-6   600 pages

PROTECTING SHAREHOLDER VALUE

A Guide to Managing Financial Risk

Abraham M. George

Protecting Shareholder Value discusses the risk that shareholders face from exposures of their companies to foreign exchange and interest rate changes. It also discusses how management can effectively deal with the uncertainties in financial markets to protect the value of the firm.
ISBN: 0-7863-0439-1   500 pages

INTEREST RATE RISK MANAGEMENT

The Banker's Guide to Using Futures, Options, Swaps and Other Derivative Instruments

Benton E. Gup & Robert Brooks

As banks invest more and more in mortgage-based securities and other interest-sensitive products, their exposure to interest-rate risk increases proportionately. Now *Interest Rate Risk Management* tackles this important issue . . . presenting simplified, non-technical examples of how to use derivative securities to protect against swings in interest rates, explaining why some interest rates are more volatile than others, and demonstrating how to use derivative securities effectively in any financial services business.
ISBN: 1-55738-370-7   275 pages